A BREED APART

The inside story of a
Recce's Special Forces training year

JOHAN RAATH

and
South African Special Forces Cycle 86/01

Delta Books
Johannesburg • Cape Town • London

All rights reserved.
No part of this publication may be reproduced or transmitted, in any form or by any means, without the prior written permission of the publisher or copyright holder.

Text © Johan Raath (2022)
Images © Johan Raath (2022), Scope magazine
The cover image was used on promotional material for the Special Forces in the 1980s. Front: Anton Retief. Middle row (left to right): Martiens Verster, Dave Tippett, Koos Moorcroft. Back row (left to right): Ben Loots, Harry Botha.
Published edition © Jonathan Ball Publishers (2022)

Published in South Africa in 2022 by
DELTA BOOKS
A division of Jonathan Ball Publishers
A division of Media24 (Pty) Ltd
PO Box 33977
Jeppestown
2043

ISBN 978-1-92824-824-8
ebook ISBN 978-1-92824-825-5

Every effort has been made to trace the copyright holders and to obtain their permission for the use of copyright material. The publishers apologise for any errors or omissions and would be grateful to be notified of any corrections that should be incorporated in future editions of this book.

www.jonathanball.co.za
www.twitter.com/JonathanBallPub
www.facebook.com/JonathanBallPublishers

Cover by Johan Koortzen
Design and typesetting by Johan Koortzen
Set in 11 on 16pt Bembo Std

CONTENTS

Acknowledgments	iv
List of abbreviations	v
Introduction	1
1. The Crux	9
2. Basics – The Recce Way	32
3. Special Forces Orientation	60
4. Special Forces Selection	70
5. Special Forces Individual	87
6. Seaborne/Water Orientation	96
7. Know Your Enemy (Dark Phase)	105
8. Parachute Course	118
9. Air Operations (Air Orientation)	131
10. Demolitions and Mine Warfare	140
11. Bushcraft, Tracking and Survival	153
12. Minor Tactics (Guerrilla/Unconventional Warfare)	170
13. Urban Warfare	199
14. Life after the Basic Recce Cycle and Beyond	209
Conclusion (1988 to 1990)	243
Epilogue	267
The Members of Recce Cycle 86/01	275
Rest in Peace (Others)	291
South African Special Forces Mission and Vision	292
Index	294

ACKNOWLEDGEMENTS

Writing a book about events that occurred more than 36 years ago is no easy feat. And the Recces were/are a secretive lot at the best of times, so written accounts of these events are few and far between.

Fortunately, the 'cycles' that did their training together are a tight-knit bunch, and each member remembers certain events that were burned into our DNA through blood, sweat, tears and dust. I am therefore indebted to my buddies and the entire cycle of SF-86/01 for their contributions. Each man's recollection spurred a flurry of memories within the group, and between us we mapped it as accurately as possible. Thank goodness we were selected for our intelligence – among other things – and there are some smart fellas in our ranks. I particularly want to thank the following members for their added-value contributions: Barry Visser, Chris Serfontein, Brian Harris and Matthys 'Diff' de Villiers.

Photos were also hard to come by, but fortunately a few brave souls sneaked cameras onto training courses. No one particular Recce can lay claim to the photos of the organisation, as it was a collective effort. Fortuitously, a number of photos were taken and kept by the Recce training wing. Many of the photos in the book are drawn from that combined collection, which some members obtained copies of before they left Special Forces.

Finally, the greatest acknowledgement must go to my Creator, for giving me the ability and strength not only to become a Recce but also to write this book.

We Fear Naught but God.

LIST OF ABBREVIATIONS

ANC African National Congress
DZ drop zone
E&E escape and evasion
EMT emergency medical technician
Fapla People's Armed Forces of Liberation of Angola
GPS Global Positioning System
HAHO high altitude high opening
HALO high altitude low opening
HE high explosive
HF high frequency
IED improvised explosive device
IV intravenous
LMG light machine gun
LN local national
LZ landing zone
MK Umkhonto we Sizwe
MMA mixed martial arts
MPLA Popular Movement for the Liberation of Angola
NCO non-commissioned officer
NSAID non-steroidal anti-inflammatory drug
NVD night-vision device
NVG night-vision goggles
OC officer commanding
PMC private military contractor
POW prisoner of war
PT physical training
PTSD post-traumatic stress disorder
RLI Rhodesian Light Infantry
RP red phosphorus

RPG rocket-propelled grenade
RSM regimental sergeant major
RV rendezvous
SADF South African Defence Force
SAI South African Infantry
SAM surface-to-air missile
SAP South African Police
SAS Special Air Service
STF Special Task Force (SAP)
Swapo South West Africa People's Organisation
Swapol South West African Police
Tac-HQ tactical headquarters
TAD tricyclic anti-depressant
TL team leader
TTP tactics, techniques and procedures
Unita National Union for the Total Independence of Angola
UNTAG United Nations Transition Assistance Group
WO warrant officer

INTRODUCTION

Special Forces. These two words instil respect, admiration, esteem, reverence and mystique among the general population but create fear, anxiety and distress in the hearts of insurgents, warlords, criminal syndicates, drug lords and any wrongdoers who find themselves in the crosshairs of Special Forces teams. Unfortunately, these two words are also sometimes hijacked by wannabes who dream up fantasies in order to boost their own low self-esteem. We call it 'stolen valour'.

The South African Special Forces was established in the early 1970s and in a short space of time became operationally active. To this day it is a prestigious and vital unit of the South African National Defence Force (SANDF). The first Special Forces unit, 1 Reconnaissance Commando, was established in 1972 at the highly respected South African Infantry (SAI) School in Oudtshoorn. 1 Reconnaissance Commando then moved to the coastal city of Durban in 1974. Two more operational Special Forces units and the Special Forces Headquarters (known as Speskop) were spawned in the late 1970s.

Selection and training doctrines were initially based on those of the British Special Air Service (SAS), with some influence from the French Special Forces, particularly on the combat diving and seaborne operations side. Air capabilities were drawn from the highly esteemed 1 Parachute Battalion, based in my hometown of Bloemfontein in the central highlands of South Africa.

It wasn't long before Special Forces operators were being referred to as 'Recces' – an abbreviation of Reconnaissance Commando. From the outset these Recce operators were involved in hair-raising and difficult operations in Angola, Rhodesia (today Zimbabwe), Mozambique and other sub-equatorial African countries. After Angola and Mozambique received their independence from Portugal in 1975, communist governments were installed in both countries. The National Party government in South Africa perceived these black majority-ruled states as a threat to white minority rule but also as part of the so-called Red Peril – the threat posed by communism at the height of the Cold War. The United States (US), through the Central Intelligence Agency (CIA), encouraged South Africa to take a stand against communism in southern Africa.

South Africa also faced an insurgency in the then South West Africa (today Namibia) by the South West Africa People's Organisation (Swapo). At the time, South West Africa was governed by South Africa as a protectorate. The National Party government also had to deal with the threat from Umkhonto we Sizwe (MK), the armed wing of the African National Congress (ANC), and from the Azanian People's Liberation Army (APLA), the armed wing of the Pan Africanist Congress. From the viewpoint of the apartheid regime, these groups were insurgents or terrorists, but as I point out in my book *Blood Money*, one person's insurgent is another's freedom fighter or liberator. These armed groups were fighting the apartheid system for the independence of South West Africa, on the one hand, and for a democratic South Africa, on the other.

The first South African Defence Force (SADF) soldier killed in action in Angola, in March 1974, was Lieutenant Fred Zeelie. It is probably significant that he was a Recce operator from 1 Reconnaissance Commando. The Recces were very busy from 1975 onwards after Angola and Mozambique gained their independence and received backing from the Soviet Union and its satellites, while the white-minority regime in Rhodesia faced an onslaught from liberation movements. From the mid-1970s until 1980, when Rhodesia became independent, the Recces often worked with the elite Rhodesian SAS on operations in Rhodesia, Zambia and Mozambique, where the insurgents/freedom fighters had training camps and from where they launched attacks against the Rhodesian security forces. By then the Special Forces of both South Africa and Rhodesia were experienced and hardened bush fighters with a wide variety of skills and specialised tactics derived from operations against numerically larger enemy forces.

In 1980, the old security forces of Rhodesia were discontinued and

Introduction

a number of SAS, Selous Scouts and Rhodesian Light Infantry (RLI) operators joined the South African Reconnaissance Commandos. The amalgamation of the Recces with these Rhodesian special operations formations created one of the finest Special Forces organisations the world has ever seen.

By the late 1970s there were three South African Special Forces units: 1 Reconnaissance Regiment (Durban), 4 Reconnaissance Regiment (Langebaan) and 5 Reconnaissance Regiment (Phalaborwa). The Special Forces HQ was located in Pretoria. Although all of the operators were schooled in bush warfare, parachute deployments, demolitions, basic seaborne operations and urban warfare, each unit specialised in certain kinds of deployment: 1 Recce became experts in urban warfare, 4 Recce in seaborne operations, attack diving and underwater demolitions, and 5 Recce were masters of larger-scale bush warfare operations, often expedited through fast strikes delivered by light armoured vehicles.

Military or police conscription for all white males between the ages of 17 and 65 became compulsory from 1976. Initially, this duty had been performed over a nine-month period. In 1972, the conscription period was increased to one year, and from 1977 to 1993 all white South African males had to do two years of military service. In the early 1990s this was reduced to one year after Namibia became independent and the ANC and other liberation groups were unbanned. Conscription was abolished in August 1993.

Roughly 600 000 young white men were conscripted. Military service might have been mandatory, but it turned out to be the thing that would define my life and who I became as a person.

I was born in 1968, in the city of Bloemfontein, in the Free State province. I come from a modest middle-class family: my father was a teacher and my mother was an administrative secretary at the local municipality. Both my parents grew up on farms in the Free State, and our family comes from a community of farmers, or Boers in the Afrikaans language.

From an early age I was interested in military matters. I had a particular interest first in toy guns, then in real firearms. Fortunately, one of my

My first drawing depicting life in the military, 1974.

Wearing my uncle's army boots and beret.

Ready for cadet camp during high school.

Introduction

uncles allowed me to stay on his farm in the mountainous eastern Free State during school holidays. He taught me how to shoot a rifle and how to hunt small animals such as rabbit, dassie (rock rabbit), meerkat and various birds. I quickly progressed from a .22 long rifle to a shotgun, and later to larger calibres, which we used to hunt various species of buck (antelope). Like many Afrikaner boys from farming communities, I excelled at shooting.

I also enjoyed fishing, which my father and uncle taught me, and I learned to ride a horse. I really loved being outdoors in the veld. At the time I did not realise it, but these skills were in my DNA, as they were for the Boers who trekked from the Cape into the hinterland during the 19th century. The Boers' military prowess and skill at survival in the veld would later become famed through the actions of the Boer commandos in various wars against local tribes and two wars against the British Empire.

One of the subjects my dad taught at high school was history, and he was particularly interested in the Anglo-Boer War (1899–1902) and its battle sites around the country. I enjoyed all things military, and I loved to hear more about my upcoming military service, as well as news from the border (between South West Africa and Angola), where the SADF was engaged in battles against Swapo guerrillas and the People's Armed Forces of Liberation of Angola (Fapla), the armed forces of Angola's communist government.

During this time I heard tales, and sometimes rumours, about the secretive Recces and what an outstanding group of combat soldiers they were. In my early teens I developed an interest in becoming a Recce and took part in the cadet camps that young men of the era were encouraged to experience during the winter holiday break.

When I turned 16 I had to complete my 'call-up' papers for my compulsory military service. There was a standard set of administrative questions covering personal and family details, and a short informative summary about the Special Forces. You could indicate there if you were interested in attempting the selection/s and training cycle required to become a Recce. By this time in my life, I was sure that I wanted to become a soldier and had it in my mind that I really wanted to be a

A Breed Apart

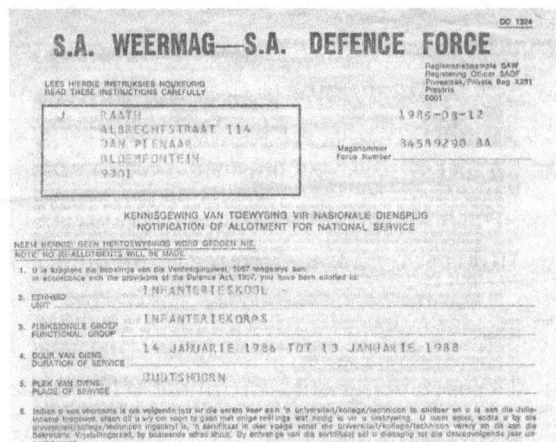

My conscription call-up papers.

The information booklet that came with my call-up papers.

Introduction

Special Forces operator. I indicated as much on the form and the papers were sent off. Around six months later, my mother received my call-up instructions in the post.

With the instructions was a letter from an army general applauding my enthusiasm to join the Special Forces but also informing me that applying was not as simple as writing a letter. He did, however, indicate that he could arrange for me to be called up to the Infantry School at Oudtshoorn, where the Recces had kicked off 14 years earlier.

I was not particularly interested in school. Rugby, cricket, parties, girls and a regular bar fight were the subjects that I excelled in. In my matric year, I was ambushed by a bunch of national servicemen who had crashed a party I was attending. I punched one of them and then the rest of the cowardly gang ambushed me from behind. They pinned me down for their mates to kick my face in, to the extent that I had to undergo facial reconstruction surgery.

I missed a couple of months of high school and could not play rugby anymore, something that was hard to accept at the time. But this episode made me much stronger mentally, and in a way motivated me even more to become a Recce. My call-up papers had also stipulated that conscripts who wanted to join Special Forces had to meet certain criteria. For example, you had to have no criminal record, be medically fit and sound, and have a matric certificate. You also had to be able to communicate in English, which would be a bit of a journey for me. (When I arrived at 1 Recce in Durban, I was still a raw Dutchman from the Free State, and only knew three English words – 'yes', 'no' and I battled with 'thank you'. But being in Durban, working with the black operators and ex-Rhodies, I struggled along and learned. Then in 1989 I moved in with the woman who turned out to be my life partner, and she was English. I was furthermore transferred to the Recce training wing and had to present classes in English. It was a long road, but I taught myself to the point where it became easier and to where I could start writing documents in the language of the oppressor.)

The need for a matric certificate inspired me to turn my attention, ever so slightly, to academic matters in order to pass my final exams and go to the army. I wanted to attempt the Special Forces selection and progress to the one-year basic training cycle.

I passed matric and received my high-school diploma – mission accomplished. After spending the summer vacation with my two best school friends at Margate on the east coast – a period that can be summed up by the word 'debauchery' – it was time to go to the army. I was supposed to arrive in Oudtshoorn on 14 January 1986, which meant I would leave Bloemfontein by train in the early hours of 12 January. After saying my goodbyes to my mother and sister, my dad and I thought it prudent to spend a good couple of hours in a hotel bar close to the station. It turned into a serious drinking session, to the extent that I almost missed the train to Oudtshoorn. Fortunately, I made the train and was sent off to military duties. I was 17 years and 11 months old.

1
THE CRUX

You've never lived until you've almost died. For those who have fought for it, life has a flavour the protected shall never know.
– Guy de Maupassant

We deployed from one of the Recces' forward operating bases in northern South West Africa, outside the town of Ondangwa. These bases were called 'forts', and this one went by the name of Fort Rev. It was a reference to a certain kind of combat engagement where you walked into a firefight and the enemy 'revved' you properly with incoming fire, or you did some 'revving' of your own.

What an apt name for a Recce forward base, I thought. The Recces had a few key personnel and operators stationed at Fort Rev, with 5.1 Commando from Phalaborwa deployed there on a semi-permanent basis. There was also a detention facility where captured Swapo insurgents or other enemy combatants were held.

It was almost a year since I had signed up for Special Forces training, and my first operation was set for the first week of December 1986. Our force of approximately 40 operators deployed in four Puma SA 330 helicopters, which took off from the runway next to the camp and dropped us off in the afternoon north of beacon 16. This was about 70 km north of Ondangwa on the Angolan side of the border, and approximately 100 km as the crow flies from the area where we were to lay our ambush.

The contact point was to be about 20 km south of the town of Xangongo, which in turn was another 120 km northwest of our position. Xangongo, the headquarters of Swapo's northwestern front, was protected by a brigade of Fapla troops. A Romeo Mike (*reaksie mag*, or 'fast reaction') team from 101 Battalion was to receive us at the drop-off point. Major Chris

Cycle 86/01 walking out to board the helicopters for Operation Nigel.

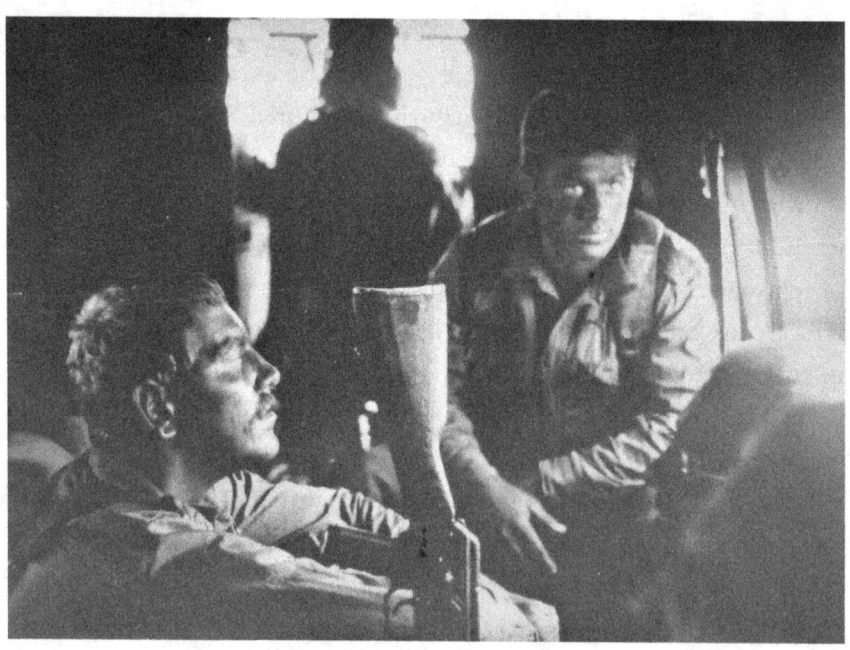
Dries Coetzee and Hennie 'Croucs' Croucamp during the chopper flight.

Greyling, a senior officer from 1.1 Commando acting as the operational and tactical commander, together with his signaller, joined up with the Romeo Mike team, who travelled in Casspir armoured troop carriers.

Greyling had arranged a rendezvous (RV) with an element from Unita, the rebel faction opposed to Angola's Marxist governing party, the Popular Movement for the Liberation of Angola (MPLA)· (Unita, or National Union for the Total Independence of Angola, was backed by the South African government, originally also with help from the CIA.) The designated Unita component joined our armoured column north of beacon 16, as they rarely went south of the border.

Many years later I learned that instead of relying on a system of messages, Greyling had flown to the operational area about month or so before the operation to personally liaise with Unita commanders based at Jamba in southern Angola. He requested their assistance in the operation, and the Unita high command eventually gave him the go-ahead.

The mobile tactical headquarters (Tac-HQ) was run by Greyling from 1 Recce's operational 1.1 Commando, at a safe distance from the target area. On the ground, the officer in charge was Major Dave Jenkinson, who had been our cycle course leader during basics, aided by some of the best sergeant majors (warrant officers) our Special Forces units have ever seen. The attack mortar team element consisted of qualified operators and non-commissioned officers (NCOs), also from 1.1 Commando: sergeants Ian Strange (RIP), Gary Yaffe, CJ 'Oosie' Oosthuizen and 'Swapo' Prinsloo, and Corporal David Hall, who was also the dedicated signaller for the operation.

Some of our instructors from the Minor Tactics, Guerrilla Warfare and Bush Warfare training phases, who now also formed part of our combat team, were integrated in the attack force. These operators included Major Jenkinson, Sergeant Major Johan 'Boats' Botes, Sergeant Major Bruce Laing (RIP), Staff Sergeant Ray Godbeer and Sergeant Wessel 'Jorrie' Jordaan. The Unita troops were going to give us a ride to the target area, and their troops were to assist the team in carrying the 81 mm mortar pipes and ammunition to the attack point. They would also act as a rearguard for the main ambush group.

Preparing and loading kit onto Unita trucks.

Moving to the target area on Unita trucks.

We did not move far from the drop zone (DZ) before we went into an overnight hide position. We were now inside enemy territory, and this was the real deal – the culmination of a year of specialised training. The operation, dubbed 'Nigel', was intended to disrupt enemy forces in Xangongo with a barrage of 81 mm mortar fire. We expected Fapla to send out search teams, which we would then ambush on the road stretching southwards from the town.

The *ou manne* (older, experienced operators) in the team spoke of a 'KSP patrol', or *kak-soek-patrollie* (shit-seeking patrol). KSP patrols were used to harass the enemy and draw them out to fight with you. This was a useful way of christening Special Forces recruits with their first contact and fire initiation with enemy forces. We were shown our all-round defence positions, teamed up in buddy pairs, and our arc of fire was pointed out to us by the instructors.

Our guard shifts were relatively short, as we were a medium-sized fighting force. I pulled my sleeping bag out but could not sleep due to the excitement of participating in my first Special Forces operation behind enemy lines. When I woke up at around 05:00 I discovered to my amusement that I had had an erotic dream during the night ... I put it down to the excitement of an 18-year-old high on adrenaline and testosterone. This was a day and a half before our planned ambush operation, which was to take place at first light on 3 December 1986.

We departed shortly after first light, sitting on the back of captured Russian Ural and GAZ military trucks and Mercedes-Benz 110 five-ton trucks that the South African military had given to Unita. Bearings were indicated and the column moved slowly towards the target area, Xangongo, where there was an airfield and brigade-sized military concentrations with tanks, armoured vehicles, field artillery pieces and surface-to-air missiles (SAMs).

We bundu-bashed (drove overland) for many hours until sometime before last light. Travelling through the African bush on the back of a truck was no fun at all. It was a hard, bumpy and dusty ride due to broken or missing spring blades on the trucks. Bear in mind that southern Angola had few developed roads, and the directive from the SADF high command was not to travel on established roads in enemy territory because of the risk of landmines. The dusty, spine-crunching trip felt like a lifetime but probably only lasted around eight or ten hours.

That night we were to lie up around 25–30 km from our planned ambush point. Very early the next morning we would start moving on foot to infiltrate silently towards Xangongo.

We prepared to move as one formation at sunrise, as we had to walk 20–30 km to a lying-up area close to the ambush point. We were then supposed to be in our ambush position the following morning before sunrise, which was at 05:48. Our formation included two former Angolan insurgents who had been caught and 'turned' at the detention facility at Fort Rev. They had been convinced to work for the Recces as informants and scouts in their former area of operations. These scouts were to lead us into our ambush position, as they were familiar with the area around Xangongo.

It was sweltering hot, and we were carrying heavy Bergens (large, sturdy backpacks) full of the weaponry and munitions needed to rev the enemy properly. Most of our Bergens weighed in excess of 80 kg; mine came in at around 84 kg, as I carried a 60 mm mortar pipe and first, second- and third-line mortar ammo, totalling 12 bombs. Our webbing and tactical gear with all the necessary military equipment, plus pistol, AK-47 rifle and eight 30-round magazines, weighed an additional 15–20 kg, which placed most of our loads well over 100 kg.

It was December in southern Africa, and in the fairly thick bush and humid conditions, some team members started to become dehydrated. We carried sufficient food and water for a five-day deployment, but with the heat and some unplanned additional walking, our water supplies started to run low. At one point a senior team member had to be infused with an intravenous (IV) saline drip by the medics on our team, as he was badly dehydrated. The IV bag did the trick, and the team soon moved on again.

We must have been walking for ten or twelve hours before we noiselessly went into our all-round lying-up formation. We were close to a large military complex and on foot, so we simply could not afford to be compromised. We were ready to get on with it and spring the ambush on the enemy. The night dragged on, and finally we received word that we should prepare to get moving.

We moved off in the early hours of the morning in a box formation, with Unita at our rear, and the two scouts leading the way. At some point the team leader (TL) and senior Recces realised that the two scouts had disappeared. The operators leading the mission concluded that the scouts must have panicked as we neared Xangongo. Should they be caught by their former comrades, they would most likely be tortured or executed for joining the enemy.

With the attack team now without their lead, we had to navigate to the ambush point. None of the team members had been here before as the mission timings had not permitted an advance reconnaissance, or recce, of the area. Bearings were worked out by the instructors and seniors and we navigated by compass and map. After two to three hours of moving silently through the bush, we arrived at the ambush spot between 04:15 and 04:45. Sometime earlier, the mortar attack team had peeled off to the north to set up their 81 mm pipes. They were assisted by the Unita fighters, who helped them carry the heavy baseplates, mortar pipes and substantial ammunition required for an 81 mm setup.

THE MIGHTY MORTAR TEAM

After leaving the rest of the force at the lying-up position, the mortar team navigated through the scrub in the dark, carrying the two 81 mm mortars and their personal combat equipment. According to Gary Yaffe, the mortar team eventually arrived at a point they were fairly sure was the right one – it was as close as they could get – and where Xangongo would be within range.

In preparation for this deployment, operational testing of 81 mm red phosphorus (RP) rounds had been conducted at the Kentron range at the Special Forces training area known as Hellsgate in northern Natal. Yaffe recalls: 'Not only did the new rounds have an increased range but the RP airburst rounds were quite impressive when raining down over Lake St Lucia during the testing phase. The mortar load for the operation was a 50/50 blend of good old-fashioned HE (high explosive) and the new RP rounds.'

The operation required that the mortar team attract the attention of the enemy by bombarding the Xangongo garrison. Yaffe continues: 'This action had to be completed with enough time for the mortar team to withdraw to the ambush site. We would then leave a trail heading generally southwards which was to pass through the killing zone of the ambush site before silently moving in to our positions with the rest of the 60 mm patrol mortars.

'The idea was that the enemy, having been fired on by our mortars, would be suitably pissed off and would launch a follow-up on the mortar team at first light. They would then be drawn into the killing zone of the ambush site, which would be initiated by the new operators, providing them with their initiation to enemy fire. I don't recall the total number of rounds carried, but someone later commented that is was around 80, split 50/50 with HE and RP rounds. This was more than enough to create the disturbance required.

'No GPS (Global Positioning System) devices were available those years yet, and navigation was done by compass and map in the dark of night. We realised that we had been navigating on foot in the dark for about ten kilometres and that we now had to set up our mortars and fire on a town that was still approximately five kilometres to our northwest.

'Sergeant Ian Strange was in charge of mortar pipe no 1 and I operated pipe no 2. We set the mortars up in the fairly soft southern Angolan soil and aimed them towards the town. The rest of the team assisted, and the mortar rounds were prepared and positioned for quick firing. We were going to fire one HE followed by an RP and continue until the ammunition was finished.

'When the first two rounds were fired, the sound burst through the quiet of the bush. They were followed by the rest of the mortars in rapid fire. The sound and the muzzle flash of the two pipes firing was definitely going to provide the enemy with an ideal starting point for their follow-up to eliminate us. Although we were not aware of it at the time, subsequent radio intercepts indicated that we had been successful in landing at least one of our mortars on a troop concentration, which resulted in 18 enemy forces killed in action.

'When the last rounds had been fired, both mortars had sunk into the soft soil and it took a considerable effort from the team, assisted by the Unita soldiers, to get them out before we could leave. With the dawn sky fast approaching, we moved off towards the ambush site. The mortar team was led by a Unita soldier who was supposed to know the way back towards the road that ran almost directly south from Xangongo.

'Unfortunately, or fortunately as it turned out, our team was led directly into the northern side of the ambush position past the northern stopper group. We then walked around the back of the position, past the killing zone and group, and then into position behind the killing group and near where the 60 mm mortar positions were set up. The ambush team had time to prepare shallow shell-scrapes but no extra time to provide the main mortar team with any prepared defensive positions.

'The enemy follow-up force must have made good time on our tracks and, if the ambush position had been a few kilometres further south, they may well have caught up with us before we could join the rest of the force. We had just arrived when the first contact was made between the Unita protection element and the enemy follow-up force. After a short but sharp contact the enemy withdrew and attempted what to them would have been a classic flanking movement of the engaged force, but was in fact a movement into the prepared kill zone of the ambush position. There was a lull in fire for almost half an hour and that's when the shit really hit the fan.'

THE AMBUSH TEAM

The rest of the team were briefed by the team leaders and instructors on where to deploy to ensure that we took up the right positions for the planned ambush. The stopper groups sneaked to the furthest ends of the ambush area, approximately 500 m on both sides of the main group, where they set up the claymore mines that would initiate, or perhaps end, the contact. Operators carrying machine guns, rocket-propelled grenades (RPGs) and 40 mm grenade launchers were shown where to lay down, behind their backpacks, with each soldier's arc of fire pointed out and explained to them.

Without making any noise, the entire team moved into place, just like we had been taught by the experienced instructor-operators during our combat training in the Caprivi in the months prior to this deployment. I formed part of the three-man light mortar team (not to be confused with the main attack mortar force that would lure the enemy forces to come looking for us). Our tasking was to use our 60 mm 'commando' mortar pipes – a crude Russian-made light mortar with a leather strap instead of bipod supporting device – to hit the enemy forces once they came looking for us. We were stationed 15–20 m behind the team members, who were lying prone facing the road, which was another 10–15 m in front of them.

I was on the left flank of the mortar team (south), with lance corporals Tjepeppa and Bezuidenhout (RIP) to my right. We were spaced approximately 15 m apart, and we dug shallow foxholes where we set up our mortar pipes and prepared our rounds. This involved turning the nose safety fuses to 'armed', and placing the rounds with the nose cones facing upward/forward, ready to be slid into the mortar pipe. We were just about ready when we heard heavy gunfire behind us. It was shortly after first light and the contact went on from 05:20 to 05:30. There was some radio chatter and verbal shouting going on, and we realised that an enemy patrol must have run into our force. Fortunately, the Unita fighters who had helped us carry the heavy mortars and ammunition cases were deployed on our six o'clock position, facing east, where they would have waited while the main force sprung our ambush on the enemy, and where they now acted as the rearguard for the formation.

There were some serious bursts of gunfire and it sounded as if the enemy was very close to us. I remember our TL, Major Jenkinson, shouting commands at us, the mortar element, to turn our pipes around and fire towards our rear, where the enemy had run into the Unita fighters at the back of our formation. I had no idea how far away the enemy was, but I realised they were close.

Using the commando mortar involves anchoring with your left foot (if right-handed), holding the pipe with your left hand and then sliding the mortar round into the pipe with your strong hand. I used the markings on the leather strap, which start at 100 m, increasing by 100 m denominations up to 800 m, and fired my first two HE rounds approximately 100 m to

The Crux

An operator using a 60 mm Russian commando mortar.

our rear. The Unita fighters were about 50 m behind us, thus placing the enemy forces anywhere from 20 to 50 m behind them.

Through the gunfire and explosions of the mortars, I heard Major Jenkinson shouting that our mortars were landing too far out and that we should bring the next salvo closer. I duly obliged and saw my fellow mortar team element raising their pipes to deliver a closer barrage of fire, hopefully on top of the enemy. We had to be careful not to land our fire on the Unita element, as the HE rounds apparently landed very close to their positions. Our salvo helped to drive the enemy forces away, as they split up and started circling around to both our left and southern flanks, with some moving to the right of our position (north).

The next thing, we saw Ian Strange charge towards one of the mortar operators shouting, '*Gooi, gooi!*' (Throw, throw). He then grabbed one of the 60 mm mortar pipes and operated it himself. After the second salvo, the shooting faded out a bit, and it seemed that the gunfire was now coming from my rear left. The enemy forces apparently thought that they had run into an ambush, and they were now circling around our left and right flanks, probably thinking they could hit us from the rear once they moved around us.

When the enemy broke contact at our rear and moved past our main ambush team's position on our left (south), a new contact occurred, initially with the Unita elements behind us. Then there was another tiff with the stopper team members on the left side of the ambush. Unbeknown to the enemy, they were not circling to our rear but were on their way to face the main ambush group head-on.

THE SOUTHERN STOPPER GROUP
Corporal Matthys 'Diff' de Villiers was with the southern stopper group that day. He explains how the day started with a crisis of a different kind: 'We had just finished setting up our positions and foxholes when Braam, with some urgency, whispered to Sergeant Major Bruce Laing, "Samajoor, Samajoor, I need to go and take a shit." He got permission to go and was told not to move too far back behind the stopper group.

'The rest of us took up our positions behind our rucksacks, weapons loaded, ready and facing the road. As the first rays of light broke through the African bush, we saw that our killing group was set up at an area where the main road had a secondary road that split the road into a Y-junction. We were about to inform the main ambush/killing group about the split in the road when all hell broke loose behind us.'

They were rather confused to hear a firefight behind them to their right rear since the action was supposed to be in front of them, where the enemy was supposed to move in from our right to left (north to south) from their stronghold in Xangongo. Diff takes up the story again: 'We jumped over our rucksacks and laid down behind them, now facing 180 degrees in the opposite direction than originally planned. We heard bullets flying overhead tearing into the trees, with leaves raining down on us, but we could not initiate fire as we did not know exactly what the deal was, and also knew that Braam was out there somewhere performing his morning rituals. I remember someone shouting, "Where the fuck is Braam?"

'The next thing we see through the dust and the rain of lead was a curious sight – Braam sprinting back towards his comrades, his overalls down on his ankles, his lily-white body with blackened face and hands from the black camo cream. He had his webbing in one hand and his rifle in the other, and scrambled back into his foxhole as quickly as he could with his clothing around his ankles. His white body stood out like a lighthouse on a dark night, but luckily, he did not eat any lead from the enemy and made it back to his position.

'Braam and I got into a tiff, but the sergeant major's voice quickly brought us back to reality. "Stop bickering and shoot, you bastards!" he screamed.

'The contact that broke out behind us quickly moved closer and around our left, as the enemy was under the impression that they were circling us and would now be attacking us from the rear. The enemy appeared metres away from us in the bushes. They advanced, took cover, shot at us and advanced even closer.

'The moment was too surreal for me to grasp. During all the months of training we shot at different targets, but never at a live target. I wanted to shoot but it seemed too easy. I shouted to our senior, "Samajoor, may I shoot?"

'And just like that the command came, calm and goal-oriented: "Fire at will."

'I let rip with bursts until smoke started coming from the PKM (Russian-made general-purpose belt-fed machine gun) I was manning, and by now I was relieved that I had carried 45 kg of PKM ammo in my Bergen. I remember thinking, "Surely it can't be that easy?"'

When the contact was over, they were ordered to withdraw. Only then did Lance Corporal De Beer have time to put on his overalls. He had got through all three firefights in his birthday suit.

Diff also discovered that his pack was wet, and upon quick inspection saw that bullets had punctured the outside, where the water bottles were packed. It was an important lesson: even a shallow foxhole with some type of cover in front of you (in this instance his Bergen) and a very low profile can indeed save your life in a firefight.

Diff's group now needed to move towards the kill group and merge with them to withdraw: 'For the first time in my life, I understood what the instructors had taught us throughout our Bush Warfare phase when they said to look through cover, not at it. It felt like I had developed an extra pair of eyes and that I could see through every shrub and bush. Nothing escaped me. Good training combined with a healthy dose of adrenaline and aggression works miracles for a soldier.

'Later, as we withdrew, Samajoor Bruce always remained calm, in control, and a perfect example for us youngsters, as did Samajoor Boats on the other end. They were professional soldiers with vast experience in bush warfare and other specialised operations.'

It was a lucky day for De Villiers because the next moment the enemy fired an RPG into the bushes surrounding them, but the rocket did not detonate. The projectile lay smouldering in the sand. It was a dud.

THE NORTHERN STOPPER GROUP

This group operated under the very experienced leadership of Warrant Officer (WO) Johan Botes. Boats explains that it was standard procedure to plan an operation after the Special Forces recruits had completed their Minor Tactics (Guerrilla/Unconventional Warfare) training phase. Chances were good that they could come under enemy fire during such an operation: 'Wooden targets do not shoot back during training and this also gave us an opportunity to gauge the students' reaction under enemy fire. This operation had all the elements required for a *vuurdoop* (baptism of fire). Navigation in the African bush without a GPS was not easy and had to be accurately calculated by the human factor to ensure success and the team's ability to survive. You had to trust your map-reading, compass training and navigational skills to navigate accurately. During the Recce training cycle the students are constantly taught, tested and evaluated on their navigational skills.'

Botes did not trust the two Angolans who had to lead the group to the target area. Consequently, as the group moved towards Xangongo he used his own dead reckoning (DR) map and navigation table, with compass bearings, timings, distance and outstanding features as a backup. This proved to be a wise move after the two scouts absconded during the night.

'After the firefight we had to get out of the area as quickly as possible,' he recalled, 'because the enemy was busy with a follow-up and the 122 mm Katyusha rockets got quite close to us. After the contact, my DR map assisted us to take a compass bearing to the RV with armoured vehicles that were on their way to extract us. Thank God we had no casualties.'

The northern stopper group team members were Christo Roelofse, Chris Serfontein, Mark de Wet and De Wet Human. De Wet recalls: 'I don't think I will ever forget that morning. The initial attack came from our side and I was the person who had put out the claymore mines. We were dug into our foxholes with a string attached to each individual so that we could warn each other of any possible danger. Then all of a sudden bullets started flying all over with dust and leaves everywhere.

'It was at this point that WO Boats looked me in the eyes and said we were going to have to move and that I had to go and recover the claymores. I do not think my legs ever felt that heavy and my sphincter muscles were sending some kind of Morse code I did not understand. I dragged myself out of that cosy foxhole and started my walk into the unknown. That is when WO Boats tapped me on the shoulder and said, "Come, I am with you." What a man and what a soldier WO Boats was!

'After repositioning, the stopper group took part in a firefight as some of the enemy were circling north and around the stopper group in their attempt to get behind us for a sweeping attack. All soldiers in our patrol and formation eventually were shooting at the enemy who ended up right in our sights as the whole team – stopper groups, killing group and mortarmen – faced the enemy head-on.'

Back to the rest of us in the killing group. Once the enemy forces completed their 180-degree movement around the ambush team, via the left and right flanks, they were facing us head-on (still under the impression they were attacking us from the rear). This was the third contact with enemy forces within a 50-minute period. Sometime during the initial phases of these contacts Major Jenkinson reported the actions back to the Tac-HQ via radio as follows: '*Kontak-kontak, lyk my hulle het lus vir ons – uit*' (Contact, contact, looks like they are spoiling for a fight – out).

The ambush team opened fire, and us mortarmen received instructions to redirect our fire to the enemy, who were approximately 150 m from our position on the opposite (west side) of the road. There was a lot of incoming and outgoing fire from all the weapons systems available, including mortars, RPG-7 rockets, PKMs, 40 mm grenade launchers and AK-47 assault rifles. I remember explosions close to the enemy and realised that our mortars were doing their job.

The next thing I registered was a very loud detonation to my left. An RPG-7 had slammed into a tree trunk about seven metres to my left, at a height of around two metres. The explosion rocked me where I was lying in my foxhole, and my ears were hurting quite badly. Although I was closest to the exploding rocket, I was fortunate not to have picked up shrapnel. Lance Corporal Wolfgang Tjepeppa was hit by a small piece of metal that penetrated his left shoulder. I saw him briefly touch his shoulder and there was a spot of blood on his overall, but he was fine and quickly returned to his mortar duties.

By this time everybody was shooting at the enemy, and they returned volleys of rifle fire, rockets and mortars. There were bullets flying thick and fast, over us, striking the trees and bushes, shredding leaves and twigs, which rained down on us like snowflakes.

During this contact I observed a few things that have stuck with me to this day. Major Jenkinson wanted to get on the radio to call for air support of sorts. With the volley of incoming fire Sergeant Jorrie Jordaan took a leaping dive, with his rifle, kit and all, to get to cover behind a tree where another Recce student was already lying. It only really supplied cover for one soldier but somehow it grew into enough cover for two.

To my right, Lance Corporal Barry Visser got up into the kneeling position, unloading his drum-fed 40 mm grenade launcher. The firepower and gait of this action was enough to send Arnold Schwarzenegger's *Terminator* character back to school! Another observation was Lance Corporal Nicky Fourie getting onto one knee and unleashing the 200-round belt from his PKM.

The mortar guys unloaded our second- and third-line mortar ammunition on the enemy, who were by then very close – our commando mortars had to be positioned almost upright in order to get the bombs on target. This was a proper contact and a good shootout.

Brian Harris recalls an incident that involved the late Ian Strange. As the enemy launched their frontal attack, an RPG flew past Ray Godbeer and Harris and exploded close behind them: 'Things were really heating up at that stage and I even recall a pencil flare being fired in our direction. Ian, despite the firing intensity from the front, stood up and went sprinting back, grabbed a 60 mm mortar pipe from one of the students. He must have thrown six to eight bombs in close and rapid succession on the fuckers. I clearly recall a lull in fire after his salvo.

'I also recall that Major Dave Jenkinson wanted to hang in there a little longer, and distinctly heard Ray Godbeer and one other instructor shouting, "*Majoor nou moet ons fokken onttrek!*" (Major, we need to get the fuck out of here and withdraw).

'We had pinned the enemy down, but they obviously also had radio contact with their forces at Xangongo, where a very strong brigade-sized force, with airfield, artillery and tanks, was stationed. At one point in time our group heard the rumble of armoured vehicles in the distance, with the sound moving closer to our ambush position on the road. It was time to get out of Dodge.'

We increased our fire rate, and somewhere between 06:30 and 07:00 the call came from Botes and Jenkinson to withdraw. Our force started with a hasty tactical withdrawal movement – moving in buddy pairs backwards while your buddies would lay maximum fire on the enemy, ie fire-and-movement backwards. After we successfully broke contact, we formed up in a box formation and teamed up with the Unita element that was covering our rear. Three of them were wounded but fortunately their wounds were not critical, so it was hastily treated with bomb-bandages (field dressings), and one was placed on an SADF brown canvas groundsheet with handles for carrying the wounded. The Unita soldiers carried their wounded comrade, and the entire group withdrew in a box formation.

We had been on the move in enemy territory for more than 56 hours, carrying heavy packs in the sweltering heat, and had had three contacts with enemy forces, who were now deployed in armoured cars to look for us. We withdrew by running at a slow pace for around an hour, until the TL indicated that we could stop, in our formation, for a quick water break.

The wounded Unita soldiers and the 1 Recce 81 mm mortar team were in the centre of the large box formation. The rest of us chose spots behind trees or shrubs, weapons facing outwards in case of another contact with the Unita element, and some of our PKM gunners covering our rear in the direction we had just travelled. Then we heard a new and frightening sound, which the older operators and Unita soldiers both immediately recognised – the 'shooooooshing' sound of Katyusha rockets, or 'Stalin Organ' – fired in the direction we had come from and where we had set up our ambush position (the enemy underestimated the speed at which we had withdrawn). Many years later, as a private military contractor (PMC) in Iraq, I would hear all too often the familiar sound of the Katyusha.

By then we were familiar with the sound of flying mortar rounds and direct rocket fire from RPG-7s, but the sound of a rocket flying indirectly through the air was a new one to us aspiring Recces. I soon learned that a mortar bomb comes down with a whistling sound, whereas a rocket emits a 'ssshhh' sound as the propellant burns and spins the projectile forward.

Although adrenaline made our bodies resilient, we were grateful for the break, as we were exhausted and dehydrated. I was positioned on the left flank and towards the rear of the formation, and my closest teammate, who would go down with me in a buddy pair, was Lance Corporal Braam de Beer, who started basic training with me. In addition to his AK-47, Braam was also carrying an M79 grenade launcher, known at the time as the *snotneus* (snotty nose). The weapon was strapped to the right side of his Bergen.

We found a spot with a tree and some long grass for cover and decided to go down there for our water break. I squatted with my Bergen towards the tree, intending to use it as a backrest to get out of the shoulder straps. I could then take up my defensive spot, lying down behind my pack and facing outwards, keeping a lookout for possible enemy movement. Anyway, that was the plan in my head …

After placing my backpack against the tree, I reached for my water bottle, which was in a pouch at the bottom of the pack. As I raised it towards my mouth with my right hand, I heard a loud 'ka-doenk' sound. The next thing, the water bottle was knocked out of my hand and I felt a hard punch to my solar plexus.

I faintly heard some of the squad guys shouting 'contact-contact'. I was slightly dazed but recovered quickly, before spotting the projectile that had knocked the daylights out of me lying in the sand in front of me. It was the golden, egg-shaped 40 mm HE grenade from Braam's M79 launcher!

It didn't take me long to work out what had happened. An M79 grenade launcher automatically cocks itself when the barrel is closed. In our contact and before the withdrawal, Braam had loaded the launcher with an HE round (thus carrying one-up) so he could readily fire the M79 if we hit a contact again. He had strapped the M79 with the barrel facing skywards next to his Bergen. The launcher remained loaded and cocked while we were running from the contact area. However, when we went down for our water break, a strap from his Bergen caught the trigger as he took his pack off, pulled tight and fired the weapon.

Fortunately, I was in the way of the projectile and only about three metres from my buddy when the HE round hit me. I say 'fortunately' for two reasons. First, I was too close for the HE projectile to arm, as the 40 mm rounds we used had an arming distance of around seven metres. Second, if I had not been in the way, the grenade would have armed, and it was pointing straight to the front of our formation where our leader element was. It could have been a disaster. Later, Staff Sergeant Ray Godbeer drily thanked me for getting in the way of a grenade that would otherwise have flown his way.

Jokes aside, I was very lucky that day, early on in the game, and thank the Good Lord I seemed to remain lucky throughout my entire career in the military and as a PMC.

My hand was hurting, and it later turned out that my pinkie and ring fingers on my right hand were broken. My chest was also on fire due to a hairline fracture of my sternum where the 40 mm HE round, travelling at 450 ft/sec, had hit me. At that point, the adrenaline that was coursing through my body helped a lot, but later on I hurt like a motherfucker.

Once the word was sent to the leader group that it was an accidental discharge, the formation took a ten-minute water break and Braam kindly offered me a couple of sips from his bottle.

Gary Yaffe moved towards me and asked me if I was okay. Looking at the grenade lying in front of me, he said, 'No man, look what you guys have done – now I will have to walk all the way back here after the ops to blow (destroy with explosives) the piece of UXO (unexploded ordnance).'

I gave a wry grin, but I was much too exhausted to offer a smile. Gary had the presence of mind to mark the HE round with some toilet paper so that those in the rear of the formation would not step on it.

The enemy kept firing rockets in a sequence, a battle plan of sorts, trying to pin us down. Fortunately, they did not think we could break out so far so quickly and the rockets exploded to our rear and our former ambush position. The qualified Recces in the team informed us that the distinctive sound came from a Katyusha, a mobile rocket launcher with rows of 122 mm launch tubes or pipes mounted on the back of a sturdy Ural truck. The Katyusha launcher can fire as many as four dozen warheads distances of more than nine kilometres in a single ten-second burst. During World War II German soldiers gave it the nickname 'Stalin Organ' because of the unmistakable (almost musical) wailing sound the rockets made when they were fired. Of course the name is meant ironically, as its effect is anything but music to the ears! Katyusha rockets carry a warhead of around 30 kg of HE inside a metal casing that is designed to splinter upon detonation, creating a devastatingly effective hail of shrapnel.

After being on the run for an hour, carrying heavy Bergens and equipment, we were told that the ops commander, Major Greyling, was on his way with a 101 Battalion Romeo Mike team to fetch us. I guess using the Casspirs, which packed serious firepower in the form of .50 calibre Browning machine guns (some even had 20 mm anti-aircraft guns mounted on top), was a better and quicker option than getting permission to scramble the helis, and perhaps our position was too close to the contact area for an aerial extraction.

After ten to fifteen minutes we set off at the best speed possible. It was a slog, as we were tired, hungry and quite dehydrated. We could still hear the enemy's motorised vehicles in the distance, frantically searching for us. The small broken finger on my right hand and the part of my chest where the grenade had hit me were on fire. My heels also hurt badly, a result of the physical abuse I'd had to endure during Special Forces training, without receiving proper medical care.

After about another two hours of rapid movement, we heard the diesel engines of 101 Battalion's Romeo Mike Casspirs. It was the sweetest sound. Our formation went down in an all-round defensive configuration while the TL talked the Romeo Mike team in to our position. A smoke grenade was deployed, and we were elated when we saw the Casspirs breaking through the bushes.

These light armoured personnel carriers were backbone equipment for a few highly specialised and deadly fighting units, including 101 Battalion, Koevoet (the South West African Police's counterinsurgency unit) and some 5 Recce teams, who used them in vehicle operations in enemy territory, mainly for base attacks, where speed and firepower during an attack was essential. The Unita element also had to catch a lift with us to just north of beacon 16, so it was a tight fit. The Romeo Mike team started moving and for the first time in 48 hours we could finally allow ourselves a minor sigh of relief.

We were heading back to Fort Rev, next to the Ondangwa airfield. Puma choppers were sent to collect us from the area north of beacon 16. The Unita soldiers stayed behind, as some of their own vehicles would be sent to collect them.

It was almost 96 hours from when we first deployed in the Puma helicopters to when we arrived back at Fort Rev. I was so tired that the next few hours are a bit of a blur, but I do remember how someone taped my broken pinkie to my ring finger. As part of the demobilisation after the operation, squad equipment such as mortars, RPG-7s, machine guns and sensitive equipment such as radios, night-vision gear, claymores, grenades and medical bags were secured. Team members cleaned their AKs and machine guns, and I cleaned my mortar pipe before handing it in to be stored.

While this was going on, some guys nibbled on ration packs (rat-packs) and a lot of liquids were consumed. We started with water and Cokes but soon progressed to a brew or two ... And then of course everyone had a long shower, because it took forever to scrub ourselves clean of the 'black-is-beautiful' camouflage cream we had put on our faces, necks, forearms and hands. It often required a couple of scrubbing sessions to get it all out of your pores, as it stuck to the skin like glue.

We were exhausted but also thrilled because we had taken part in our first operation in foreign territory and behind enemy lines. It was a serious contact with the enemy, and we were happy to still be alive. I closed my eyes and thanked my Creator for sparing my life. I took some time to reflect on the events of the past four days, and deep inside I knew that one way or another a career in soldiering would work out for me.

Shortly after the operation, the intelligence section intercepted enemy radio chatter that led us to believe that apart from the 19 enemy soldiers killed in Xangongo by the main mortar team, our ambush team had killed about another 17 enemy soldiers. Furthermore, they had sustained at least 30 or more wounded. Later radio intercepts indicated that the forces in and around Xangongo beefed up their defences as they did not think that an attack force could get so close to their stronghold on foot. In military terms, this was a successful operation and the best way for us youngsters, and some of the older soldiers who were part of our Special Forces training group, to be baptised as Recces.

During Ops Nigel it became clear to me what the Recce *ou manne* brought to the mission. Their experience was invaluable. The mortar team operators from 1.1. Commando did an outstanding job, and the experienced instructors from 1 Recce's training wing, 1.2 Commando, brought calmness and strong leadership to a team of mostly very young men. These Recce operators led by example, and this made a lasting impression on me.

Good leadership and experience makes the world of difference in a combat situation. I have seen this throughout my career, first in the military and afterwards in the private security sector. These qualities particularly held true when we were forced to fall back on our soldiering

Group photo before Operation Nigel.

skills when things went south in places like Iraq, Afghanistan, Libya and other war zones where former Recces worked as PMCs.

I believe that from the mid-1970s to the end of the Bush War in 1989, 1 Reconnaissance Regiment, or 1 Recce, was one of the best Special Forces units in the world. This sentiment was often silently confirmed by the global special operations forces environment. As the mother unit, 1 Reconnaissance Commando spawned two more units in the late 1970s – 4 Recce and 5 Recce. Very soon these regiments also morphed into some the best units in their respective specialist fields.

2

BASICS – THE RECCE WAY

*Discipline is the soul of an army. It makes small numbers formidable;
procures success to the weak, and esteem to all.*
– George Washington

The Recces came into being in 1972 at the SAI School in Oudtshoorn, after the legendary Colonel Jan Breytenbach assembled a squad of 12 men, himself included, who became known as the 'Dirty Dozen'. He recruited some of the finest soldiers of his generation.

For the next decade, recruitment for Special Forces was a fairly secretive affair. Recruits were drawn from the ranks of the SADF, with the bulk coming from 1 Parachute Battalion and various infantry units, and some men joining from the Engineer Corps (Sappers) and Intelligence community. Back then you had to be 21 and to have served at least three years in the SADF before you could apply to join the Special Forces. This meant that you had to be a short-term or Permanent Force member, as conscripts were not allowed to join the Special Forces straight from school and without a few years' experience in the army.

However, because of growing demand for Special Forces soldiers, in the early 1980s the Department of Defence allowed the unit to recruit young men who were doing their national service. They would do their basic training in the Special Forces, and should they pass 'Recce basics' they would be eligible to attempt the Recce selection course. In the 50-year history of the South African Special Forces, this happened on only five occasions.

The first time the Special Forces offered a Basics course was in 1982. The second time was in 1984 when they even allowed civilians, or 'civvies', who had not yet done their national service to do their basic training in a Recce unit. The third occasion was in 1986, which was when I signed on.

On the eve of my departure for military duty in January 1986, my dad and I eventually managed to get to the train station after our 'celebration' session. I won't easily forget the train journey, as I had a hangover and headache from hell. The Infantry School corporals who were accompanying us barked out orders and were intent on keeping us occupied. They told us recruits to line up in the hallway outside the train compartments, squatting with our backs an inch from the cabin wall, legs at 90 degrees and horizontal at the knee, with our arms stretched forward at 90 degrees, while we had to crunch our hands into a balled fist and open again, repeatedly.

Then there was the universal troop-torturing exercise – the dreaded push-up. It does not matter how young, strong or fit you are; your legs and arms eventually conk out when you can't handle the fire in your muscles and ligaments anymore. We were ordered, in very strong language, by an over-zealous corporal, to hit the deck – more push-up time! And here your upper body muscles and shoulders would eventually burn and hurt even more. Then it was back to the squatting position, rotating back to push-ups, and so it went, without stopping, all the bloody way to Oudtshoorn.

On the train we met other school leavers from further north in the country who had boarded the 'army train' at various locations, and I also met other guys from Bloemfontein who had been at different schools than me. De Wet Human was a Bloemfontein recruit who would become a good buddy of mine. I also befriended Barry Visser, who would become my close buddy and party partner when we were NCOs in 1 Recce, as well as a lifelong friend.

Barry's father, Major Nick Visser, was a Recce himself, and had been involved with the unit since its inception. Major Visser was described as a 'man among men' by the seniors of his era. Sadly, he had died in an aircraft incident in Angola in 1977. (Many decades later my father passed away on the exact same date, which is also my mother's birthday.)

Barry followed in his dad's footsteps by rising through the ranks and becoming the OC of 4 Special Forces Regiment, based at Langebaan on the west coast. He went on to Speskop in Pretoria, where he serves in a senior command capacity to this day. The Vissers were the second of a few father/son members who both became qualified Recces.

We arrived at the station in Oudtshoorn and were taken to the Infantry School in the back of five-ton Samil trucks. By now we thought that we had an idea of what an *opfok* (army slang for a really hard physical training [PT] session) meant, but clearly these infantry corporals and lieutenants had other ideas …

From the moment the troop-carrying trucks stopped, we were chased around like it was nobody's business: we had to run everywhere, and were ordered to do push-ups and other physical exercises for just about anything – even just for looking the wrong way at a corporal or lieutenant.

The first stop was the barber shop, where my longish hair ended up on the floor in minutes. Then we were sent to the stores where we were issued with so-called browns, the standard military fatigues of the day. (The army's colour of choice was referred to as 'nutria brown'. All clothing, gear, vehicles and apparel were this kind of mud brown.) Our kit included all the clothing and footgear you would need in the army: leather boots, a pair of flat running shoes with thin soles, two sets of trousers with large belt holes and side pockets, two short-sleeve shirts with collars and front pockets, two T-shirts, two vests, a brown military-style jersey with patches on the elbows, two brown overalls (in which we did most of our training), three sets of underpants and socks, a green beret with *bokkop* (springbok head) insignia, a *boshoed* (field hat), a webbing belt that fit the loops on your trousers, two running shorts and a roll-up shaving bag to keep your toothbrush and toothpaste, bar of soap, razor blade and shampoo. Note the absence of a comb or hairbrush (thanks to the buzz cut given to us by the army barber).

Next up we were assigned to our companies; I was placed in Charlie Company, or C Coy. We were shown the bungalows (barracks) where we would sleep. Each man was assigned a small iron single bed with two sheets, a thin grey army blanket, a pillow with a pillowcase, a small metal cupboard and a *trommel*, a rectangular green-painted metal box with a lockable lid – for storing your gear. We were issued with a *varkpan*, a silver metal tray into which our food would be dished up, and a *pikstel*, a set of metal cutlery that fitted together.

Basics – The Recce Way

Our beds had to be made, repeatedly, to square perfection. Uniforms had to be ironed to military crispness, and boots had to be polished to a level where you could just about see your reflection. Furthermore, our berets had to be broken in so they would slant towards the right ear at the precise and correct angle. The *bokkop* had to sit above your left eye, and the brim of the beret two fingers above your eyebrows.

Our boots were made of hard, tough leather that was not easy to break in. Someone in the squad mentioned that you could break them in more quickly by soaking them in warm water before wearing them. This advice worked, even if it took a while. During the breaking-in process, and before our boots adapted to our feet, we had to endure blisters and aching feet as a result of all the running around and marching we had to do.

A week or ten days must have passed before we were told that the pre-selection team from the Recces would soon be at the base to check us out and decide who would move on to do the Basics course at the 1 Recce base on the Bluff in Durban.

Pre-selection for the Special Forces mainly concerns your medical state and fitness levels. The Special Forces training wing, or Special Forces School, operated out of the 1 Recce base. The training wing had an OC and a senior warrant officer, with different sections or 'wings' run by ex-operators who rotated through the Special Forces School every few years. Instructors for certain courses were drawn from 1, 4 and 5 Recce, and each instructor would report to the Special Forces School for the duration of the course, after which they returned to their respective unit.

Over the next couple of days, the Special Forces selection team, consisting of Major Kobus Human and Major Frans van Dyk, ran a number of trials to sift through the hundreds of recruits. Initially, we thought that only those who had indicated on their call-up papers that they wanted to try out for the Special Forces selection would be put through these physical tests. Then someone higher up decided that the entire new intake at the Infantry School – around 700 young white males, mostly fresh from high school – had to do the tests. They had no say in the matter, because when the army tells you to do something, you don't argue.

After you passed your medical check-up you had to pass a few basic physical exercises. These included: a 15 km route march with a 30 kg backpack in two hours; a 5 km run in 20 minutes; eight pull-ups (military style, straight up, no swinging, chin above the bar, no stopping); 80 sit-ups in two minutes; 50 push-ups (again, in military style with straight back and chest or chin touching the ground with no stops); 20 x 20 m shuttle runs in two minutes; a 200 m *skaapdra* (fireman's carry), meaning you had to transport a person the same weight as you on your shoulders in one minute; and 85 *hurkskoppe* (squat/flutter kicks) in one minute.

You were also put through a Cybex Isokinetic Test, which measures the maximum strength of a joint throughout its available range of motion. You also had to pass the Dynavit Test, which measures the strength in your legs and hips, and is often used by skiers and other athletes.

The pre-selection tests were not that hard to pass if you had a fair to good level of fitness and strength and could withstand the temptation to stop when your body was hurting a bit. This also put you in a military-medical rating category of G1K1, which meant you were medically and physically fit and able to serve in the infantry, and hence to be sent to do battle for your country.

After the final bunch of troops had gone through the above tests, around 120 recruits passed and were accepted to do their basics at 1 Recce. It felt like a first, small victory, and I remember how proud I was for the next day or two, until we were trucked to Oudtshoorn station to be put on a train to Durban. At that point I discovered that with our selection for basics came a new level of *rondfok* (getting fucked around) and PT.

The corporals and instructors reminded us that if you wanted to become a Recce, you had to expect to get stuffed-up more, and harder. The train trip took around two days, and we were grilled by the corporals and lieutenants from the minute we left Oudtshoorn. We were supposed to stop briefly in Bloemfontein, and De Wet devised a plan to get us some alcohol. He told the corporals that it was his birthday and that he was going to receive a gift from his girlfriend Melanie, at the station. She would gift-wrap six cans of beer and hand it to him when we stopped. The plan worked, but De Wet had to pay a bribe to one of the corporals who got wind of the scheme, so he lost two beers in the process. He kindly shared his beers with me and Barry van Aswegen, another Bloem trooper, and we finished them eagerly. I was 17 at the time and still not legally allowed to drink, especially not in public spaces such as on a train.

As if we hadn't endured enough on the train journey, it was more of the same on arrival at Durban station, with orders to do squats, push-ups and short sprints. Finally, trucks arrived and we each loaded our *balsak*, the brown duffle bag containing all our clothing and gear, into the back.

The Bluff military complex is around 15 km from the city centre, around Durban's port – the largest in southern Africa, and South Africa's main importation point for oil, gas and container goods in transit. After half an hour's drive the trucks slowed down and somebody informed us that we were close to the Bluff military area. This consisted of a lighthouse, the navy's main ammunition storage facility – mostly for its strike craft and for the naval guns on the Bluff – a limited amount of government housing and the 1 Recce base. The Recce facility included the 'old base', with a rugby field and the nearby para-stores, where various items of equipment were stored, including the unit's rigid-hulled inflatable boats, or RHIBs. The 'new base', around one kilometre north of the old base, was the unit's HQ.

As the trucks cleared the entrance gate, I stuck my head out and got my first glimpse of the 1 Recce base. That image remains with me to this day. There were a lot of shrubs and bushes, which flourished in the subtropical coastal climate, and a white signboard with the warning 'Careful, troops running' in black letters. After a few minutes the trucks turned right into the old base complex, where there were a number of buildings and barrack blocks.

The lieutenants and corporals who had escorted us from Oudtshoorn were not our designated basics instructors, and they were sent back to their units after handing us over to our course trainers. On the Bluff, six lieutenants and another six corporals from the Infantry School took over our bunch of raw young recruits. We were ordered to get out of the trucks and '*Tree aan!*' (Get into formation). We were then divided into five platoons – I was placed in platoon 3 – and shown to our barracks, where the same standard items as at the Infantry School were awaiting us.

We were set to start basic training the Infantry School way, under the watchful eyes of qualified Special Forces operators and Recce course leader Major Dave Jenkinson. His right-hand man was Lieutenant Rob Jennings, another product of the Infantry School's officer course. Rob would later join us for the Special Forces selection after he assisted in presenting the Basics course and the Infantry Individual course, which dealt with infantry platoon tactics and the use of platoon weapons.

The senior NCO chosen to make our lives miserable, and to ensure that the corporals kept their feet firmly on the gas (us), was Staff Sergeant Chris Oosthuizen, a career infantryman renowned for his bull's-horn moustache. We kept our Infantry School clothing, boots, helmet, etc, which we had to pack carefully in a metal locker.

One of the first new and really exciting military pieces of equipment issued to us was our assault rifles. We had to run to the weapons store at the 'new' 1 Recce base where we were issued with an R4 assault rifle, six magazines and a military rifle-cleaning kit rolled up in a canvas bag. The R4 is a South African-produced version of the Israeli Galil assault rifle, which in turn is based on the faultless AK-47 assault rifle's working parts. The major difference is in the calibre, as the R4 is chambered to take a 5.56 x 45 mm (.223) bullet instead of the AK-47's 7.62 x 39 mm. We were also issued with green 'Niemoller' webbing to carry our mags and water bottle, with a few pouches for other military equipment.

There was no downtime, and we were kept busy 14 to 16 hours a day. We walked absolutely nowhere, instead running in a squad wearing overalls, leather boots, wide canvas webbing belt and an SADF M63 *staaldak* (steel helmet). The helmet had an inner plastic liner, and was kept in place by a canvas-and-leather strap contraption that hardly ever worked. The damn helmet was always moving around on your head and hanging over your eyes. And of course we had to run holding our assault rifles in the high-ready position.

The old base was exactly one kilometre from the troop mess hall inside the 1 Recce base, which is not far, but it caught up with you after a day of being drilled and fucked-up from sunrise until well after sunset. Durban has a very humid climate, and the worst months are between January and the end of March. By the time we arrived at the mess hall, our overalls were sopping wet. What followed next was the stuff of nightmares. A pull-up (chin) bar was erected right at the entrance to the mess hall, and us basics troopers had to earn our meals by doing pull-ups the military way – straight arms and body, chin well above the bar, straight down again and with absolutely no swinging.

We started with eight chin-ups before each meal, and over a number of weeks worked our way up to 20 per session. If you got tired, or if you 'gypo'd' (tried to cheat by swinging), you would be sent to the back of the queue again, to start from zero, regardless of how many 'good' ones you'd managed to execute before your arms and upper body conked out. Therefore, towards the middle of our basic training we did a minimum of 60 pull-ups a day in order to qualify for three meals per 24-hour cycle. If your efforts were not 100 per cent correct you could easily end up doing 80-plus chin-ups a day.

We were all slim, fit, strong and very athletic, but this was still a tall order, especially after a long, hot and physically taxing day. By the time you completed your running and pull-ups, your body would try to cool itself by giving off buckets of sweat. I will never forget how the salty drops would flow from my head and face onto the plate, to the extent that the cabbage and cauliflower seemed to be floating in perspiration.

From the time you arrived at the mess hall you had 30 minutes to pass your pull-up torture, stand in line to be served your food, eat it and then fall into a squad again to run back to the old base to continue whatever training/discipline/physical exercises were awaiting you. Our corporals revelled in our torture and anguish, while we battled to do the requisite number of pull-ups in front of the mess hall. But justice is a bastard. A few months later some of them joined us for the Infantry Individual course when we were busy with our final preparations for the Special Forces selection, and there they battled to keep up with us troopers when it came to PT, especially when it was time for the chin-up bar. The old adage that 'practice makes perfect' rings true in most scenarios.

In week one we had our first lectures on military security, subversion, physical security of a military base, securing of documents, etc. During the initial lectures we were taught who the 'enemy' was, and thus began,

Rifleman De Wet Human, Corporal Coenie 'Tropics' de Jong and Braam de Beer during basics.

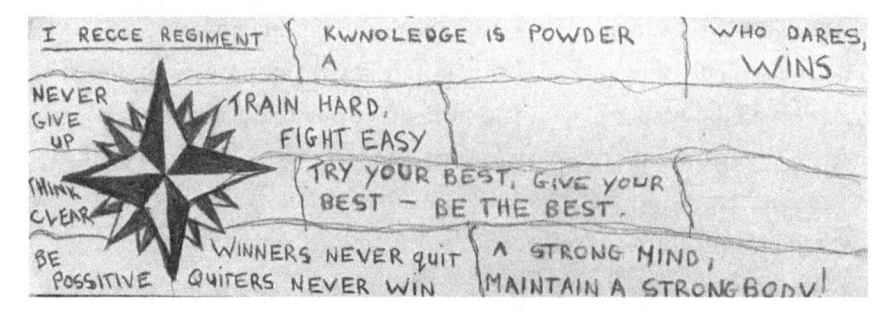

A bookmark made by the author during basic training.

De Wet 'Wetta' Human doing *opfok* rifle PT.

rightly or wrongly, the indoctrination and programming of our young minds. At the time it did not matter much to me who the enemy was. I was there to be trained as a weapon of war and then to be pointed in the direction of the enemy, with a set of mission orders, to defend my country and to disseminate (destroy) our foes, regardless of who they were.

Over the next few weeks, the lectures included understanding unit standing orders (which were further broken down into different parts), dress regulations and understanding how orders were given to a soldier by his commander. Most of our teaching took place not in the lecture room, but on the periphery of the rugby field in semi-open classrooms. One side of these wooden structures was completely open, and the other three sides were constructed from planks with wooden seats on stilts for the students. The lieutenant or corporal giving the lecture would have a blackboard on an easel with some white pieces of chalk, with perhaps a paper flipchart with different-coloured Koki pens. During these lectures we were taught the principles of patrolling, formations, fieldcraft, observation techniques and many other infantry subjects.

The regimental sergeant major (RSM) of 1 Recce at the time was WO1 PP 'Pep' van Zyl, a mountain of a man and a true legend. The 'Samajoor' (Afrikaans army slang for warrant officer) had started his career in the 1960s at 1 Parachute Battalion, where he quickly developed a reputation as a hard but fair soldier who knew how to sort out unruly troops. However, he gained the respect of troops, NCOs and officers alike. WO Pep was also instrumental in the formation of 32 Battalion in the mid-1970s, and joined the Recce formation in 1980 where he took over as RSM at 1 Recce from WO Trevor Floyd (RIP), another legend who was one of the founding members of the Recces.

Our morning parade and drilling rituals took place at the old base, mostly on the rugby field and also around the old buildings itself. The members of 1 Recce held their parades on the open area behind the HQ building at the new base, where we were being blooded in the art of drilling.

One morning, either on the way to the unit or returning after breakfast, two of our members of the 'soutie' (English-speaking) squad had their first run-in with the RSM. Samajoor Pep was holding his pace-stick (a long, hinged, brass-tipped stick, used to measure the pace of marching troops) as it was around parade time for the Permanent Force members of 1 Recce. Craig Leppan and Mark de Wet were so intimidated by the RSM's squat, mountain-man demeanour that Craig decided to salute him. This was the ultimate insult to this weathered, no-nonsense soldier. In his famously deep, thunderous voice, he bellowed that he was 'not a bloody officer' and that he 'worked for his money'!

At the time, we were only wearing the plastic inner liners of our M63 helmet, also known as a 'doiby' (the helmet without the outer steel shell but with the chinstrap). The next thing, he took his pace-stick and smashed it over Craig's doiby, causing it to crack open, while shouting a number of obscenities. Mark was under the impression that he had escaped the wrath of the RSM, but before he knew it he had been hammered over the head with the pace-stick as well, and so hard that his doiby also cracked.

The RSM told him that the famous Anglo-Boer War general Christiaan de Wet, would turn in his grave if he had to hear someone with such an Afrikaans surname speaking English! That evening their platoon corporal, Diff de Villiers, had to buy a '*strafdop*' (round of drinks) for all the NCOs in the pub for allowing these English-speaking members of his platoon to work up the RSM to such an extent.

At the main unit, like any other military unit, there was a duty room with an officer and NCO on duty after hours and on weekends to deal with general unit standing orders, for example ensuring that guards were on duty, patrols were conducted and all was well within the unit lines. The old base within 1 Recce was not permanently in use, but when there was a basics group stationed there, the instructors and course personnel had to man a duty room at the old base to keep an eye on the troops in the barracks, and to ensure that these youngsters did not interfere with the main unit's activities or personnel.

During these initial weeks of our basic training, Corporal Coenie de Jong was appointed the platoon corporal of platoon 4. He was on duty one night when two troops who later turned out to be regular *kakbakkers* (shit-stirrers) had to wash his scrambler motorbike. Braam de Beer and De Wet

'Wetta' Human duly washed the bike, but when Coenie went on his rounds they decided to lift the bike onto a desk in the duty room like some kind of trophy. Unluckily for them and their corporal, the NCO on duty at the main base was a senior Recce operator who duly did his rounds, including going by the old base, where he came across this spectacle. He scolded De Jong, who in turn took it out on the two troublemakers.

Corporal De Jong's nickname among his men was Tropics, after a nightclub in Langebaan (where 4 Recce was based) that he frequented, since he had grown up in the area. In our bungalows the walls were painted with motivational slogans such as 'Winners Never Quit; Quitters Never Win', 'Train Hard, Fight Easy' and others. The same two *kakbakkers* then got hold of some paint, and in a less frequented spot in their bungalow came up with a slogan of their own, something to the effect of: 'Cpl Tropics could not make them any stronger, but he sure did make them tougher.'

During bungalow inspection one morning, the beady eye of Staff Sergeant Oosthuizen caught a glimpse of this new and unusual slogan and he inquired who Tropics was. The cat was out of the bag and Braam and Wetta had to wash Corporal Tropic's motorbike a good number of times again. The upside to all of this was that the corporal's motorbike shone most of the time, especially when it was parked close to the old base duty room, in case some of the operators from the unit came by to see what the troopers and their instructors were up to.

One of Corporal Tropics's favourite ways of sorting a trooper out was to make him do 50 push-ups with his hands on his helmet. It was not unusual at all to *sak* (go down) for 50 push-ups, as we were doing it day in and day out, many times a day, but doing a push-up while balancing your upper body weight on your smooth and round helmet was a bit trickier. Often the manoeuvre went awry and then you had to start all over again.

The instructors also constructed a metal clock that had only one hand, which was manually moved from one position to the next each time a trooper made a wrong move. When the hand reached 12 the entire basics group would get *'opfok'* PT. We feared and dreaded the damn clock that could not even keep time but that led to our pain and misery!

Our PT sessions were hard and frequent. Whatever the troops at the Infantry School and the paratroopers at the Parachute Battalion did, we had to do harder, faster and further. By now the reader should be aware of our pull-up talents (or lack thereof, in the case of some troopers). Other PT included running 2.4 km, 5 km, and 10 km all the bloody time.

Then there was the infamous 'rifle PT', an exercise that Lieutenant Rob Jennings excelled at dishing out. He found some sadistic pleasure in giving it to us long and hard. The R4 rifle weighs slightly over four kilograms, which might not seem much, but try holding the darn weapon by its barrel and buttstock, arms straight in front of you, or with raised arms above your head for hours on end … It quickly starts to hurt, causing a burning sensation that resembles an open flame being sprayed with flammable liquid.

This piece of machinery could never leave your side and had to be carried around *everywhere*. This makes sense, since a soldier on duty needs to be trained to have his weapon at his side. But during basics the bloody thing had to accompany you to the bathroom, toilet, everywhere. You even had to sleep with the cold piece of metal as if it were your newfound girlfriend. But we couldn't complain; it was a matter of 'you're in the army now'.

To this day I still cannot understand why we were not allowed to have a sling on our assault rifles. It would have made matters so much easier, and would have freed our hands to get on with other tasks instead of clutching the weapon in one or the other hand. Most conscript infantrymen and other two-year national servicemen were never allowed a sling on their weapons. Even when they deployed operationally to the border, the basic rule stood: have your weapon in your hand at all times. What a load of crock. In the Special Forces we fixed slings of all kinds on our weapons, and most were modified by the individual users to suit their needs.

Other PT sessions included '*paal-PT*' (pole PT), which entailed five or fewer troops having to carry a ten-metre wooden pole weighing around 50 kg. All sorts of torture could be extracted from the pole: doing military press exercises above the head, doing sit-ups with the pole across your chest, running with it on your shoulder, squats, arm curls, the lot. The thing about *paal-PT* is that it requires small teams to operate together

Basics – The Recce Way

Mark de Wet and DEM Laubscher doing pole PT, Dukuduku.

in unison to make it work. The trouble starts when one or more of the troops get tired and start to lag, making it harder on the rest of the squad. It doesn't take long for resentment to build up towards the weaker links in the squad as the stronger guys have to carry more of the load to escape the wrath of the corporals or lieutenants.

Then there was the dreaded 'marble', which was a square piece of concrete weighing 25 kg. This damn man-made rock was designed to break a trooper's will and spirit, or to transform him into a tough, strong and enduring soldier. The marble was used for all the normal kinds of strength exercises as with *paal-PT* – military press, bench press, arms curls, squats, sit-ups, running around with it on your shoulder and then putting it into a rucksack to be carried around during route marches.

The marble broke the skin, tore muscles, ripped tendons and sometimes caused grievous bodily harm when it was not handled with respect. Do not be fooled by the weight of 'only' 25 kg; it weighs a ton when the reps are non-stop and the PT is day in, day out. Somehow the instructors came up with a plan to create a shorter running route for a quick *opfok*. It was decided that we troopers had to bundu-bash a route, carrying the damn marble, through the dense vegetation and shrubs behind the instruction huts on the eastern side of the rugby field.

On top of that, all the PT sessions were a competition of sorts between the lieutenants and corporals to see whose platoon performed the best. One day towards the end of February, when Durban was at its most humid and hottest, one of the troops keeled over during a heavy PT session. He started pissing blood and ended up being diagnosed with heat exhaustion. The instructors' answer to this was not to slow down the PT but rather to make us down litres of water from our water bottles, in front of an instructor, to the point that some troops started vomiting. What a solution!

Then there were the inter-platoon boxing matches, where we pummelled the daylights out of each other. Fortunately, boxing was a sport I enjoyed and had been practising since a very young age.

Despite the hardship, a number of us actually took some pleasure in pushing ourselves physically and mentally. We were super-fit and embraced all the hardships the instructors could throw our way. Although we did not realise it at the time, by enduring these kinds of tortures we ended up having the right attitude and mindset to become Recces, which was still my dream.

While the PT was gruelling, it could be performed by fit and strong young men such as one would find in the paratroops, infantry units and other specialised warfare elements. However, the one area where the Recces really had to excel in was the ability to walk great distances carrying very heavy packs and gear.

Keep in mind that in the 1970s, 1980s and the early 1990s, South Africa was a pariah state due to its apartheid policy. Therefore, virtually none of the African countries where Special Forces operations took place would give their consent for the South African military to use their airspace or territory to establish logistics or forward operating bases to support their teams. The Special Forces teams were on their own once they left South African or South West African territory. When deployed in enemy territory, the Special Forces teams often had to cover long distances on foot and were deployed for weeks, and sometimes months, on end, having to survive and resupply themselves from their Bergens.

The weight of these large backpacks would range from 75 kg to well over 110 kg in the case of the 'small team' operators, known in international

Basics – The Recce Way

Two legends: Neves Mathias and Andre Diedericks with 110 kg packs.

military terms as 'long-range reconnaissance patrols' or 'deep-penetration recon teams'. Some of the older Recces referred to an exclusive club called the Gunston 500, to which quite a few of them belonged. At the time, the Gunston 500 was South Africa's premier surfing competition, held in Durban during the holiday season. The Recce version of the Gunston 500 did not refer to a good ride on a surfboard, though, but to the fact that club members had covered 500 km on foot on an operation or in continuous follow-up missions.

Let's just consider this for a minute: imagine having to walk stealthily in hot, humid conditions through the African bush in enemy territory, where running into the local population could compromise your operation and get you captured or killed. You have no close military support for weeks on end, you get very little quality sleep and you have to survive on meagre rations or live off the land, while covering 500 km on foot, with packs and tactical gear weighing well over 100 kg! Whenever I see television programmes about how some or other personality tries to survive in a jungle or on an island in apparently rough conditions, I cannot

The eastern side of the Bluff, looking towards the Indian Ocean.

The perimeter fence and running trail at the old base, the Bluff.

help but smile. To me, the old warrior soldiers in whose giant footsteps we were to follow were the ultimate hardmen and true survivors. They were ordinary men with extraordinarily strong minds and exceptional endurance capabilities.

From the very first week in basics, aside from all the other tough PT and *opfoks*, we had to take part in route marches carrying packs that became increasingly heavy. During the first half of our basic training we did route marches around the Bluff military complex, which is essentially a gigantic sand dune covered in lush green vegetation and criss-crossed with footpaths.

We started with five-kilometre marches and backpacks weighing 30 kg. For the roughly eight weeks we were stationed there, the distance and the weight increased each week by increments of five, if memory serves me right. When we moved to the 1 Recce training base at Dukuduku in northern Natal, the marches in the vast woods of Zululand became even longer. Carrying a heavy backpack while moving fast under pressure tires the body in a way that messes with your mind. It takes a strong will to live through the pain inflicted on your shoulders, spine, hips, legs and feet.

It did not take us long to figure out that guys with large muscles struggled with this form of endurance activity. We had some *kragvarkies* (literally, power pigs) in our squads who had made the initial pre-selection tests in Oudtshoorn at the Infantry School. But soon enough they started falling short of the required times and goals set for these route marches. I remember how one big strong dude who had national colours in bodybuilding – the type who could walk around like he was carrying a piano under each arm – broke down during one of the longer marches. He actually cried and complained that his body was not built for this type of shit. Then there was another trooper, nicknamed 'Rambo', who had strong arms and a deep voice and an attitude to match. He also ended up crying like a baby in the humid woods of Zululand during a really challenging route march.

In general, the short and stocky or thinner but athletically built guys fared much better with this particular type of torture than the Rambos of this world. I saw this throughout my military and PMC careers: large, overly muscled men can seldom endure a lot of pain. Their overall endurance threshold seems to be lower due to the muscle bulk they carry around, which also makes them more prone to injuries and exhaustion, especially on a meagre diet with no protein shakes, and particularly in an escape/evasion/survival scenario.

One of the troopers I later befriended kept score of all our route marches and worked out that during our basic training we walked around 600 km with backpacks weighing from 25 to 50 kg. And this was just the warm-up phase of our preparation for the selection course. The pressure increased during the route-march exercises – the final preparatory phase before tackling one of the toughest Special Forces selection processes in the world.

We had very little downtime, but Sundays were usually reserved for church service, which allowed you an extra hour's sleep if you were crafty enough. Then there was some personal time out if you had not accrued a 'dirty' or two. When a trooper messed up during the week and owed an instructor a stuff-up session that could not be done during the already long hours of training from Mondays to Saturdays, he would get his 'dirty' or punishment on a Sunday during downtime.

Corporal Diff ended up with platoon 5, which consisted mostly of English speakers, including Mark de Wet. I've mentioned, Mark had a natural affinity for making trouble and was a very energetic character.

Platoon 5 during basics on the Bluff.

Diff would chase him around and give him *opfok* PT all the time, but it did not seem to help much, as Mark did not tire easily.

After a while, the corporal came up with a genius idea for how to punish rifleman De Wet. He was instructed to write letters to Diff's mom on his behalf – in Afrikaans – just about every Sunday! This was a serious form of punishment. Diff's mom, however, was very pleased to hear from her son so regularly. Many years later, Diff told his mom the truth about the letters, and when Mark met Diff's parents, his letter-writing skills were a favourite talking point.

Among my few personal belongings was a Walkman, a small portable cassette player that at the time was the latest thing in technology. I had two mix tapes, with mostly hard rock and heavy metal, that I would listen to on Sundays after church parade while executing trooper duties such as washing and ironing my clothes, cleaning my rifle, shining my boots and, of course, cleaning and polishing the barracks for the thorough Monday-morning inspection.

Corporal Dolf von Mollendorf was our platoon 3 NCO. I made friends with Japie Celliers, a staunch farm boy from Ermelo in the Eastern Transvaal. Someone in our bungalow had a little FM/AM receiver radio and sometimes we would listen to the hits of the day by the likes of Lionel Richie, Billy Ocean and Dire Straits. The song 'We Built this City' by Starship still takes me back to the old base at 1 Recce and our basic training there.

Sundays also gave us an opportunity to get to know our fellow platoon troopers and fellas from the other platoons better. I made friends with a few Afrikaans guys but ended up having almost as many English-speaking friends – including Mark de Wet, Craig Leppan, Craig Davies and Grant Shaeffer. While I was writing this book, it occurred to me that the few friends I made during basics all passed Recce selection, and most finished the one-year Special Forces training cycle. Was it a coincidence, or do individuals with the same attitude and level of determination subconsciously attract similar personality types?

We were all still teenagers, and sometimes our conversation was about girls, music, sports cars and bars. But mostly the talk was about military matters, and the Recces specifically. Would we pass the selection and training cycle? Which unit would we end up going to? How soon would we take part in operations? And what type? Which weaponry and tactics would be used?

We were a bunch of 17- and 18-year-old kids talking, very enthusiastically, about *war*. This is the most powerful three-letter word (after God), whose full meaning I would learn at first hand. It is a word that carries more weight, through blood, sweat, tears, hardship, sorrow, destitution, destruction, hatred, persecution, devastation and ruin, than any other word I know. Yes, we were excited at the prospect of going to war for our country, knowing so little about the human cost and physical mayhem of war. We were still unaware of its tragic consequences. All that mattered then was our goal to become Special Forces operators – Recces.

Our first eight weeks of basics flew by, although at the time I felt it was dragging a bit, probably because I was looking forward so much to the next phase of the training. It would take place at the Dukuduku training base in Zululand.

However, before we got to Zululand, the powers that be decided that we had to do a long route march carrying heavy packs, to put our bushcraft and navigational skills to the test. This exercise would take place in the Richmond region of the Natal Midlands, approximately 38 km southwest of Pietermaritzburg. This is a farming area with a high average rainfall, where timber, sugar cane, poultry, citrus fruit and dairy goods are produced. I am not sure if the exercise was held on government forestry land, or on private farms, but it was a wooded, bushy area.

We all have different memories of this route march, but there is one thing everyone remembers, and that is how wet it was, and right from the start. We were taken there in Mercedes five-ton trucks, complete with tents, equipment and logistical supplies. It was a pretty uncomfortable ride, as these trucks have a hard suspension and we had to sit on metal fold-down benches. Some guys lay on their kit, which was packed into our brown army duffel bags.

When we arrived at the point where we would erect the base camp, a soft, misty rain was falling on earth that was already quite soaked. It was our first encounter with putting up the nutria-brown/greenish army canvas tents, something we would get accustomed to in the months ahead. Fortunately, the lieutenants and corporals knew how these field accommodation units had to be erected, and they cracked the whip for us to do it in a speedy and organised manner. It was a muddy affair, with the only benefit being that the bloody tent pegs could be driven into the ground quite easily.

Over the next four or five days, we were kept busy, in wet and very damp conditions. We were not yet fully schooled in the art of advanced navigation. That was to be addressed in Infantry Individual, the course that followed Basics, and in Special Forces Orientation, the course that follows the selection phase. In Special Forces circles this course was also known as SMORIE, the Afrikaans abbreviation for Spesiale Magte Oriëntasie. Still, we were taught how to read a map, how to use a compass and how to march on a specific bearing while counting your steps to calculate the distance covered.

We marched with packs weighing upwards of 35 kg in the muddy and moist conditions to prepare us for the next training phase, where we would carry heavier packs more regularly and farther in preparation for the selection phase. After this exercise we were transported to the training base at Dukuduku.

DUKUDUKU

The Dukuduku Special Forces training facility was located in a vast state forest area 50 km north of the town of Matubatuba (today Mtubatuba), and the journey there took around two and a half hours. The facility was on the eastern side of the base; the opposite side was occupied by 121 Infantry Battalion, which at the time consisted mainly of Zulu speakers. The area is rife with exotic and very poisonous snakes, but more on that later on.

The first thing I noticed at Dukuduku was the smell. The place had the wet, damp odour of composting soil and leaves. This was due to the extreme humidity, and all the fallen leaves and tree bark form a kind of carpet under the thick shrubs and dense pine forests. I heard that in Zulu slang, Dukuduku means 'the place of groping in the dark'. I understood this description better after our first route march through the forest, where the canopy is so dense that little light reaches the ground. The humidity in the area is almost unbearably high, often in the 90 per cent range, and it is properly hot throughout the year, with February being the worst month of all. Something else that we quickly got acquainted with in this subtropical wooded area was the snakes, the black mamba and the Gaboon viper in particular.

It is a given that soldiers, on occasion, suffer from diarrhoea due to field catering. We referred to severe diarrhoea as 'gyppo guts'. The word 'gyppo' was army slang for being lazy, or sliding along, and gyppo guts meant that your asshole was lazy and allowed the contents of your stomach to 'slide along', resulting in constant runs to the toilet or shitting your pants.

When you got gyppo guts, your problem was compounded by the fact that we trained in overalls, which, unlike trousers, can't simply be pulled down. When you got caught with gyppo guts during field training, the best thing was to get rid of the damn overall as quickly as possible, step into the veld, bush or woods, and let things slide along. Gyppo guts became part and parcel of daily life during military training, so no one even looked up when someone took a few paces into the wilderness to relieve himself. Our training carried on, with the instructors pressing ever harder with rifle PT, marble PT and a lot of pole PT. Of course, diarrhoea is something that must be stopped in its tracks with medication and the right food, as you can become dehydrated very quickly, particularly if you sweat a lot – like we did.

Our route marches were getting closer to the 50 km and 50 kg mark. At some point, I started to feel a burning sensation in my ankles, particularly after a route march, but I downplayed it, thinking it must be a natural consequence of carrying heavy loads and other strenuous activities.

A trooper in our basic squad called 'Mil' (not his real name) put himself through the Special Forces pre-selection phase in Oudtshoorn with the sole aim of returning to his home city, Durban. Mil was of slender build and barely survived the gruelling PT sessions on the Bluff, and he had a hard time in Duku. Later, it became apparent that he had a plan to get himself 'slightly' injured so that he could be returned to the base in Durban, in the hope of getting a support position or being transferred to another army unit in the area.

One morning, during marble PT, Mil saw his opportunity. I was two rows behind him while we were doing military presses with the 25 kg concrete blocks. Doing ten or twenty of these marble military presses was easy enough for a fit young man, but when the instructor made you hold it up above your head for minutes on end, your shoulders started to burn. During one of these drills, I saw Mil's arms start to tremble and I thought he was going to throw the marble down on the ground and face whatever punishment would follow from the corporals. But Mil dropped the 25 kg square rock on his bloody head!

Thank goodness we were wearing our helmets during this *opfok* as Mil's head would otherwise have been split open. The bang on the head caused him to fall down, and he was removed from the squad to be checked out by a medic. This antic had the desired effect: Mil was placed on light duty and had to wear the traditional white helmet indicating that the wearer was injured and should abstain from physical activity until cleared by the medics or a doctor. Mil never made it past basics and was detached to another unit in Durban, which would have located him close to his mother's house – exactly where he wanted to be.

Between all the running around, PT drills, thrice-weekly route marches with heavy packs, and lectures, we also spent a lot of time on the shooting range. Here we were taught the basics of infantry marksmanship with our R4 assault rifles, from 50 m to 500 m in the standing, kneeling and prone positions. The instructors were on hand to show us the finer tricks of the trade.

One morning our course leader, Major Jenkinson, decided to visit the range to see the progress the troopers were making. I remember him producing an R5 rifle, the shorter and lighter iteration of the R4, walking to the 100 m firing point and going down in the prone position to shoot with the troopers spread out on the line. He fired a good couple of shots in rapid succession before making the weapon safe and slowly standing back. It was time to go and score and see who had shot the best. The major's grouping was very good and in the centre of the target.

I was terribly impressed. Apparently, Recces shoot straight and fast, and from that point on I started shooting faster, or rather as fast as I (accurately) could. As I learned, also in my PMC career, it helps to shoot fast and accurately. Be quick or be dead.

Our marksmanship improved, as we shot often and used a lot of ammunition on the range. The farm boys excelled in the use of a long gun, and the holidays I'd spent on my uncle's farm stood me in good stead when it came to firing a rifle accurately.

We eventually moved on to training with machine guns, which form part of the infantry platoon weapons. The standard light machine gun (LMG) issued to the SADF was the Fabrique Nationale (FN) LMG, which used the NATO 7.62 x 51 mm round. This old warhorse was belt-fed and normally came with a spare barrel. We were taught how to operate the machine gun in a buddy pair, with one trooper shooting it and the other to his left feeding the linked belt at a 90-degree angle into the feeding plate. The number two was also responsible for assisting with the barrel-change procedure when the barrel got really hot. Later on, we were taught how to operate an LMG as individuals, as the Recces normally did not have the manpower to waste on a number two.

Machine-gun belts are normally loaded with four ball (full metal jacket) rounds and one tracer as every fifth round. The tracer allows the gunner to see where his rounds are hitting in order to shift his aim onto the target. It is particularly effective during low light and night-time shooting scenarios where the trail of the tracer is like an aiming laser indicating exactly where to dispatch your rounds. Psychologically, it is also intimidating when you are on the receiving end of it as you actually see the darn bullets flying your way.

An old Rhodesian war veteran once told me about parachuting into so-called hot zones at night when enemy forces were firing from the ground with tracers. He described the feeling of helplessness that takes hold as you slowly descend to the ground on a static-line parachute, with tracer rounds from machine guns streaming past you, while your rifle is strapped to your back or side. The most you could do was to fire phew-phew rounds with your pistol from a few hundred feet up in the air!

Tracer rounds also have another devastating effect: they cause fires to break out where there is dry grass, twigs and scrubs. This happened on a few occasions during basic training when there was grass growing on top and behind the dirt wall, or berm, at the back of the shooting range. When this happened, the 'cease fire' command was shouted by the instructor in charge, which in this case happened to be Staff Sergeant Oosie. We then had to grab the '*vuurplakke*' (literally, fire swats), run to where the veld fire had broken out and extinguish it by beating the shit out of it. These *vuurplakke* consisted of a long broomstick-like wooden pole with a piece of rubber conveyor belt attached to the front. Once the fire was out, you would stomp on the smouldering grass with your boot soles, or kick a bit of sand over it, to ensure the wind did not reignite the fire.

The veld was getting drier as we entered the third month of our basic training and the summer rainy season was tapering off. During one of our LMG exercises a fire broke out, and after the 'cease fire' command came through, the machine guns were made safe and a bunch of us were dispatched to put out the fire. Before we got to the berm to attack the flames on top and beyond, we heard the bark of a machine gun and heard the crack of bullets flying overhead. We scrambled to get over the berm, and the bloody LMG burst seemed to have no end. After firing dozens of rounds, the gun fell silent.

I peeped around the berm and saw Staff Oosie beating the shit out of a trooper's doiby on the far left flank of the shooting line. He was wielding the long, heavy screwdriver that was used to set the sights on the R4s, and was kept close by to stop a runaway belt on a machine gun. I later heard that this particular trooper, who had a knack for landing himself in trouble, had been battling to clear a jam when the command to cease firing came through. He should have raised his hand or a leg to request help from the instructors but instead fiddled with the LMG, trying to clear it on his own. The cocked weapon fired and, in the process, rushed through an entire piece of whatever amount of linked ammo was left in the belt.

This kind of fuck-up is called a 'runaway' belt, and the only way to stop it is to grab the rapidly moving belt with a hand and twist it so that it jams, or to ram a metal rod – in this case a screwdriver – into the belt on the feeding side to force the gun to stop firing. This was exactly what the staff sergeant did once he realised what was happening. Thank God the weapon's buttstock was on the ground when the trooper fiddled with it, as the barrel was pointing slightly upwards, which caused the rounds to pass over the berm.

The poor dude who caused the runaway belt was punished hard and long with a marble, among other punishments by the corporals under the instruction of Staff Oosie. I have never seen people move as fast as I did that day, myself included. It was a scary moment, and one that we had to absorb and conquer, as this was what happened in actual Special Forces operations, with the difference being that when you are shot at during operations it is normally by the enemy.

We were getting towards the end of our basic training cycle. We could drill well in a squad; we had been trained to maintain ourselves and our environment; we had been schooled in basic infantry combat basics; we could handle assault rifles and machine guns; and we were fit and strong. At the end of basics, our numbers were reduced to 75.

I had succeeded in the first phase of becoming a Special Forces operator. I was now earmarked to advance to the next step of the selection process,

The author during his first weekend pass,
April 1986.

which was a month-long course in infantry platoon weapons and combat techniques, plus a lot more preparation for the final Special Forces selection phase. This meant that more route marches with heavy packs, harder PT and some interesting dietary challenges awaited us.

When we got back to Durban we were allowed our first weekend pass. I hitchhiked home to Bloemfontein. In those days, the SADF encouraged members of the public to pick up military personnel who were hitchhiking, and there were designated collection points along the major routes. We had to wear a triangular orange plastic belt device that clipped around your waist and one end over your shoulder. This campaign was called the '*ry veilig*' (drive safe) initiative and it worked well, since many people wanted to show their appreciation to national servicemen for defending their country.

During the next year, I hitchhiked home a few times and met quite a few colourful and weird people along the way, including black truckers, which was unheard of in those years. I spent a weekend at home with my mom and sister, and of course my dad and I celebrated my first homecoming in appropriate fashion. I was (barely) old enough to drink legally so we bar-hopped a bit – something I had done from time to time, albeit under cover, while still in high school.

3
SPECIAL FORCES ORIENTATION

I'm convinced that the infantry is the group in the army which gives more and gets less than anybody else.
– Bill Mauldin

Our basic training was done, mostly the infantry way but with a little Recce spicing and Special Forces oomph. Our next course before we attempted selection was to be trained in the use of infantry platoon weaponry and more relevant navigation, fieldcraft, radio comms, basic ropework, basic first aid (aimed at being able to help a buddy or team member), battle procedures and general combat tactics while working in an infantry platoon setup.

In many ways this was part of the selection phase, much like the US Army's 30-day Delta Force pre-selection phase in the mountains of North Carolina. It was a hard training course where you are pushed and tested in preparation for the Special Forces selection course to follow. We remained at the Recce training base at Dukuduku in the forests of Zululand.

The course instructors were a mix of qualified operators and instructors who had completed previous Special Forces selections. The senior instructors were Major Dave Jenkinson (course leader), Captain Rob Jennings (second-in-command [2IC]), Staff Sergeant Chris Oosthuizen (chief instructor) and Second Lieutenant Chris Serfontein (platoon commander).

Some of our basics instructors now joined us, as they also wanted to attempt the Recce selection and cycle training. Corporals Matthys de Villiers, Coenie de Jong and Stephan Muller, all instructors during our Basics course, were now students with us. We were joined by other SADF members who had completed their basic training and passed earlier pre-

Special Forces Orientation

selection phases. In a way, the month-long course also formed part of a further selection phase, as you had to pass a range of assessments before you could attempt the selection course.

When I think of it, there are actually four phases (in our case five, as we had to pass Recce basic training as well) before you could qualify as an operator. We underwent the first part of the sifting process in Oudtshoorn, which we can call the Special Forces 'entrance selection'. This was followed by the SMORIE course, which can be seen as a 'pre-selection' course, after which you had to pass the main selection phase. Thereafter you had to pass all the basic Recce 'cycle' courses as part of the official selection course, although I have grouped them together in one phase. Finally, there was the year-long actual training as a Special Forces operator, after which the Recce trainer review board would make the final call about whether you were selected. It was a long, intense, tough and complicated journey to become a Recce, but we were ready to do what was needed to qualify.

Some of the new students who joined us, and who had passed the 'entrance selection' at their various units, were older soldiers who had either first completed their tertiary education or were Permanent Force members from established combat units such as 32 Battalion, 1 Parachute Battalion, the School of Armour and infantry units all over the country. Under them were the likes of captains Brian Harris and William Mutlow, lieutenants Sybie van der Spuy, Renier 'PP' Hugo, Hannes Lintvelt and Chris Serfontein. Our numbers grew to 75 and our ages ranged from 18 to 34, with me one of the youngest members in the group.

The goal of the SMORIE course was to acclimatise the students to the climate in Zululand, to prepare them physically for selection and Recce training, to apply 'artificial' and steady pressure on the students to cope better with the upcoming selection, and to set a baseline standard for soldiers from different branches of the military to be able to fit in with the Special Forces training that would follow selection – for the few who made the cut.

WEAPONS TRAINING

In basics we had only trained in the use of the R4 assault rifle and the FN LMG. We were now introduced to pistols, which was a first for many of us. Growing up, we had only been taught how to shoot rifles and shotguns. We covered two military handgun workhorses, namely, the Beretta M92 9 mmP (for Parabellum), and the Browning Hi-Power, also in 9 mmP. Both were semi-automatic handguns, the Beretta a double-action, and the Hi-Power a single-action. We continued to use our R4s, and were introduced to its shorter younger brother, the R5, which would later be issued to us for urban warfare training and operations.

We had to be able to operate each weapon safely, know how to field-strip them while disassembling and assembling all systems, sometimes against time or blindfolded, mimicking night-time conditions, and how to clean and maintain them, and we had to be able to accurately fire them all. Then there was the darn M79 (Y1) 40 mm grenade launcher, which cocked automatically when the barrel was locked closed, and which had no safety catch. (This was the weapon that would punch the daylights out of me during Operation Nigel.) We also covered the MGL (Y2) 40 mm multi-grenade launcher, which had a rotating drum magazine containing six grenades. This weapon often caused stoppages, but was also very effective and devastating at delivering small 'flying bombs' when you got it going, as Barry would show us during Ops Nigel.

We also received instruction in the use of M16 and AK-47 assault rifles fitted with a 40 mm grenade-launch tube. These were dubbed the '203' models. When operating in an infantry squad you also require a rocket launcher and a light mortar, in addition to the team LMGs and assault rifles that we carried. The rocket launcher of choice was the evergreen Russian RPG-7, first designed in 1961, a reusable and unguided rocket-propelled system and an exceptionally destructive weapon. In later years, Barry would recall how, during the 1989 'Nine Day War' in then South West Africa, so many RPG rockets were fired during contacts with Swapo fighters that it sounded as if the launcher had a magazine filled with rockets. From 2004 onwards I also saw the destructive force of this weapon when I encountered it in Iraq and Afghanistan where it was used against PMCs.

Later that year we would learn why the rocket head was so devastating, when the theory of shaped charges was explained to us in our Demolitions course. Essentially, the RPG-7 has a conical-shaped charge that allows the rocket to penetrate armoured steel. Because of its deadly effectiveness, it became the most-used shoulder-fired anti-tank/armour weapon ever, and is still in use globally.

The RPG-7 arsenal consists mainly of an anti-tank shaped HE (PG-7) round, and an anti-personnel (OG-7) fragmentation warhead designed for causing maximum damage to humans. The RPG-7 launcher has no recoil, but it creates a massive 'back blast' that can potentially kill, or severely injure, anyone positioned directly behind or within a few metres of it. We were shown the arcs of safety behind the device, and learned that it was the gunner's responsibility to look back and ensure nobody was wrongly positioned, and then to shout 'RPG' as loudly as he could before firing the launcher.

In a typical 12-man squad we would often have two LMG gunners, one 60 mm mortar (typically, the light, man-portable Russian commando mortar) and an RPG-7 operator, with another member carrying the 40 mm MLG grenade launcher (drum version), or an M79 single-shot launcher, and some team members carrying AK-47 203 models. Every squad member would carry their assault rifles, unless you were an LMG gunner, and as a last resort everyone carried a 9 mm pistol. But the above model differed from operation to operation as the criteria for each attack and mission differed.

We first received theoretical instruction on these weapon systems in the field classroom at Dukuduku, where we also stripped and reassembled each system. These theoretical classes included the theory of small arms fire, ensuring an understanding of all the factors that might influence accurate fire, and would be followed by a session at the range, where we conducted a lot of practical shooting exercises. We shot at distances ranging from 50 m to 300 m with the assault rifles and machine guns, while the mortar could be deployed up to 1 050 m in skilled hands, and the RPG-7 effectively to around 400 m – the rocket self-destructs after 910 m (1 000 ft). There were various different types of mortar ammunition, for example practice, HE, smoke and illumination (illum) rounds.

On this course we were also trained in the use of hand grenades, small handheld explosive devices with a time-delay detonating device. First we trained with the locally available ones and, after selection, also on foreign ones, mostly Russian. These various-sized 'hand-bombs', as the Iraqis called them many decades later, came with different HE loads and fragmentation methods. After the training cycle, and during the rest of my military career, I figured out that there are three golden rules when it comes to the use of grenades. First, they never detonate exactly on time or as indicated – be prepared for anywhere between 2.5 and 5.5 seconds. Second, ensure there is hard cover between you and the device when it explodes; if no hard cover is available, then hit the deck in the 'grenade drill' fashion – turn away from the grenade, fall down on your stomach, close your legs and boots together, arms covering your head, which must be turned away from the blast, and keep your mouth open. (We would be taught this move during our Urban Warfare course.) Third, always be ready to follow up with gunfire, directly after detonation, as an enemy attacker throwing a hand grenade might use it to get you down and follow up with small arms fire if you were not killed.

Grenades are mainly thrown by hand but can be delivered by some military rifles. Rifle grenades are fitted onto the muzzle of a special blank rifle; when fired, the gases created propel the grenade up to 300 m indirectly through the air. Rifle grenades can be deployed much further than grenades thrown by hand.

The above weapons, training and skills would enable us to deploy in a squad, or as a Recce team. We had to undergo combat drills, and some more advanced exercises, before we could use these weapons in combat. It was time to exercise 'grazing cover', which was sometimes also called 'snap shooting'. This is where you fire your first shot as quickly as possible in the direction of your enemy to put him on the back foot and to get his head down, which gives you time to take a second, aimed shot, or more shots, and hit the target. We practised on the shooting range, and thereafter in the bush where static and moving (sliding, swinging and pop-up) targets were hidden behind branches, twigs, leaves and shrubs. We also practised in 'bush lanes', which are small footpaths in the veld through the bushes.

This culminated in an exercise where we had to walk/stalk though the bush and observe for targets behind cover, and engage in 'grazing fire' exercises to eliminate the targets as quickly as possible. This exercise was often done against the stopwatch to track our progress in future exercises. This was great training, and exciting to execute, and fortunately we did it often and eventually very well.

FLARES

As part of our combat infantry training we had to understand and know how to handle and deploy 'pyrotechnics' during combat situations. The term comes from the Greek words *pyr* (fire) and *tekhnikos* (made by art), and refers to self-contained and self-sustained chemical reactions designed to make heat, light, gas, smoke and/or sound.

One pyrotechnic device was the 15 mm pencil flare, which had to be carried on your webbing. When fired, it created a trail of light towards the area you directed it to. There were different-coloured pencil flares to indicate that a TL should organise his men in a certain manner, or to indicate predetermined signal/s when required. To my surprise, during Ops Nigel later that year (see Prologue), the enemy used coloured flares to direct small arms, mortar and RPG fire against us while they were busy with their counterattacks.

Next up was the so-called 1 000 ft flare, a device that shooshed up in the air to a height of around 300 m. This was often used to indicate your position to aircraft, or to another ground team who were some distance from your location. The flare could also be used to create light at night, as the illuminated version has a small parachute that deploys at the maximum height. The flare then slowly drifts down to earth. The same principle is behind the illuminating mortar, which when fired provides light to soldiers on the battlefield to manoeuvre or shoot at the enemy.

We were also trained in using the trip flare, a canister on a metal leg that was stuck in the ground and connected to other such devices, at around ankle height, with a thin metal tripwire. When the tripwire was engaged, it set off the flare it was connected to, which would burn intensely bright to illuminate the surrounding area. These devices were often placed at a safe distance around a patrol when they went into a 'hide' (a defensive position, using geographical features such shrubs, rocks and trees and camouflaging techniques to conceal your position) when resting or lying up overnight to indicate activity close to your patrol. During training, illuminating and trip flares caused several veld fires, requiring hours of firefighting, especially in savannah-type terrain.

Apart from flares, we learned to use No 83 R1M1 smoke grenades, which came in red, green, and yellow, as well as R1M1 white phosphorus grenades. These devices are very handy for organising concealment where there is little or no cover, as they create a smokescreen to hide your movements, particularly in tight situations where you are on the back foot, such as when withdrawing from a firefight.

TACTICS AND DEPLOYMENT

After a few weeks of training, we were ready to be taught battle procedures, which included understanding the sequence and detail of the 15 deployment drills. These drills are the foundation of sound tactical procedures, which all the teams had to follow during our Minor Tactics training phase later that year and in future operations. We also focused on acquiring more technical combat skills, which included the fire-and-movement drills that are so critical for the infantryman while on an operation or patrol. These manoeuvres entail moving and firing while fighting to get to the enemy by frontal or flank attack to outmanoeuvre and destroy him, or to withdraw effectively if the enemy surprises or overwhelms your team.

We were taught the theoretical basis of fire-and-movement manoeuvres. This included the positions of the different platoon gunners, how to move in short legs past one another, arcs of fire and safety aspects, followed by demonstrations on the range. We then had to go through these moves while executing dry drills, first at a slow pace and then faster as we improved.

Then, finally it was time for the real thing. For many of us it would be the first time that we would be shooting and moving alongside our buddies. The prospect excited me. At the time, the Recce instructors did not use training aids such as blank rounds, laser-system rifles with compatible vests, or 'airsoft' guns, which weren't available back then. Nope, we did it all with live full metal jacket or, in military terms, 'ball' (ballistic) ammunition. There was no latitude for mistakes, or a lapse in safety procedures, otherwise you might clobber your buddies, or get shot in the back of the head.

The secret to success with fire-and-movement drills is to keep the distance that you move forward relatively short, around ten metres or as the terrain dictates. This means that you have to hit the deck every 30 seconds or so, look through your sights, aim and fire at the target, get up, sprint around ten metres in a low-down profile and hit the deck again. This cycle is repeated until you reach the objective/target in a move that was called 'dash-down-roll, crawl, observe, sights, fire'. When conducting fire-and-movement for long stretches your body starts aching, and you breathe heavily, which makes aiming and hitting your targets more challenging. There are reasons why most soldiers in war are young, and this is one of them: combat soldiering takes its toll on your body.

PUTTING IT ALL TOGETHER

SMORIE was expertly planned and executed to build all the candidates' physical fitness, grit (perseverance of effort) and ability to endure individual and team hardship over extended periods within a military context. We still had to take part in route marches, and often walked distances of 10 to 50 km, with packs weighing between 25 and 50 kg. For we youngsters who had just finished basics and had done several route marches in the woods of Zululand, the going was initially a bit easier, but the corporals and Permanent Force members who had joined us soon caught up and were walking fit before long.

Our daily PT sessions were hard and heavy, and usually consisted of an early morning and a late afternoon session, which frequently included marble and pole PT. But the regime worked, and we became really fit and strong. The expression 'the wheel turns' became true for the corporals who did our basic training. We still had to do 20 pull-ups before each meal, but now they also had to join in. They battled to keep up with us – justice was done! Eventually they caught up, since they were also fit, young and strong.

We expanded our navigational knowledge and did a lot of route marches involving map-reading and taking compass bearings. The concepts of magnetic north, magnetic declination and true north were explained to us in greater detail. I found this topic fascinating as my dad taught geography to high school students and had told me a lot about it. In general, he was a man who understood maps, compasses and direction-finding. The Dukuduku plantations and the coastal landscape west of St Lucia were ideal for laying the foundations of, and practising, sound navigational skills, as the dense bush created numerous challenges and forced me to trust my compass.

Signals also formed part of the SMORIE course. Although we had learned the elementary use of radios during basic training, it was during this phase that we really learned about military communications through the use of high frequency (HF), very high frequency (VHF) and ultra-high frequency (UHF) radios. The HF radios could communicate over very long distances if the antenna was 'cut' to the correct length and erected properly. This referred to restricting the length of antenna required (not physically cutting it), which was predetermined through certain calculations, by 'binding' it around a non-conducting (plastic or wood) square or object. We were trained to use the Racal Syncal 30 HF radio, which allowed a deployed team to communicate over hundreds, sometimes thousands, of kilometres with their Tac-HQ.

We covered radio procedures and had to learn the phonetic alphabet used in the military to spell words over the radio, for example Alpha (A), Bravo (B), Charlie (C), and so on. After qualifying, many operators underwent advanced training after being nominated for the Regimental Signals course. There you were taught Morse code, how to use a data encryption device (DET) to encrypt radio communications and how to use an array of radios, including ground-to-air units used to call in choppers or airstrikes.

The weeks flew past. We were fed a lot of potatoes, in mountain-sized portions, to ensure that we consumed the same amount of calories as we were burning, which was a lot, and to 'beef up' before the selection. Maybe the meals we ate supplied us with more calories, but we stayed thin and athletic.

The time for the Special Forces selection was fast approaching, and a SMORIE selection board confirmed our progress according to the set requirements. Yet again, a number of men failed to make the cut, but the board informed me that I would be going on the selection course.

Another milestone had been achieved, and a humongous new goal lay ahead. I knew that many would start but only a few would succeed. Some of the students in our group shared stories about their previous failed attempts, and it didn't help when we heard that only six men had made the selection in October 1985.

4
SPECIAL FORCES SELECTION

The hardships that I encountered in the past will help me succeed in the future.
– Barbara Castle

The South African Special Forces selection is widely recognised as one of the toughest tests of its kind. If you are successful, you are allowed to complete the full year-long Special Forces training cycle. Until the late 1970s, the Special Forces selection phase was conducted over ten days to two weeks and often culminated in an operation in enemy territory before you could qualify as a Recce operator. In the 1980s, the selection process was streamlined to a shorter but very intense four- to six-day exercise, which has since become the norm. Our selection phase took place between 5 and 10 May 1986.

After the Basics and Infantry Individual courses, 52 soldiers were left to attempt the selection course, which took place at the Dukuduku training base. By now we were acclimatised to the humid weather and rugged conditions of northern Natal. The few who passed the gruelling selection would then undergo the South African Special Forces basic training cycle for the rest of the year. A bunch of other officers and NCOs who had completed their basic training, or who had served in regular units and had passed the pre-selection phases, now joined us for the main selection phase.

We felt fit and ready for whatever might come our way, but needless to say the instructors and psychologists were ready to drive us past the point of physical endurance. We would undergo selection dressed in our (now familiar) brown overalls, standard SADF heavy brown leather boots, brown bush hats, our green Niemoller webbing (named after former operator Johan Niemoller), R4 assault rifles and large brown

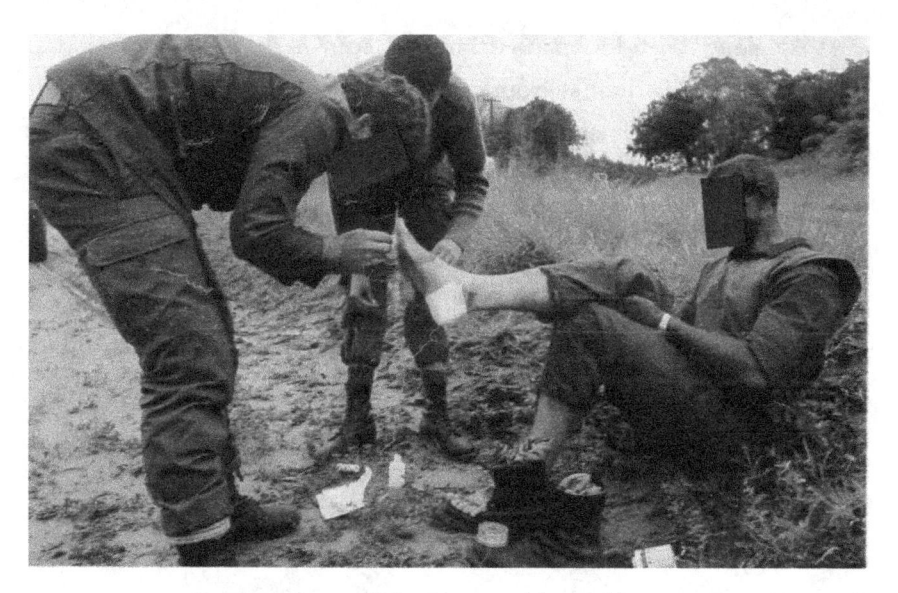

Selection candidates treating blistered feet.

SADF backpacks. (The nutria-brown SADF backpacks were made from a thinner type of canvas than the Special Forces Bergens, and the straps were not as strong.)

The candidates were split into two groups, Alpha and Bravo, and we received numbers. We enjoyed our last hot Sunday lunch on 4 May, after which we had final inspection of our kit to ensure the candidates did not sneak in food, pain meds or other items that could confer an unfair advantage. We stood around naked as the instructors searched even our overalls, boots and headgear. Then our backpacks were weighed to be 45 kg and each candidate was issued his Day-Glo orange selection number. This was stitched onto two pieces of canvas, with one strapped on your backpack to be visible from the rear and one hung around your neck to be visible from the front.

From now on, all candidates were equal. We were like troopers without an identity, with no ranks and no names; you could only respond when someone called out your selection number. From 16:00 to 18:00 we underwent a memory test, with 25 items that were used on the Infantry Individual course on display. You had 60 seconds to memorise the items laid out in front of you, without noting them down.

At last light we had to camouflage our faces, neck, chest, arms, hands and the rest of our bodies from a ten-litre drum of 'black-is-beautiful' camouflage cream, which had to be reapplied throughout selection. Then we moved to the point of departure, where we settled down for the night.

Note that the following account is a summary of the average number of exercises completed during the different selection courses in 1985 and 1986. The exact sequence of events might differ from one selection group to another, depending on how the instructors and training wing personnel organised it on the ground at the time.

DAY ONE

On day one, we were rounded up at 03:00 for roll call, after which we warmed up, stretched and did some serious PT training for an hour. At 04:00 we started our individual route march; this was over a distance of 45 km, and the physical walking had to be concluded in 11 hours. A couple of extra hours were permitted to allow for the tests and exercises we had to do during and after the march.

Day one is designed to physically exhaust candidates, especially in the very humid conditions and soft sand in certain sections of the Dukuduku forest, which make the route march even more taxing. The cut-off time for the exercise was 15 hours and we therefore had to keep moving at a steady rate of almost 4.5 kph to make up for time lost on psychological tests and just generally getting stuffed around.

Staying hydrated was crucial to completing this exercise successfully, and the SADF water bunkers became our frequent oasis. Our bottles also had to remain full because we had to maintain the 45 kg minimum weight of our packs. Barry recalls that one of the students asked another troop to jump on his knee so that he could say he was injured and drop out of selection. He probably did this to avoid indicating that he could not take it anymore.

After a few hours my left Achilles tendon was on fire and my heel hurt like hell, which caused me to start walking with a slight limp. When the instructors noticed it, they asked if I wanted to bail out. I gave it some thought but decided I was not ready to give up on my dream of becoming a Recce. I declined and kept marching.

This was a different experience, as we were constantly tested by psychologists and instructors, and a lot of additional exercises were thrown in where you had to endure psychometric tests. Unlike marches, there was no nutrition allowed, and here you had to work in teams where marches had previously been individual. Also, in the past if you failed the time, you could try again, but here you only had one chance. This was it – now or never.

JJ Raath, who had done his selection the year before but had been injured during his last cycle course, was deployed as an assistant on our selection. He drove the Mercedes five-ton truck and picked up the candidates who had thrown in the towel or who were injured to such an extent that they could not continue. At more than one point JJ pulled up to me and told me that, as a Raath, I needed to keep going. He encouraged his namesake, even though he is not a direct relation. He even told me that Staff Oosie had made a comment that I was not going to make it. This just spurred me on.

It was never a given that any of us would make it. Diff recalled later how amazed he was when a soldier who had always finished first on the SMORIE route marches, and always had lots of war stories to tell, fell off during the first day of selection.

The cut-off point was getting closer. I was really battling to walk – the tendons and heel of my foot were giving me hell. At one point I remember crawling for a while, with JJ encouraging me, and then finally the RV came within sight. What a relief!

Stumbling and crawling like a wounded animal, I made it in time to the instructors, where our next test was awaiting us. We were dog-tired, but of course we were not allowed to sleep. Instead, we were lined up for another memory test: sitting by the road, an instructor would ask us to name the 25 items we had been shown in 60 seconds on Sunday afternoon. It was a serious challenge to recall more than 60 per cent of the items when you were utterly exhausted, and partially dehydrated after 11 to 14 hours of hard walking while carrying a 45 kg backpack that went up occasionally to 75 kg or more (such as during a casevac situation). The psychologists also conducted individual problem-solving exercises, creating scenarios to

Hooded candidates undergo interrogation session during selection.

Waterboarding during interrogation session.

test the candidates' concentration and spatial orientation, as well as their problem-solving and communication abilities.

We underwent medical inspections, especially of our feet, knees, hips and shoulders. JJ arranged for the medics to strap my ankles with some tape, but it did not really help much. We had to strip down to our underpants to be weighed, and blood was drawn. We were never told what the tests were for, but apparently it had to do with our diet, where they tried to determine if the extra food and Ensure nutritional shakes that we had received in the month leading up to selection actually helped us fare better.

Quite a few of us were experiencing severe muscle cramps. Corporal Diff came up with a plan to alleviate cramping: before selection he poured salt into the hollow metal H-frames attached to the back of his backpack and sealed the ends. In the dark, Diff would sneak from one soldier to the next and offer each a bit of salt. It was a lifesaver, especially since the night turned out to be a long one …

Part of Special Forces selection and training involves what to do in the event that you are captured and interrogated behind enemy lines. You also need to know how to escape from such a situation and how to evade your foe. This is called escape and evasion, or E&E for short. At about 19:00 all candidates who had survived the selection thus far were rounded up, and our hands were cuffed behind our backs. Our overalls were pulled down to our waists to expose our bare chests and then a canvas bag was pulled over our heads.

The canvas hoodies each had our Day-Glo numbers on them. They were shaped to fit over the candidates' heads and shoulders with tie-downs under the arms. The hoodie had a small hole in front of the mouth area, allowing you to breathe, but anyone who felt claustrophobic would be in serious trouble. We were pushed to the ground and instructed to sit with our legs straight in front of us and hunched forward.

Then the shouting, screaming and slapping started.

Along with the verbal abuse came buckets of ice-cold water, thrown over us at every possible opportunity. The hood got so wet that the water made you choke at times. I was just happy to be able to rest my aching tendons and burning heels for a while. Nicky Fourie remembers being kicked backward by an instructor onto his cuffed hands, after which he pulled himself up into a sitting position again.

At about 22:00 a heavy thunderstorm soaked us completely, and soon most of us were sitting in hip-deep water since we were placed in a depression in the ground. The instructors continued to throw fire buckets filled with ice-cold water over us.

None of us expected what came next. Our 'interrogators' started using the waterboarding technique on us. We were flung onto our sides and an instructor would lift up part of the hood and start to pour water into it. The water would go up into your nostrils and into your mouth as you tried to breathe. This technique fools the brain into thinking that you are about to drown, inducing a state of complete panic and helplessness. If you were lucky you could gulp down some icy water, but it was not easy as the water also went into your nostrils and you mostly choked as you breathed it in. This shit was repeated every half an hour or so for hours on end. The aim, as I later learned when I became an instructor with the Special Forces training wing, was to establish which candidates could control their fear. Waterboarding is one of the most effective techniques to induce fear.

We were instructed to stand, then to sit, and the next moment to kneel or lie down – all in an effort to ensure that we never became comfortable in a single position or got any kind of rest. At one point they took us one by one to an interrogation tent where the hood was removed and a very bright light was shone into your eyes. Our 'interrogators' then aggressively asked a multitude of questions, including who you were and what unit you served in, and about operational capabilities and training. You had to answer without giving any information away, remain quiet or withdraw from selection if your aching body and soul could not handle the abuse any longer.

Several candidates threw in the towel during the interrogation phase as it was the last straw after the gruelling first day. It really felt as if it would never come to an end. However, by the time the sun rose the next morning, our 'interrogation' was finally over. Sure as hell, I had survived the night!

DAY TWO

At 05:00 the next morning we again started the day with a PT session to warm up and stretch our now cramping muscles. Then we were divided into groups of four for the day's first test: a ten-kilometre group exercise. We carried the same packs, weighing 45 kg, but totalling 50 kg with webbing and rifle.

It was time for the 'granddaddy' of *afkak* exercises (meaning to get seriously stuffed up) – the 'iron cross'. An article in *Scope* magazine in 1988 described the iron cross as 'a masterpiece of frustration, a small piece of malicious genius, designed by a sadistic ex-Rhodie sergeant major'. It consisted of a square metal frame with thick chains hanging from each corner. Attached to the chains were four lengths of railway steel, each weighing 25 kg. The chains also weighed 25 kg in total, so the whole thing weighed in at 125 kg!

Over the course of a route march of approximately 30 km, a four-man team had to carry the iron cross for the first 15 km. Our instructors put together the teams so that each would have two stronger candidates and two others who had really battled the previous day. Of course, this was done to test the candidates on teamwork, communication, leadership skills, problem-solving and perseverance.

The 'iron cross' exercise.

Almost all the teams first tried to balance the 25 kg steel bars on top of their already heavy backpacks. The problem is that due to the small space between the bars and the centre square – each bar was attached to the square by a short length of chain – the troopers tended to trip and fall over each other's feet, causing a lot of frustration and at times aggression. Try playing twinkle toes with a 70 kg backpack pulling on your shoulders – causing your back, hips, legs and feet to burn like coals – while walking in formation and in step, with the metal pieces doing their best to obey the law of gravity!

The teams could carry the iron cross any way they wanted, but it was not allowed to touch the ground or be dragged. Nicky recalls that his team rigged the iron cross to one of their backpacks and carried it one team member at a time! The contents of the backpack were divided between the other three team members. Needless to say, they didn't get far with this scheme.

Dries Coetzee was a tall, strong *boerseun* (farm boy) who had grown up on a farm in the Kalahari. We later learned that when he did his selection the previous year, he carried the iron cross alone for a long period of time. Very few candidates ever managed this.

Next, Nicky's team decided to rig the four arms of the cross to each man's backpack with the short lengths of 'kinetic rope' we used as part of our gear. They then walked in a four-man formation and very close together. This plan did not last long either, because the candidate in front of Nicky moved away from the formation, which caused a 25 kg railway steel bar to come loose, and it dropped on Nicky's foot. Fortunately, it only grazed the fleshy parts of his toes, and he was able to continue.

Arnold Human, who had qualified as a doctor before deciding to become a Recce, recalls how within the first few minutes a trooper withdrew, and shortly after that another, leaving him and PP Hugo with one railway bar each, still attached to the centre square. They could barely move. Eventually, an instructor removed two of the bars so that they each had to carry 'only' 25 kg on top of their packs.

Along the way, the teams had to endure further 'challenges' that they had to pass or risk falling off selection. These included memory and 'stress' tests, and being questioned and assessed for any sign of irritability, all while the older operators acting as 'evaluators' watched our every move and emotional reaction.

The whole time the '*kopdokters*' (psychiatrists) circled like vultures, ready to pounce on us with their psychometric tests while we were hungry, aching and tired beyond exhaustion. Initially, each four-man group had one experienced operator and one psychiatrist who followed our every move looking for signs of irritation and aggression among the team members. They also assessed how adaptable the candidates were, how well they communicated under pressure and how they solved problems.

Once the first man in the team decided to pull out, things got more challenging, as one of the metal bars was removed and the already tricky squad-shuffle turned into a triangular formation. On surviving the first five-kilometre team exercise, we entered a phase where the iron cross was dismantled and each candidate was given a railway bar. This is called the 'individual' phase and involves carrying the bar on your backpack, on one shoulder or in your arms – if other parts of your body were hurting too much – for the next five kilometres.

In the late 1980s, the iron cross was reworked into an even more

Major Sybie van der Spuy and WO2 MP Viljoen with 'octopus' balls.

torturous device when the 25 kg railway bars were exchanged for iron balls. This new contraption was aptly named the 'octopus'! Apparently, it was the brainchild of RSM Pep van Zyl, which makes sense, since he was a master at devising ways to fuck up a soldier.

Needless to say, the absence of food contributes greatly to your level of agitation, especially when your body aches and you have had little to no sleep. At some point during the march, we were pulled over and asked to build items out of Lego blocks that lay littered on a metal folding table. Under different circumstances, this might have been fun, but believe me, it wasn't.

When we were done with the iron-cross torture we also had to take part in a mind-bending puzzle that involved candidates threading coloured chains through colour-coded holes in a very specific manner. By then I hurt so much I thought I would collapse, and both my Achilles tendons were giving me hell. On top of that I had a couple of blisters. But I couldn't afford not to focus on the task at hand, otherwise I would be disqualified. After a gruelling 75 km where we were laden like pack mules, these tasks were anything but easy and required you to draw on inner strengths that you did not know you had.

Negotiating an obstacle on the 'letra' course during selection.

Candidates cross an obstacle on the 'letra' course.

Rope challenge on the 'letra' course.

Our physical fitness, grit and ability to endure individual and team hardship started to show. There was no way to fake it: either you had these qualities or you didn't. Of course, this was the point of it all – to find out which students were able to dig deeper in terms of their physical and spiritual resources, and who would surpass all 'normal' limits of human endurance. It also showed that certain individuals can actually go further and harder under very trying circumstances if they are mentally strong and resilient enough.

A number of guys fell out during the iron-cross exercise, but the ones who made it faced yet another arduous phase. We were in for a 12 km night route march in the jungles of Zululand with the route indicated by Lumisticks (chemical lights). Those damn Lumisticks are quite deceiving; when you spot them you get very excited because you think you are close to your next assignment. However, this is just an illusion. In reality, they are visible from quite far away in the total darkness of the woods and the distance to the next navigational point is in fact a long way off.

During the night route march the instructors subjected us to 'chats' in which they subtly probed our minds and emotional states. We were also subjected to exercises such as stripping and assembling weapons against the clock and doing radio transmission talks and physical exercises. The older, qualified operators looked for signs of irritability, snappiness and how well we worked in a team under pressure.

After the route march we were asked questions on what we had observed along the route. Some of us saw or heard nothing, but the ones that maintained their concentration under very difficult conditions could hear people talking over a distance, see and smell a small campfire 50 m from the road with guys sitting next to it, hear a weapon cocking in the distance, see heavy drag marks over the road in the waning half-moon's ambient light, see the fluorescence of a compass lying next to the road, and more.

We were kept awake for the rest of the night – by now we had not slept for 48 hours. There was method to this madness, though, because one of the selection objectives is to evaluate the candidates' ability to perform under stressful conditions and when faced with sleep deprivation. By now both my Achilles tendons and heels were killing me, and most of us had blisters under our feet. We were completely drained, but somehow we made it through day two of Recce selection.

DAY THREE

In the early hours of the morning, in between exercises, Barry Visser and Henk van Wyk found a spot where they could roll out a sleeping bag one of them had access to. They climbed in it together to keep each other warm. However, they were spotted by Sergeant Major Bruce Laing, who laid his boot into them. Barry absorbed most of the kicks as he struggled to get out of the bag.

At around 04:30 of day three, the instructors got us together again to do stretching exercises to warm up our aching muscles and tendons. This was extremely painful since our bodies had cooled down, and for the first few minutes we looked like chameleons performing a dance. It was time to start marching again … The few of us who were left were absolutely knackered.

Somewhere along the route we were directed to the 'letra' course, which resembles the games from the television show *Survivor*. There were various wooden contraptions, ropes, sandpits and some items made from concrete. We were divided into teams and given challenging tasks to do together, such as moving over and through the obstacles. The psychiatrists and instructors watched us closely, noting our interactions with our teammates, while looking out for individuals who showed initiative and leadership, and identifying those who showed signs of irritability, pig-headedness and extreme fatigue.

After completing this course, we were given a heading, or RV, to navigate to. This consisted of three legs of navigation, of three kilometres each, designed to test our ability to focus and concentrate despite severe tiredness, hunger and pain. These exercises kept us busy until around noon when we were rounded up for a kit check to make sure we had not ditched any weight, to inspect our webbing and assault rifles, and to have us checked out medically.

This was followed by a ten-kilometre casevac (casualty evacuation) exercise in which five men were grouped together to carry one trooper at a time using a groundsheet with loop handles on the corners. The exercise mimicked a situation where you might have to carry a wounded buddy from the battlefield. This exercise often creates some disarray in the group because the ones who are weaker and/or hurting the most have to be assisted, and thus carried throughout the exercise by their buddies. The only good thing about it was that it distinguished the stronger candidates from the weaker ones.

Towards last light we had to undergo another medical inspection. You only had to whisper to the doctors that you could not take the pain anymore and you would leave the course immediately. Mentally and physically, I was drained. Again, I had to dig incredibly deep into my inner reserves to continue despite the sharp pain in my ankles and heels, and the soul-destroying overall hurt in my body.

For the night of day three we had to undertake a 21 km individual speed night route march. The route had to be completed in three hours and fifteen minutes, still carrying your hefty backpack, webbing and rifle. We had to walk at around seven kilometres per hour, which seems like an impossible pace after what we had been through on the previous days. Once again, we had to follow Lumisticks to stay on the route – the bloody chemical lights never seemed to end. Some of us made the cut-off time but some fell out.

We were kept awake throughout the night. By now it felt like a lifetime had passed since we started the selection process 72 hours before.

DAY FOUR

On the morning of day four we started at 05:00 warming up our sore bodies, followed by stretches and a heavy Special Forces-style PT session. Diff recalls seeing that a number of us had bleeding feet due to broken blisters. Sybie van der Spuy sucked up the pain and kept walking, albeit with a limp, and this served as inspiration for Diff to get going again.

At 06:00 the candidates left for the shooting range for tests measuring weapon agility, shooting accuracy and the handling of a variety of weapon systems. The goal was to test the candidates' ability to use their weapons effectively under stressful conditions. This went on until 11:00 whereafter the candidates had to pitch a field base. Lunch time came – not that there was any lunch for the guys on selection.

At 13:00–14:00 we were again subjected to individual problem-solving exercises set by the psychologists. We resumed the erection of the field base, which consisted of various-sized army canvas tents. This went on from 14:00 until 19:00 under the close watch of the operators, who continued to evaluate us in terms of leadership, perseverance, mental toughness and patience. At 22:00 we were finally left to sleep, but at this point most of us were too far gone. I for one battled to fall asleep. The pain in my body, and particularly in my lower legs and heels, kept me awake. I have subsequently learned that chronic pain tends to be more profound at night. It turned out to be a long night, and shortly after I eventually dozed off, we were rounded up again.

DAY FIVE

We started day five at 05:00 and did PT exercises until 06:00. We then proceeded on a speed march where we had to cover ten kilometres in two hours on a marked route. What would've been a fairly easy task under normal circumstances was now pure torture. Again, a few guys did not make the mandatory cut-off time and were thrown off selection. It was heart-breaking to see after they had come this far, but that was the way the selection course was designed.

By 10:00 there were around 20 candidates left and we were sent on another route march. Unbeknown to us, it was a short distance to the base area and would see us complete the 110 to 120 km required for the selection process. The march was the last straw for one of the candidates, and he threw in the towel, not knowing that we were basically done.

We were steered towards the camp, and close to the base we were told to remove poles, marbles and tyres from the back of a Samil 50 truck. Our hearts sank because we knew what the Recce instructors would have us do with these items! Then, when we opened the back of the truck, we saw cold drinks, beers and some snacks. And, just like that, our Special Forces selection process came to an end.

Once I realised what was happening, I found a quiet spot and went

Lieutenant PP Hugo (shown fourth from left in the back row) with 'youngsters' after selection. The author is second from left at rear.

down on my knees to thank God for giving me the courage and strength to have passed this test among tests.

After we had some refreshments, we made our way back to our bungalows, where we took hot showers, scrubbing the 'black-is-beautiful' camo cream out of the pores of our faces and necks, allowing a minute or two for the hot water to run over our beat-up bodies and fucked-up feet. A few of us who had passed selection got together for a photo that I cannot even remember being taken.

We proceeded to clean our rifles, webbing and gear, and then, finally, we could pass out on our beds. Sometime later I was woken to go and eat at the dining facility. We ate slowly and a little at the time, as our systems were too run-down to absorb and digest large amounts of food.

RSM Pep van Zyl was known for making hot (as in spicy) potatoes. Barry overfilled his plate with the potatoes and the beady-eyed sergeant major spotted it. Barry's eyes were bigger than his shrunken stomach and soon his mouth was on fire, but he had to force the potatoes down as the RSM was tracking his progress. The RSM had known Barry since he was a boy, as he and Barry's father had served together in 1 Parachute Battalion.

'Did you make it?' he asked.

To which Barry replied, 'Yes, RSM.'

To this the old soldier simply replied, 'We shall see.'

Barry realised that passing the Special Forces selection does not mean you suddenly become an operator. A lot of water still has to flow under the bridge.

In total, 21 of us had made it. Of the 700-odd men who had attempted pre-selection at the Infantry School at the beginning of the year, and the 118 who went on to do basic training, only 12 were left (the other nine who made it were from the Permanent Force). During the coming six months of the Special Forces training cycle, a further number of this group would fall out due to injury, illness or other factors. We returned to Durban, where the unsuccessful candidates were returned to their units and those of us who had made it were given a weekend off to go home and lick our wounds.

5

SPECIAL FORCES INDIVIDUAL

'A weapon is a tool,' she repeated, a little breathlessly. 'A tool for killing and destroying. And there will be times when, as an Envoy, you must kill and destroy. Then you will choose and equip yourself with the tools that you need. But remember the weakness of weapons. They are an extension – you are the killer and destroyer. You are whole, with or without them.'
– Richard K Morgan, Altered Carbon

A Special Forces soldier must be able to use any weapon system, from a .22 pistol to a .50 calibre. Guns from all parts of the world awaited us in the Special Forces orientation course – handguns, shotguns, rifles, assault rifles, machine guns, sub-machine guns, sniper systems and larger anti-aircraft and anti-materiel weapons.

This phase of our training would address many of these requirements, particularly the foreign weapons (mainly Russian and East Bloc) used by our foes. Those weapons not covered in this course would be dealt with later in the year in other specialised courses. By the end of the year, we would be well versed in correctly deploying the applicable weapon system required to kill an enemy effectively and quickly. It was programmed into you as part of your subconscious muscle memory.

The Special Forces Individual orientation course was, and still is, known to operators as SMIND, which is the abbreviation for its Afrikaans name, Spesiale Magte Individueel. The student had to have passed SMORIE and Special Forces selection in order to continue with the year-long training cycle. Our ranks now contained a number of older career soldiers who had passed selection, specifically the guys from the second selection at the end of 1985 and those who had been injured in the previous cycle. In total, 35 soldiers started the Special Forces orientation course. It was good to mingle with the older soldiers, some officers and others who had been around the block a few times.

The course was presented at Dukuduku, which we were by now familiar with. Our instructors were all operators from the various Recce units and were mostly NCOs, including sergeants Ian Strange, CJ Oosthuizen and Billy Faul, staff sergeants Johan Sheffer and Marc van der Merwe and Warrant Officer Bruce Laing. The heavy PT sessions continued: there was a lot of running, marble PT, pole PT and some field exercises where we had to carry heavy backpacks. To our relief, the constant route marches with heavy backpacks, and the exercises aimed at messing us around, were replaced by more purposeful and targeted PT. It was still hard going but everything made more sense.

We were now also introduced to unarmed combat, which was taught to us by Master Chung, who hailed from South Korea and was a sensei in fighting techniques. Back then there was no Ultimate Fighting Championship or mixed martial arts (MMA), or its forerunner, shootfighting. The fighting techniques he taught us were, I guess, a mixture of karate and taekwondo, with a sprinkling of jujitsu. The unarmed combat exercises were conducted with a minimum of chat because it was a practical subject, but also because of Master Chung's limited English.

One command that Master Chung often shouted was 'fighting-stance Chung-i', which meant we had to get ready for combat by turning sideways, bending the left knee slightly and bringing up our firsts into a type of boxing stance. Another command, which took some time for us to decode, was 'halazem'. After a while we figured out he was trying to say '*haal asem*', the Afrikaans for 'breathe'.

This was exciting stuff and great fun. Each morning at 05:00 we had to be on the parade ground – the same one where we got fucked-up during basics. We would line up in two rows, facing one another, about two metres apart, ready to be told the different ways to punch and kick an opponent. The guys who had done basics were used to being thrown into regular boxing matches, where we pummelled each other properly, but now we had to practise our punches and kicks many times in the air, stopping just short of an aiming point on the man opposite you, before we got on with the real deal of punching, blocking, and so on.

Every so often, one of the students would land a punch on his opposing buddy, which often led to bloody noses, split lips and painful body shots. True to our alpha-male character, the man who was punched would retaliate with some punitive measures of his own! For the next four weeks we practised unarmed combat every day, either before or after the PT sessions. It would not be the last time we saw the athletic sensei.

We had daily instruction on the types, characteristics, specifications, parts and use of foreign weapons, and had the opportunity to shoot all that were available. I remember how thrilled we were when we were told in the course overview about all the weapons we would handle. It started with a small .32 calibre pistol fitted with a silencer – it was supercool, a bit like James Bond. We covered the Soviet Makarov and Tokarev pistols, then the Colt 1911 .45 ACP, which I took a liking to for many reasons.

Next we covered the sub-machine guns of the era: the Israeli Uzi was first, also fitted with a silencer, then the Ingram .45 calibre, then the Sterling-Patchett (Mk 4 and Mk 5), with its characteristic side-fitting curved magazine. There was the Italian Beretta PM(P) and the Russian-made Scorpion, which was used by guerrillas and freedom fighters all over Africa.

We then progressed to assault rifles: the Heckler & Koch G3, an old warhorse still found in many parts of Africa; the American M16; the Italian Beretta AR70/90; the AK-85 (5.56 mm calibre); the AK-74 (5.45 mm calibre); and then the various types of AK-47s that were floating around Africa. We covered their markings and where each hailed from.

Next up were the light machine guns (LMGs). We covered the RPK, which was an AK-47 with a longer and heavier barrel, a squarish solid wooden buttstock and a foldable bipod. The calibre was the same as the AK, but it was not belt-fed and could operate with the standard 30-round AK mags, although the longer 40-round version was preferred. It could also function with the circular 75-round drum magazine designed for the RPD machine gun, which is a totally different and older design, but of the same calibre as the AK. These weapons were used extensively by the North Vietnamese during the Vietnam War, and by some African countries, as well as in Rhodesia. In later years I would also encounter a number of these old warhorses during my travels in Africa and in the early days in Iraq. It works very well if properly maintained and kept fairly clean.

I was so impressed when the Recce who gave the lecture, Staff Sergeant Marc van der Merwe, told us what the letters RPD stood for that I remember it to this day: Ruchnoy Pulemyot Degtyaryova (Degtyaryov light machine gun). This soldier really knew his subject, like all the Recce instructors did, in a time when you could not quickly Google something and become an overnight expert. These men knew their guns, their application and their tactics intimately, since they actively used them.

Then it was time to get acquainted with the king-of-the-ring when it comes to LMGs, namely, the Russian PKM. This machine also fired a 7.62 mm bullet, but it was a heavier and faster round as the casing was longer than the standard NATO 7.62 mm. It was one of the few machine guns where the belt fed from the right, which caused the empty casings to be ejected onto your left arm, which hurt quite a bit when firing from a standing position.

The PKM was the LMG of choice for the Recces during operations, but it was also used by the enemy forces as the Soviet Union flooded Angola, Mozambique and the rest of Africa with these guns. Rugged and incredibly reliable, the PKM could get wet, muddy and dusty, and the barrel seemed to take a hammering better than any other. The square 200-round metal-box-type magazines also seemed to work better than the mags used by the rest of the pack. The PKM packed some serious firepower, and we would get even better acquainted with it later in the year during our unconventional warfare training phase, and in the operation that followed the course.

The weapons training progressed well, and shooting guns from all over the globe, particularly the machine guns, was a great experience. There was a lot of after-hours cleaning and maintenance to be done after shooting the daylights out of them. This was also a sort of downtime for us, as we would sit in groups and talk about a range of topics. As a youngster, it was great for me to listen to the stories of the older guys who had been in the military for a while.

As we progressed through weapons training, it was time to get acquainted with foreign, and particularly Russian, grenades of all shapes and sizes. There were small egg-shaped ones called the mini-Arges, which were great for training exercises as they were not that powerful. Still, they were the real McCoy because they had small ball bearings as fragmentation. Then there were the different Russian hand-bombs, such as the F-1, RGD-5, RG-42 and various 'stick grenades', which had a type of handle like a short broomstick to improve the thrower's grip. The handle also allowed you to throw an armour-piercing version at armoured vehicles. (The grenade part was heavier than the handle and would therefore make contact first. On impact, the grenade detonated a shaped explosive against the armour to ensure maximum penetration.)

These devices were also handy for fighting on a hillside or other incline, as the grenade is less likely to roll downwards to your position than the round ones. Soon we were familiar with tossing these hand-bombs different distances from a sandbagged position, where the instructor and his student could take cover while counting the seconds until the device exploded.

During this Special Forces course we also got acquainted with night-vision devices (NVDs), which were often used during Special Forces operations. An NVD is an optoelectronic device that allows images to be produced in levels of light approaching total darkness. The military had a trio of such devices, designated by the Afrikaans abbreviations LOT, MOT and KOT.[1] At the time, these NVDs were highly classified and we were sworn to secrecy about their existence.

NVDs were also very expensive to replace. Diff de Villiers recalls how one of the instructors at the Infantry School explained that if a trooper broke one of the NVDs, then that trooper would have to serve for 17 years to pay it off!

The most versatile model at the time was the night-vision goggles (NVG) used by drivers and pilots during night operational manoeuvres. The device consisted of a headband that could be set to different sizes to fit over your

---

1 Langafstand Observasietoestel, Medium-afstand Observasietoestel, Kort-Afstand Observasietoestel, respectively.

head, with a clip-click connection where the NVG 'tube' is attached to the headband to position the optical tubes(s) in front of your eye(s).

Once the device is switched on, it creates an eerie, green-coloured image of the area you are looking at. This image is produced by capturing the available night-time illumination and converting it to both visible and near-infrared light. NVDs cause temporary night blindness, so we were taught to use them with one eye only, thus enabling the other eye to take in whatever is visible once the NVD has been removed.

We also received training in the NVD telescopic sights that were available at the time, and that could be fitted to the R1 assault rifle. These early-model night scopes were bulky and heavy and the picture they generated was of low quality, but if tuned correctly, and with a bit of practice, they worked well enough.

We did a lot of practice shooting because there were no budgetary constraints in terms of training for Special Forces soldiers. The exercises were realistic and based on the experiences of the Recce instructors who had the relevant combat experience.

SNAKES

During basics, Diff had proved that he had no fear of snakes by catching a bunch of them on the Bluff, and at Dukuduku he was truly in his element. He had a box with no less than four snakes under his bed, some of them highly venomous. One was a Gaboon viper (*Bitis gabonica*), which is very rare and deadly. One morning, upon inspection, it was discovered that the snake box was empty! Needless to say the five other inhabitants were reluctant to stay in the bungalow until all the snakes could be accounted for. Some were found in the bungalow and the rest were captured on the grounds of the base.

Another funny snake incident had occurred a month earlier on our SMORIE course. During a weapons lecture in the bush, the instructor was happily explaining something when a Gaboon viper suddenly fell out of one of the trees and onto him and the squad. The men 'bomb-shelled' and scrammed into the bushes in a split second.

The vine snake (*Thelotornis capensis*) is another rare snake that lives in trees and looks much like a twig. It was one of only two types of snake for which there was no anti-venom (the other was the yellow/black sea snake). When we were deployed in the Caprivi, we encountered many more snakes, and over the years I had a few run-ins with these slithery creatures. It was part and parcel of a Special Forces soldier's skills to be able to help yourself, or to assist a team buddy, with practical field combat medical assistance and first aid, which included the steps to take when bitten by a snake.

Dr Tinus Scheepers, who worked on the medical team for the selection course in Dukuduku in 1987, recalls how one of the students was bitten on the finger by a black mamba. They had to race with him to a hospital in a town about an hour from the base, where the soldier ended up in intensive care on a ventilator. He was one of the lucky few to survive a mamba strike.

MEDICAL MATTERS

Our medical training started during the SMIND course and would continue for the rest of the year. At the end of the training cycle, our skills were equivalent to Operational Medic, or Military Medic level II, which meant we knew how to do triage (prioritise treatment), keep a wounded or injured soldier's airway open, stop bleeding, administer cardiopulmonary resuscitation and assist with splints, general first aid and evacuation of a wounded fellow soldier from the battlefield. This was crucial training and included the all-important life-saving procedure when a wounded soldier is losing blood – administering IV fluids. This process involves inserting a thick needle into a vein, then connecting it to a bag of sterile fluid with a length of thin silicone piping.

The theory of how it works was explained to us, then demonstrated on a student, and thereafter we had to start sticking IV needles into each other's arms! It took quite a bit of practice and many of us walked around with bruised arms for a few days. We also heard stories of how the older Recces had to administer drips to wounded team members during operations. I learned in later years how critical it is to stop serious bleeding quickly and to administer a drip as soon as possible to prevent the wounded person from going into shock. This skill served me well many decades later in Iraq during mass-casualty situations following suicide bombings.[2]

NAVIGATION

Our map-reading and navigational skills were also upgraded. We were taught how to differentiate between maps, mostly topographical ones, and their scales and classifications. Then we had to know how to calculate distance on the scaled maps, and how to orientate them according to the landscape and our surroundings. Most importantly, you had to be able to determine where you were and how to work out an accurate six-figure coordinate. This was long before GPS devices were available. It involved calculating magnetic declination, orienting your map and position accurately, and using a method called 'triangulation' on your map to be accurate enough.

We also had to grasp the different types of north – magnetic, true, grid and compass north. We were sent on navigational route marches where a coordinate would be given to us to navigate to, using a compass and a map, or we would move to a position and be dropped where we had to calculate our position and navigate in 'legs' to different RV points. We were shown how to waterproof a map by covering it with a thin adhesive plastic coating, which came in a roll and which we called 'mapfolio'. Then we had to prepare the map using different-coloured, fine-tipped permanent markers to denote routes, coordinates and areas of importance for our patrol or mission. We learned how to interpret aerial photos but would later be schooled in more depth on this subject.

With the advent of GPS devices many years later, I was amazed at how easy it became to navigate, track your movements and plot your position electronically. However, I live by the motto that 'anything electronic is subject to failure'. Map-reading might seem like a dying skill to most people, but I have found it very useful to be able to fall back on the analogue way of using maps and compasses.

The SMIND orientation course greatly expanded our soldering skills.

---

2   See Blood Money, pages 44 and 82.

When I was transferred to the Special Forces training wing in later years and had access to the curriculum, I learned that one of the chief aims of the course was to stimulate the students to such an extent that they would develop a love for weapons. Our instructors were successful in this goal, and to this day many of us have a love for guns, of all kinds and applications.

This makes me think of a famous quote by the gangster Al Capone: 'You can get further with a kind word and a gun than a kind word alone.' We were now equipped with the knowledge to add a variety of international weapons to a kind word, should we have to persuade someone to cooperate with us ...

6

SEABORNE/WATER ORIENTATION

4 Recce unit emblem

You can't calm the storm, so stop trying.
What you can do is to calm yourself. The storm will pass.
– US Department of the Navy

It was now time to become acquainted with seaborne and riverine operations. The South African Special Forces equivalent of the British Special Boat Service (SBS) and the US Navy Seals was 4 Recce, based in Langebaan, around 120 km north of Cape Town, on the country's west coast. The motto of these seaborne fighters is 'Iron Fist from the Sea',[3] and they are highly specialised in closed-circuit and attack diving, underwater operations that include demolitions, deploying from the navy's strike craft and submarines, and using small fast attack boats to infiltrate and exfiltrate target areas during operations. Many Recce operations were facilitated by the navy and the use of 4 Recce's attack boats, and therefore all Special Forces members had to be oriented for such occasions when members of the different units, particularly 1 Recce but also members of 5 Recce and the secretive Civil Cooperation Bureau,[4] had to deploy by boat to reach their targets.

After our long stint in the woods of Zululand, we returned to Durban.

---

3   See Douw Steyn and Arnè Söderlund, Iron Fist from the Sea: Top Secret Seaborne Recce Operations (1978–1988). Johannesburg: Jonathan Ball Publishers, 2018.
4   The Civil Cooperation Bureau, better known as the CCB, was a covert counterinsurgency unit whose members were drawn from both the SADF and the South African Police.

We then flew to Langebaan from the military side of Durban's Louis Botha Airport. To many of us 'inlanders', and particularly the boys from the Free State, the sea was a largely unknown entity. Fortunately, I could swim well – in a pool, that is – and had spent family vacations on the east coast in the warm and fairly calm Indian Ocean. But a shock awaited us. We landed at Langebaanweg Air Force Base, around 21 km from the scenic holiday town of Langebaan. We boarded five-ton Merc trucks, which the Recces seemed to have a healthy supply of, and travelled into town. At a jetty on Langebaan's beach, we boarded 4 Recce's ferry, *The Viking*, to cross over to Donkergat (Dark Hole), a rocky peninsula where the unit's training and operations were run from.

The Donkergat facility was fairly new, and included boathouses, jetties, classrooms, bungalows, a mess hall, a large pool, dive tanks and a shooting range. There was also a 'red line' that could not be crossed by students and support personnel; only operators from the unit and personnel with 'secret' clearance could go beyond this line to where the sensitive and clandestine operational equipment for seaborne operations was kept. All operations were run from this facility, and no equipment, maps or other operational gear were allowed to leave the peninsula or be taken to the unit buildings on the Langebaan side.

During this phase of the training we were joined by a few guys from 2 Recce, who were doing the training cycle in phases. 2 Recce was an Active Citizen Force (reserve) unit, and its members were civilians who held 'regular' jobs. These guys were super and quite a bit older than us youngsters. (One of them, Stephen Cockroft, enjoyed the seaborne orientation course so much that he stayed in the business after his military service; he became an expert in catamarans and now runs a successful business, Catamaran Guru, in Florida.)

Chris Serfontein recalls how on arriving at our accommodation area, to our surprise we were informed that the unit commander, Colonel Hannes Venter, had decided that the officers and warrant officers would be accommodated in 16 x 16 canvas army tents, while the NCOs would stay in the newly built accommodation quarters. This was in lieu of some 'special' treatment for the young officers as the winter weather was terrible,

View of 4 Recce's base and training facility at Donkergat, on the west coast.

with continuous rain. The officers stayed in the tented accommodation for the duration of the course, while we troopers and the corporals stayed nice and dry in the new barracks. This is about the only time that I can recall that the NCOs had better quarters than the officers. Kudos to the unit commander for this small victory.

During our first classes we were taught about seamanship, the different parts of a boat, movements on a boat and all the commands involved, anchor drills and the rules of navigation at sea. We were then shown how to waterproof all our equipment, including communications (comms) devices, munitions such as mortars and explosives, and all other individual and team equipment required to conduct Special Forces operations. Plastic bags and containers were key, but condoms also featured in the waterproofing exercises. All pieces of equipment, however small, had to be attached to your body when moving about at sea or on a river.

Then we received instruction in small-boat operations, including giving orders, protection of boats while deployed and when anchored, man-overboard drills and safety arcs when firing various weapons from these vessels. Then we were introduced to kayaks and Kleppers (two-man fibreglass canoes), how to quickly assemble/disassemble operational craft, caching procedures (storing supplies and materiel in the field), safety aspects of kayaking, operational capacity and load-bearing limits, and how to maintain these two-man-propelled deployment vessels. We

Another view of the Donkergat training facility.

also learned about formations for small team deployments, signals and the handling of weapons aboard a kayak.

Two things about our kayak training have stayed with me. The first was how bloody cold I felt during a night exercise when I was the number two, sitting in the back of the kayak. Barry Visser's paddle strokes kept spraying cold water over me. We were clad only in PT shorts and T-shirts, and the water temperature was around 12°C.

The second memorable moment was when we fired RPG-7 rockets from kayaks at targets on land at the unit's firing range. It is important for the gunner to ensure he turns 90 degrees and checks that the backside of the launcher is not facing towards his buddy. Firing rocket-propelled grenades and machine guns from rowing boats was supercool!

The use of kayaks opened up a lot of new possibilities for quick deployment and exfiltration into and out of target areas. The training gave us all the standard knowledge of procedures and characteristics, but there was additional training in the safe use of outboard engines, particularly when there are men deployed in the water, or during a man-overboard drill.

Maintenance is an important aspect of working with boats, and our training covered engine maintenance, including desalination using fresh water and rust prevention. The latter involved the application of Momar spray, which dries fast and is not affected by salt water. It was also

4 Recce boat formation.

important for us to understand the mix of fuel for two-stroke engines, and how to safely connect and use the fuel lines.

We were given demonstration rides on the Barracuda and Avalanche boats that the unit used during operations to ferry the attack teams onshore, most of the time deploying off the back end of the navy's Israeli-built strike craft. These attack boats had powerful engines: the Barracuda Mk 1 had two 90 hp Yamaha outboards, and the Mk 2 packed 115 hp, while the Avalanches had great-sounding twin inboard 400 hp MerCruiser V8 engines with counter-rotating gearboxes and props. The Avalanche could reach a speed of 55 knots (101 kph), which was not too shabby for the mid-1980s.

To operate these boats, you had to be a qualified coxswain, meaning that you were certified to steer the boat under operational conditions. You could train as a coxswain only if you had been seconded to 4 Recce and had been nominated to undergo the training.

We were taken out to sea by some of the experienced coxswains in the unit, and one such exercise has stayed with me to this day. A few of us students were on a Barracuda with Captain Alewyn 'Vossie' Vorster in rough seas when a large wave was heading our way. He looked at the wave, then at us, and said: 'Hold on.' Only then did I realise that we were not going to try and outrun the wave but go straight through it. I remember him angling the bow of the boat (nose) towards the wave,

Seaborne/Water Orientation

Seaborne training using kayaks.

pushing the throttle (accelerator) forward with his right hand and saying, 'He who hesitates, dies!' We hit the wave full on and were flung upwards, and the boat crashed down with some force on the other side of the wave. My back was hurting from the impact; we were told to sit down and hold on to the seats, but one of our group suffered a spinal compression injury that forced him to withdraw from the cycle. I learned a valuable lesson here: when facing potential hazards or life-threatening situations, make a decision quickly or suffer the consequences.

We learned about ocean currents, tides and their relation to the phases of the moon, the different types of beaches, wave action at different beaches, shallow water obstacles, how to plan operations on various coastlines and safety around such places. Then we were introduced to knots, all kinds of them, which we had to practise often, with the most difficult one being the bowline.

We did a lot of PT in the pool and we had to swim a lot, including underwater swims in the 25 m pool. These involved exercises where you had to hold your breath underwater for long periods of time to test your lung capacity. These were commonly known in the unit as 'apnoea exercises', and the seaborne operators had to do them on a quarterly basis to maintain their seaborne status or attack diving qualification.

During the training we heard stories of the *ou manne*, the older seasoned Recces who could hold their breath for up to five minutes and longer underwater. The challenge with this exercise is that at around two minutes your mind starts panicking and your diaphragm starts an involuntary jerked breathing motion, trying to force your chest to inhale. This leads to hyperventilation, so you have to focus your mind and gather your thoughts so as not to panic and start swallowing water. The instructors told us how a few men who pushed it too far experienced 'shallow-water blackouts', a sudden loss of consciousness caused by oxygen starvation (hypoxia) following a breath-holding dive.

One night during our stay at Donkergat, my friend Neil 'Bez' Bezuidenhout was being his usual self, talking non-stop, as the excellent motormouth and clown he was. So the cycle participants decided to teach him a lesson: they would lock him up in a small steel cupboard, naked, and place it outside for the night in the cold west coast winter weather! He put up a good fight but was eventually bundled into the steel box, which was then locked. The cupboard shook for a while but eventually went silent. Maybe this was finally the right way to silence Mr Motormouth ... Then, sometime in the early hours of the morning, Bez was released from captivity. But he had saved his energy for this moment and went off like a cracker, talking faster, louder and more than ever before! He was going to teach us a lesson – whenever he was subdued, he would come back harder at us. He was a classic, a person who could make you laugh most of the time, regardless of how tired and sore you were. And he was as tough as nails, our wiry, thin, athletic buddy. He was killed in action in Angola in 1993 while working for Executive Outcomes. Rest in peace, my friend.

One weekend, some of the officers on the cycle decided to go on an (unauthorised) adventure trip. Four of them got hold of some kayaks and paddled across to Langebaan, where Hannes's mother collected them and drove them to the family home for the weekend. Her late husband had worked at the KWV brandy distillery, so she had ample stocks of the five-year-old version of this excellent brandy. The quartet were gifted a full crate of brandy, which they rowed back to Donkergat after their 'busy' weekend, and hid it from the instructors under their beds.

Sybie wanted to keep a bottle for his dad, Colonel Sybrand 'Sybie Snr' van der Spuy, the OC of 2 Recce, but by the end of the course the stocks were depleted. The excuse the others had was that they had drunk the brandy at night after our night-time exercises and 'skinnies'. A skinny was the maritime version of an *opfok* in which the students who did not toe the line, or who committed an infringement, had to swim in the cold waters of the Atlantic Ocean as part of their punishment. Skinnies were held after hours, and the offending trooper normally had to jump half-naked from the 35 ft dive tower – similar, psychologically, to the 45 ft *aapkas* (ape box) at 1 Parachute Battalion (see Chapter 8) – into the cold lagoon and swim a predetermined distance. Julian Masella recalls how one of the students who joined us for this phase, a black soldier called PJ (his name was Phillip Jones), had to get on with a skinny after dropping from the tower like a plank and landing flat on his stomach with a loud slapping sound. His belly must have been stinging like crazy, but he survived and got on with his punishment.

The two-week Water Orientation course came to an end. But before we wrote our exams and did our practical exercises, we had to be orientated in the use of compressed-air diving cylinders. Instruction took place in the ice-cold dive tank at the Donkergat facility. We were not offered wet/dry suits, though their use was explained to us. No, we had to descend into this frigid box wearing only PT shorts. The crisp coldness of the water took my breath away, and I remember how I had to focus to breathe normally through the mouthpiece and collect my thoughts. I guess the instructors were looking at how well we freshmen could handle the cold water while using the diving equipment.

Another exercise that stood out was the night-time swimming session from Donkergat to Langebaan, across the lagoon. This swim was around 3.2 km (depending on the currents) through the cold water, after jumping off the dive tower, which had a scramble net in front of it.

After the exams it was time for the course party, which was held on a Friday evening in Langebaan at a restaurant owned by Gavin Christie (RIP), one of the unit members. This was one heck of a party, and we did some serious drinking with these seaborne warriors.

With the cold and wet course now done and dusted, it was time to move to the warm bushveld climate of 5 Recce's base at Phalaborwa. There we would undergo our next course – Know Your Enemy, better known as 'Dark Phase'. We were supposed to fly from Langebaanweg in two Dakota C-47 transport planes (the military version of the DC-3 airliner). Because of our numbers and the amount of basic gear we were lugging around, each man was allowed only one bag, and the maximum weight permitted was 110 kg. Most of us were athletic and lean and made the weight, but Dries and Leon, both big tall Dutchmen, were over the limit. We quickly made a plan and divided their gear between the rest of the team.

It was around 1 700 km to Phalaborwa, and the slow old Dakotas took the best part of a day to get there. All of us had a serious bout of *babalaas* (hangover), and many of us remember how cold it was in the air. It was winter in the southern hemisphere and the outside temperature was far below zero. The cabin of the Dakota was not pressurised, and therefore the temperature could not be controlled. The flight was hours and hours of slow torture. We landed at the air force base outside Bloemfontein, which was more or less the halfway mark, and the squad looked for a sunny spot to stand in to 'defrost'. At this point I was sick of being cold, and was really looking forward to the warm weather of the bushveld. I was unaware of what a torturous time we were in for next.

7

KNOW YOUR ENEMY (DARK PHASE)

5 Recce unit emblem

To know your Enemy, you must become your Enemy.
– Sun Tzu

Although the Special Forces Orientation and Seaborne Orientation courses were visibly on a different level, and more challenging and of a higher standard than what we had previously encountered, what came next was a new level of testing a Special Forces soldier's mental endurance, physical strength and survival skills in the bush. It also involved a totally different lifestyle, with a survivability factor in a more 'guerrilla' setting, in channelled 'extreme subsistence' and in dire conditions. The Know Your Enemy course was also known as 'Dark Phase' among the operators, and was named after a course that the Selous Scouts ran on so-called pseudo-operations. In the 1970s, a group of 13 Recces went to Rhodesia to take part in this course and to use the knowledge acquired there to create the foundation for a future Recce training course on pseudo-operations and on learning how to understand your enemy.

I thought the name Dark Phase was appropriate, partly because of the hardships and all the 'black-is-beautiful' camo cream that the white men had to keep applying, but also perhaps because of the gloominess of the training. Regardless, it turned out to be a challenging time on our cycle, akin to another selection phase as our actions on the course would prove to be mentally torturous. Many operators will agree that they would rather do Special Forces selection again, as hard as it was, than do Dark Phase over.

Phalaborwa is situated in the northern bushveld area of South Africa, adjacent to the famous Kruger National Park, a wildlife reserve roughly the size of Israel, where a rich variety of wildlife roam free. Phalaborwa was the base of 5 Recce Regiment, which had started off in Dukuduku in the late 1970s. The 5 Recce facility outside Phalaborwa had been established in 1979 and occupied a year later.

Although 1 and 4 Recce had some black operators – mainly former citizens of Angola and Mozambique – 5 Recce was earmarked to be manned mainly by black operators from all South African ethnic groups, and some from other southern African countries. There were a handful of white operators, many of whom had started their careers in 1 Recce, who acted as commanders and team leaders. 5 Recce's speciality was bush warfare, often expedited with mobile tactics mainly through the use of the Casspir armoured troop carrier equipped with a heavy machine gun and turret. Casspirs normally carried either a .50 calibre or a 14.5 mm machine gun, with 20 mm and 23 mm Soviet anti-aircraft guns for added firepower during base attacks and counter-ambush actions.

The unit's credo, 'We Fear Naught but God', has become an overall motto for the Recces. This great unit conducted many hair-raising and tough-as-nails operations under the command of great officers, warrant officers and NCOs. Many of the black operators and instructors on our course had been born and trained as freedom fighters in southern African countries but had been captured and 'convinced' to join the SADF, and Special Forces in particular. Their language skills and inside knowledge of the areas where the Recces deployed were invaluable, and certain operations could not be undertaken without incorporating these soldiers into the teams as scouts or point men, who would often encounter an ambush or enemy fire first.

Before I go any further, it is important to point out, as I did in *Blood Money*, that one man's insurgent is another's freedom fighter, and one side's perception of terrorism might be the other side's view of liberation –

Know Your Enemy (Dark Phase)

Unit motto of 5 Recce.

doing what is necessary to bring about change in a country, depending on what side of the fence you find yourself. But the soldiers fighting these wars do not have much say in how the politicians and their leaders play their hands. Unfortunately, we are merely pawns in a complicated game of chess where lives are at stake.

We landed at Phalaborwa in the afternoon. After we warmed up, we were trucked to 5 Recce in the now very familiar Merc trucks. At first we stayed in bungalows on the base, where we received lectures for a few days. The first order of business was to explain to us what 'revolutionary' warfare was all about, the difference between an insurgency and terrorism, how revolutions are started, the phases of a revolution and who were the enemies of the state at the time. Major Dave Drew (RIP), an old hand from the Intelligence section, seemed to revel in teaching us about the enemy. We also discussed the terror attacks that were occurring in South Africa, and looked at case studies of these.

Major Willie de Koker (RIP) gave us a talk on pseudo-operations. These are operations in which the team members assume identities, complete with uniform, gear and weapons, used by the enemy in the specific area of operations. The correct technical way to describe such an operation is as follows: 'Pseudo-operations are those in which government forces

Soviet BTR-50 armoured personnel carrier.

Recces manning a 14.5 mm ZPU anti-aircraft gun mounted on a Unimog truck.

disguised as guerrillas, normally along with guerrilla defectors, operate as teams to infiltrate insurgent areas. This technique has been used by the security forces of several other countries in their operations, and typically it has been very successful.' The mandate of the Special Forces was to attack the enemy outside South Africa's borders, while it was the task of the South African Police (SAP) to deal with internal threats, often through the secretive Security Branch. If there were hostages or an overt armed attack, the elite SAP Special Task Force would be deployed.

We were then oriented on Swapo and its armed wing, the People's Liberation Army of Namibia (PLAN), whose modus operandi was infiltration across the border from Angola to execute terror attacks in South West Africa. We also received lessons on the different armed groups active in South Africa against the apartheid system, and on their methods, tactics and procedures, flags, slogans, and so on. There was a lot of writing to do and we scribbled away in the little SADF notebooks that were issued to us.

Other lectures included the organisational layout of the armed forces of various southern African countries, their military hardware in hand and the tactics, techniques and procedures (TTPs) used by these armies, and by the freedom fighters they gave safe haven to. We were told how there were more than 35 000 Cuban troops stationed in Angola to help fight the apartheid regime, along with 1 500 East Germans and around the same number of Russian advisors.

Foreign weapons and equipment that had been captured during operations, or lifted from enemy caches, was displayed at the back of the lecture room. We had to familiarise ourselves with the equipment the enemy used. Although we had handled and fired a lot of foreign small arms during the Special Forces Orientation course in Zululand, we now learned about the heavy weapons, artillery and field combat machinery used by the enemy. One of the new weapons on display was the B-10 recoilless rifle, known as the RG82 in East Germany, which was a Soviet 82 mm smoothbore recoilless gun. It could be carried on the rear of a BTR-50 armoured personnel carrier and had entered Soviet service in 1954.

The RPG-7 on display was already familiar to us, but the 14.5 mm anti-aircraft gun was new. This devastating piece of hardware was often deployed by the enemy in southern Angola, particularly around some of their larger and more permanent bases, where the fighters were often in trenches. Apart from being an effective anti-aircraft gun, the 14.5 mm was even more demoralising and effective when deployed against ground troops and personnel carriers. It had an effective range of 3 000 m when deployed horizontally, and 2 000 m vertically, while firing a 1 400-grain explosive-laden round at around 3 000 ft per second! In the early days of the Recces, some of these devastating heavy machine guns were fitted to the rear of Unimog vehicles, and were used well into the 1980s as weapons platforms during so-called Sabre operations involving vehicles with mounted heavy weaponry in support of Special Forces teams. (In later years, I shot shoulder-fired prototype bolt-action rifles in 14.5 mm and 20 mm. These machines were designed to take out vehicles, particularly suicide car bombers in the Middle East, and the recoil kicked like two mules simultaneously. I always maintained that shooting anti-aircraft guns, with explosive heads, is overkill when deployed against humans, but, as the old saying goes, 'You can never have enough firepower nor ammo in a gunfight,' and it was great having these guns on your side during vehicle operations.)

Another favoured weapon type supplied by the Russians was surface-to-air missile systems, which ranged from the SAM-2 to the SAM-13. The SAM-7, or 9K32 Strela-2, was a lightweight shoulder-fired weapon. It was a favourite during the Bush War, and a lot of Recces later received training to be able to use it in pseudo-operations behind enemy lines. In terms of heavier weapons, we also learned about the armoured personnel carriers used by the enemy, as well as fighter jets ranging from the old MiG-19 to the 'swing-wing' MiG-23.

IN THE FIELD

During our time at 5 Recce we took part in daily unit parades, but we had to '*tree-aan*' (fall into formation) away from the operators from the unit's three operational commandos. During a morning parade, I observed something that impressed me immensely. The unit RSM, the legendary Koos Moorcroft, one of the founding fathers of the Recces, stopped

Haak-en-steek thorns.

proceedings for an announcement to be made. Everybody was quiet as the sergeant major said: 'The following members need to leave the parade and get their kit, they are going on ops.' A bunch of black operators' names were called out and they disappeared to their team rooms. I was deeply impressed and excited to actually hear the call to arms for a Recce team to deploy on an operation.

After around three days of lectures on the enemy's equipment and training, we were told to get on the back of trucks, with no additional gear other than our overalls, and were transported to 5 Recce's training area at Savong, near the Kruger National Park. The next thing we heard were a couple of very loud bangs, which turned out to be 'thunder flashes' (a pyrotechnic device that causes a loud explosion) mimicking an ambush. The trucks stopped dead and the instructors began barking at us. We had to debus and tried to scramble into the lowveld bush but were held captive by our ambushers, at gunpoint, as if we had been captured by the enemy.

This was the start of the field part of our Dark Phase training. We were ordered to strip naked and were marched through the dense bush, where thorn trees such as the *haak-en-steek* (hook and stab) tore at our skin. Better known as the umbrella thorn acacia (*Acacia tortilis*), this medium- to large-canopied tree is found all over Africa, but especially in the savannah of eastern and southern Africa. The thorns easily hook onto your skin and tear the flesh. It felt like small blades being deployed to nick your body from top to toe, and stung quite a bit afterwards.

Some students tripped and fell, whereupon an instructor/'terrorist' would kick them, while the rest of us were prodded along so fast that we fell and were in turn booted. We were marched naked through the lowveld bush for a good five kilometres before arriving at our 'camp'. This was a primitive bush lair set up with captured Russian weapons and propaganda leaflets, much like the camps the Recces would raid in Angola and other neighbouring countries.

We spent the night in our birthday suits around a fire on the soil and sand. In the morning, a bundle of old, dirty, sour-smelling enemy uniforms was dumped in a heap in front of us and we had to try and mix and match clothes that fitted our dimensions. The trousers were too short, shirts were too small and we were barefoot. We were now the enemy.

We received very little food and only a bit of water. Sometime during the night, one of the instructors yelled at us to start 'fucking the ground'. This was a weird instruction, but we had no choice but to start pounding the earth. During this spectacle Van decided to add some sound effects and started moaning and groaning. In any other setting this would be funny as shit, and at least one of the instructors complimented him on his love-making efforts!

Later in the afternoon we were lined up in a straight line, whereupon one of the instructors yelled obscenities to us while slowly walking down the line and throwing slices of bread in the dirt and dust at our feet. This was supper! One of our good corporals did not take kindly to this type of treatment and decided to stomp on the slice of bread with his bare foot. This did not go down well with the instructors, and it was the start of a very long night where we got fucked up good and proper.

From the minute we arrived we got stuffed around and barked at by the instructors, in the way that they had been treated when they were in exile. They showed us how they were trained in the bush in neighbouring countries, or where they were given refuge, to be trained in revolutionary, guerrilla and unconventional warfare. We lived in foreign camo uniforms, similar to what the insurgents and 'terrorists' wore in the African bush, and had to paint our faces, necks, arms and hands black with the sticky black camo cream. One of the black Ovambo instructors was Willy Ashipala, a young ex-Swapo fighter who had been caught during an SADF operation not long before our course started. Willy's English was not the best, but he taught us to sing a Swapo freedom song that went something like this:

> Namibian people unite in one body
> To wipe out Boeralism from our country
> To put people govern to Namibia
> Supported by their workers
> Let's carry on the struggle Comrades
> Let's carry on the struggle Comrades
> We are fighting, sacrifice, suffering any time
> O yes, Namibia is ours
> Namibia must be free
> Whatever obstacle can be
> PLAN of Namibia
> Fight till we win
> O yes, Namibia is ours

Van recalls how 'one night we sat on the ground in an open patch of earth between the trees that was our "classroom", and the instructors sat on camp chairs on the outer circles and watched us. We had to learn "Nkosi Sikelel' iAfrika", which was used as the instructors' national song by our "comrades" at the time. I remember how well Comrade Willy Ashipala sang the freedom song while the captured former freedom fighter displayed some homesickness in his voice – it was full of emotion. The nights were long, with little or no sleep as we were stuffed around and kept awake. This night we were told that if we could memorise the words and sing the complete song, we might go to sleep (first). My name during Dark Phase was "Comrade Russia". I thought about this and realised that it was going to be a long night … I remember that PP Hugo, or "Comrade Bare-ass", was the first student to sing the complete song and he then could go to bed. While all the singing was going on I moved backwards slowly piece by piece in the dark without anyone seeing me. Ten minutes later I managed to crawl to my designated bush, got under it and rested. I could hear how the men were slowly progressing to sing the song. I managed to get a good night's rest and started nice and fresh the next day.'

We had to find shelter under trees and bushes and had to flatten some grass and leaves to sleep on. I remember how bloody uncomfortable I was at first, and that my morale took a dip during this training phase. This was, of course, the instructors' intention: they wanted to show us how tough the conditions were for our enemy. During the first few days we received very little food. We were hungry and tired, yet we were woken up again and again during the night to gather and sing freedom songs and slogans. All this stuffing around was designed to break down our morale, sometimes through physical activity, or the threat of violence, and it worked well. We were told how the racist Boers kept ambushing the supply trucks, so there was no food to feed us. They turned out to be right: as we later learned, the SADF, and particularly the Recces, were masters at disrupting enemy logistics.

Then there was all the propaganda against the racist apartheid regime that we had to listen to and then sing and shout out loud. It was quite ironic that 'Nkosi Sikelel' iAfrika' became the South African national anthem in 1994. The song was adopted by many exiled freedom groups, and versions of it became the national anthems of several African nations. And to think that we learned it in 1986 – almost a decade before it became our anthem …

Although many of the instructors were former insurgents/freedom fighters, Staff Sergeant Piet 'Gif/Oppies' Opperman (RIP) took charge of the proceedings. A South African who had served in Rhodesia with the RLI and Selous Scouts, Oppies was a good soldier but a hard bastard, with ice-cold blue eyes and a serious beard. The other instructors had to follow his warped sense of humour, which got us stuffed around without end. On day two, some of our cycle buddies who were smokers had nicotine withdrawal symptoms and decided to smoke some hippopotamus dung

Student receiving pap ration (Recce archives).

that the instructors had found. They were caught and ordered to dig a hole about six feet deep, in which they were buried, standing up, with only their heads sticking out in the baking sun, and with no water in sight. After a day and a night, the two tired and dehydrated soldiers were dug up and released back into the bush.

Often during Dark Phase students had to dig a square hole that was just deep enough to squat in, naked, and then were covered with sand that left only your head sticking out. This manoeuvre had a devastating effect on morale; after a few minutes your body started cramping, and you would be left in this squatting position for hours, or even a full day, without food or much water. Another punishment was being locked up, naked, in a bamboo cage that was just high enough for one person to squat in, and then having buckets of water thrown over you.

We were also taught how to march like the bloody commies without bending our knees, almost like a goosestep. They kept telling us how South Africa would fall and that the masses of Azania would rule. Who would have thought back then that they were right?

We were fed 'slap-pap', a watery and runny version of boiled maize meal, from *pap-potte* (porridge pots). Diff remembers how on one occasion Sybie pushed his grubby, dirty and dusty hand all the way down to the bottom of the large black pot next to the fire to try and grab as much porridge as he could, pulling out a lump of pap the size of a rugby ball. Some on the course thought that this was their lucky day, as they might get some food from him. Most of us could not grab much of the watery maize with one hand (you only had one go at it). But alas, the instructors prevented Sybie from sharing his loot with us, and they made him eat the entire lump of maize meal there and then.

One day, a bag of well-worn boots was dumped in our midst. We all scrambled to try and get some footwear to protect our feet from the thorns, rocks, hardwood twigs and hot sand. The boots were mismatched, with too many lefts or rights, and the sizes, shapes and makes differed vastly. It was near impossible to find a matching pair of boots that fitted, and some of us (like me) ended up with only one boot. It was a size or two too small, but it was good enough for me, as it meant I could hop around thorny and rocky areas on one foot with the boot when required. But there was one trooper who was unfazed at going barefoot in the wild – our good buddy Diff de Villiers, as he went everywhere in life without shoes! The calluses on his feet were an inch thick and as hard as boot leather, and thorns could not penetrate our comrade's feet.

Speaking of comrades, Staff Sergeant Oppies christened PP Hugo 'Comrade Bare-ass' and Braam 'A-poes' – a reference to his blood type that sounds like a very vulgar Afrikaans word!

Another incident from Dark Phase that stands out was the night we were divided into groups and each group had to go and explore a different target and then report back to the instructors. Diff's group had to do a reconnaissance on a group of 5 Recce soldiers who were busy in the bushveld with a course-end party. It was a dark night when Dem and Diff decided to peel off, leave the rest of the team behind cover and creep closer to the bunch of happy soldiers. After a period of intense observation, Diff leopard-crawled to the generator and switched it off. The bartender rushed over to the generator to refill it with petrol. Dem and Diff crawled to the bar tent and came upon a zinc bath full of ice, water, beer and cooldrinks. They grabbed as much as they could carry, as well as a handful of T-bone steaks fresh off the grill. The team had a good time and ate and drank their looted supplies on the way back to our bush camp.

The two weeks or so spent in the bush, living like terrorists, felt like much longer. Our slow torture finally came to an end. We returned to the unit and took long hot showers to scrub ourselves clean like little piglets. It was time to write exams and be tested on how well we knew our enemy, and then there had to be a course party, as usual. We were carted down to the training area at Savong, to a site next to the Selati River (a tributary of the Olifants), where the unit had a picnic facility and where we would have a braai with some proper meat and alcoholic refreshments.

We were told to stay clear of the river, as there were crocodile and hippo in the area. Mark and Grant decided to go for a walk to check out the scenic bushveld, and Mark spotted a hole below an anthill. Upon investigation, a warthog came charging out, making hog-like grunting and squealing sounds that gave Mark a fright. He took off so quickly that one of his flip-flops came flying over his head! Nevertheless, we had a good feast, and everyone was looking forward to moving on to Bloemfontein, where we were due to undergo our Parachute course.

In the end, Know Your Enemy, or Dark Phase, as we would forever refer to it, was a difficult but worthy course, taught to us by men who actually had been the 'enemy', and who had the experience to take us through our paces. Not only did this training course prepare our minds – by helping us to understand the enemy's moves better in order to plan counterterror operations – but it also mentally hardened us so that we knew what to expect if we were ever captured. I think that learning the enemy's TTPs, mindset and living conditions, plus how they are trained and indoctrinated to kill you, is invaluable for Special Forces training, as it makes planning and executing missions against such foes much easier.

8

PARACHUTE COURSE

1 Parachute Battalion emblem

And where is the Prince who can afford to so cover his country with troops for its defence, as that ten thousand men descending from the clouds, might not in many places do an infinite deal of mischief, before a force could be brought together to repel them.
– Benjamin Franklin

Jumping out of aircraft is frowned upon by most people. But in Special Forces or special operations circles, this is one of the many distinctions that separate specialist soldiers from normal infantry and other battle formations. Jumping off a high point and using a type of cloth or chute to slow the descent has an interesting history, and the first claimed parachute jump from an aircraft occurred in 1911. During World War I, 'spotters' in hot-air balloons in operational areas were given parachutes as a means of escape if the balloon was shot down. But it was during World War II that the mass dropping of paratroopers in an offensive military role made its mark and proved its value.

Since World War II, the deployment of soldiers into combat areas by parachute has been extensively used, particularly by Special Forces. The basic type of parachute deployment is referred to as a 'static-line' jump: the jumper does not control the opening of the parachute, a function that is executed by a static line with a hook device that hooks the jumper up to a steel cable that is fixed inside the aircraft and pulls on the parachute and opens it as the soldier exits the door of the aircraft. This type of jump is normally done from heights ranging from 2 000 ft to as low as 600 ft, when rapid deployment of paratroopers is required in a combat zone and to minimise the amount of time they spend drifting down in the air, when they are vulnerable to enemy fire. Special Forces are normally schooled in more specialised forms of parachute deployment: high altitude low opening (HALO) or high altitude high opening (HAHO). Such deployments normally occur between 8 000 and 35 000 ft – beyond normal auditory and visual detection, higher than the effective range of most types of anti-aircraft gun – and allow for long-range parachute infiltration.

Altitudes above 26 000 ft (8 000 m) are considered the 'death zone' for humans without assisted oxygenated breathing. So HAHO and HALO para-jumpers deploy with small oxygen tanks and masks at high altitudes. This type of parachute deployment is one of the specialist courses that a qualified operator engages in after the initial training cycle.

We were now on our way to my hometown of Bloemfontein, where the elite 1 Parachute Battalion was based and where we would undergo the basic parachute jumping course. This would enable us to deploy, with combat gear, by day or night, with a static-line parachute, and to end the jump on land or into water.

1 Parachute Battalion was formed in 1961 and has a rich tradition as an operational combat airborne unit. Like Britain's Parachute Regiment, many paratroopers globally wear a red beret. However, South African parabats adopted a maroon beret, similar to that worn by the US 82nd Airborne Division, allegedly because South African army doctors, medics and support personnel already used the red beret. When the Special Forces were created in the early 1970s, it made sense that operators would use the maroon beret as they were also airborne soldiers, though with different regalia on the beret. Initially, the Recce beret sported a metal springbok head, but this was later changed to the compass rose – the central logo of the Recces.

It is not well known, but paratroopers from 1 Parachute Battalion's Delta

Company took part in operational jumps in Rhodesia during the late 1970s as part of training by the RLI in how to conduct so-called Fireforce operations: paratroopers were dropped, often at night, behind the enemy during attacks in order to ambush and stop them. These were risky missions, but the Rhodesians were good at parachute deployment in the bush warfare context, and the South Africans learned quickly and performed well.

It was also decided in the late 1970s to establish an internal 'special operations group' within 1 Para Battalion, namely, the Pathfinders. This was just after Operation Reindeer (May 1978), when 367 paratroopers dropped on Cassinga, in Angola, to take out an enemy base, codenamed 'Moscow'. A number of parabats were killed or injured during this very difficult operation. One problem was that the drop zone had not been reconnoitred and secured before the operational jump took place. These Pathfinders underwent some intensive training, and cross-trained on a few subjects with Special Forces. Their main role was to go in first to find, create and secure operational DZs for the paratroopers during operations.

The new hangar at 1 Parachute Battalion, or 1 Bn, had been completed in 1985, and we were one of the first groups to undergo training at the facility. It was a large warehouse-sized metal building with a high roof to accommodate para-jumping instructional devices. There was a lot of gym-mat-type padding on the floor. With these mats came metal walk-up ramps where the troopers would jump onto the mats to exercise their landing rolls.

Rounded tubelike metal structures, meant to resemble the rear end of jump planes, were also erected on the sides of the hangar, and para-harnesses hung from straps in front of these simulated aircraft. One such device was called the 'block and tackle': you got into a harness a few feet off the ground and performed your aircraft exit drills, after which you were dropped like a sack of potatoes in order to practise your landing and sideways-roll drills. The thing about hanging in a harness is that it really squeezes the shit out of your testicles! And of course there had to be a sadistic instructor or two who walked around with washing pegs in their pockets that every so often found their way to a student's nuts if they weren't performing the drills flawlessly.

Parachute Course

Candidates doing marble PT at 1 Parachute Battalion, with the *aapkas* in the background (Recce archives).

Then there were a few large fan-like devices on top of a metal ledge on the north side of the hangar. Access to this level, which was 30 ft up, was by climbing up sets of metal stairs situated on the side of the hangar. It turned out that the metal cables that clipped on to the jumping harnesses worn by the trainees were connected to the fans. The turning blades would create air resistance to slow a jumper down after he jumped off the ledge.

And then there was the dreaded *aapkas*. This large box-type room was situated on metal legs 35 ft high in the air with cables running out of it – a bit like a cable car somewhere on an exotic mountain top! Would-be paratroopers were instructed to climb up the metal stairs into the *kas* (box), where you would be hooked up to the cable, as you would be in a plane before the jump command was given. They were then dispatched and pushed out of the box to slide downwards on the cable like an adventure zipline. The height of the *aapkas* was apparently a psychological threshold – not high enough to lose the perception of height but too high for your brain not to think twice about jumping. In other words, it messed with your mind to the extent that you had no choice but to jump and believe that your parachute equipment – prepared by the packers – and your training would assist you to leap out of a plane and land safely. After our seaborne safety training in Langebaan, airborne safety now became a life-and-death reality for me, and later a personal motto – 'safety first'. Chris distinctly recalls the first time I had to jump off the ledge in the hangar with the fan, and particularly so when I took the leap of faith from 35 ft above ground level out of the *aapkas*.

On 14 July 1986, a very brisk and icy Bloemfontein morning, we initiated our first training steps to become airborne combat operators. This would become one of the greatest experiences of our lives, as we all had personal fears to overcome before we could be badged as 'airborne troopers'. The Para 8617 Parachute Jumping course routine for the next three weeks at 1 Bn involved waking up at 04:30 to do PT from 05:00 to 06:00. The para-training PT was designed to be hard, in order to distinguish the troopers from the normal infantry and other units through their physical strength and fitness. But for us on the Special Forces training cycle, men whose fitness had been honed throughout the year and who had passed the Recce basics and selection phases, the physicality of the paratrooper PT was not a problem.

We were fit and strong, and absorbed all the exercises thrown at us. These included pull-ups, push-ups, pulling yourself up and over a two-metre-high wall, running, rifle and marble PT, and climbing to nine-metre heights with thick ropes by using your arms only. I did well with the rope and in later years could ascend two ropes hanging two metres apart by grabbing one rope in each hand and climbing in a fast-swinging motion akin to Tarzan or Donkey Kong – for those readers old enough to remember either of these characters!

After PT we changed into our overalls and jump smocks with the heavy leather para-boots that gave extra support to your ankles if laced correctly. One action that will cause you to fail para-training is to land with your feet open. Many would-be paratroopers were disqualified due to not landing with their feet together, as it is a natural instinct to open your feet to shoulder width when jumping off a ledge or some height. The right way to land is with your feet together, knees slightly bent, seeing the tips of your toes, back arched, arms stretched above your head against your ears, and palms turned inwards, and then with the side of the knee, then

Para-jumpers climbing into a Dakota aircraft (Recce archives).

hip and then the side of your back, rolling over to break the landing.

Diff, who like all of us was reprimanded for landing with open feet, decided to make a plan to overcome this challenge. He very ingeniously inserted a wire loop inside the inner heel of one boot, and a hook in the other. These wire devices were supposed to clip into place after jumping and doing his checks to ensure he kept his feet together for landing. It worked well, but a beady-eyed jump instructor spotted the contraptions on Diff's boots and pulled him out for some punitive PT! Apparently, a similar trick had been tried by Sybie's younger brother Olla (Olivier van der Spuy), who had done the jump course a year or two earlier. Olla had placed a large rubber band over his ankles after executing his safety drills once he cleared the plane.

This was our first outing to a non-Special Forces unit since leaving the Infantry School after passing the pre-selection phase. The mess hall, bungalows and routine were more in line with those of infantry and other army units than with the Special Forces facilities we were by now accustomed to. It was the officers' turn to enjoy the luxury of the officers' mess at the Tempe military base while the NCOs stayed in old barracks towards the centre of the 1 Bn area.

The officers might have enjoyed the after-hours luxuries, and one officer's 21st-birthday excursion led to the Halevy House Hotel, but they really missed out on the hard-core 1 Bn culture and action. We heard the stories of the battalion *ou manne* (qualified paratroopers), who traditionally gave all new troopers an *opfok* when they arrived at the unit. We did not think the national servicemen *ou manne* from the battalion would mess with the Recce recruits, but lo and behold a squad tried to sneak into our bungalow one night after lights out. One of our regular 'colourful' corporal cohorts was ready for this panel-beating squad. When they stealthily entered our sleeping quarters, they were greeted with the cocking action of a Beretta 92 9 mmP service pistol, and were instructed, in no uncertain terms, to 'fuck off' or risk being shot. It worked like a charm.

Another incident occurred at the mess during a tea break when a group of Special Forces troopers from South West Africa mistook us for regular army recruits and ensured that we did not get to the plates with the cookies. Nicky Fourie, a staunch man himself, and assisted by Diff and Wetta, decided to give it to them, and made them understand quite clearly who we were and that we also enjoyed our cookies at teatime! The problem was solved very quickly, and this lot always ensured that there were cookies left for the would-be Recces, even if they got to the mess hall first. After the cookie incident, one of the para WOs called the three into his office and congratulated them for sorting this bunch out.

We were left alone for the duration of our stay at 1 Bn, but the stories of inter-unit fisticuffs and weaponised fights in the Tempe military complex were legendry. Troopers from 1 Para Battalion, 1 SA Infantry Battalion (1 SAI) and the School of Armour (Pantserskool) clobbered each other on a regular basis, to the extent that some troopers landed in the intensive-care unit of nearby 3 Military Hospital. The commanders, of course, pretended to do their best to avoid such bloodshed, but the unwritten code of the units was to not be overpowered by opposing units' troopers, as prestige and honour were at stake.

Little did we realise that these 1 Bn troopers would become our lifeline during operations. They would sometimes join us in combat, as part of a combined fighting force during the Bush War, and would sometimes

Parachute Course

be the linking-up force, or operational reserve, to assist Special Forces operations deep behind enemy lines.

Our ground training went well. D-day came on 22 July. This was the day we put all our ground training into practice, boarded an actual aircraft and jumped out of it. Our first jump, and subsequent static-line jumps, would be from a Dakota aircraft. This 'workhorse of the sky', in military aviation terms, has seen extended service by various countries since World War II, and remains in use today.

We boarded the old bird the same way we would exit in mid-flight, via the open cargo-section door on the rear left (port) side of the aircraft. On the runway we were divided into 'sticks' of between six and twelve men; each stick would be grouped with another to make up a 12-man jump 'string'. We did our equipment checks, ending with emergency parachutes and helmets. Each Dak could accommodate two strings, thus up to 24 jumpers, with one and sometimes two jumpmasters. The aircraft slowly took off while us would-be paratroopers slowly clapped our hands, shouting 'up, up, up' and then triumphantly crying 'airborne' as we took to the skies.

The Bloemfontein plateau is almost 5 000 ft above sea level, and it took several minutes for the Dak to attain the desired altitude of 1 200 ft above ground level for our first jump. We were seated tightly next to one another, looking towards the tail at the jumpmaster. First came the 'ten-minute' warning; at the 'two-minute from jump' warning a red light went on in the back of the aircraft, which meant we had to stand up and hook on to the thick cable running along the side of the cabin. Standing in our sticks, we conducted a final kit check; then, with our right hands over the emergency parachutes, we faced the rear of the craft. When the 'one-minute' command came, the jumpmaster yelled, 'Action stations!' In line with our ground training, we all shouted 'Action-stations!' and started the para-jump shuffle, counting out loud 'one-two, one-two' until the front of the stick moved to within a metre of the door.

The number one in the stick would place his left hand in the door frame, and his right hand over his emergency parachute. We stood ready for a few seconds, when finally the jumpmaster shouted 'Stand in the door!', which we thunderously repeated while taking one more shuffle

Static-line jump from a Dakota (Recce archives).

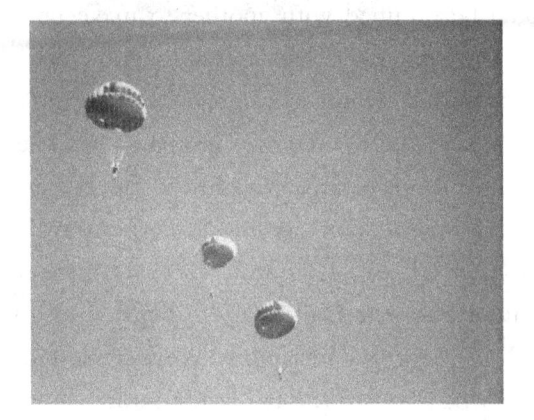

Parachutists descending.

Parachutist preparing for landing.

forward. The number one now had both hands on the door frame, with his head outside the door and the jumpmaster holding him tight. The green (jump) light was activated by the flight crew as soon as the Dak reached the DZ, and then it started: the jumpmaster screamed 'GO!' and the first jumper was dispatched with a strong but controlled leap. We took another shuffle forward each time a jumper left the plane.

Finally, it was my turn. I stood in the door, looked down through the clear skies and tried to make out what was happening below me. I did not have time to take in the 'scene' as I was pushed out the door while I propelled myself clear of the aircraft by pushing on the sides of the jump door with my arms. It was winter in the Free State and it was well below zero degrees Celsius. We were a thousand feet up in the sky in a plane that flew without a darn door, so we felt the cold good and proper.

But once I left the plane, I looked up to see my parachute deploy (to my relief), and, after concluding the 'right-low' and 'left-low' checks past my slightly bent legs, I had time to look down at my emergency parachute, where I spotted a few drops of sweat! Yeah, it's below zero and I am sweating – par for the course, I thought. But as I drifted down towards the DZ, I breathed deeply a couple of times and enjoyed the silence and the view.

This interlude was short-lived, however, as the ground and the LZ came up towards me fast. 'Feet together, feet together,' I repeated to myself. The instructors on the ground were watching our every move through special long-lensed optics mounted on high tripods, focusing especially on our landing efforts. I hit the ground hard and executed my sideways roll to break the fall. It was done: I had survived my first jump out of an aircraft. Victory!

I now had to pull the jettison cable loops situated on both breasts to release the parachute or risk being dragged by it once the wind picked it up. We had been trained to 'gather' our chutes in a very specific manner: you rolled up the canopy and rigging lines with your arms in a figure-eight motion called a 'daisy chain', and then placed the chute in an empty canvas parachute bag with closing zipper. The bags were loaded on the back of a supply truck and carted back to 1 Bn, and on to the para-stores.

Here, the specially trained packers would rearrange the chute and fold it back to a state where it could be checked and used for the next jump.

We had to conduct 12 jumps successfully in order to qualify. Some involved weapons and backpacks being rigged to your harness and placed on your upper legs when you boarded the plane. The pack stayed on your legs when you left the plane and could be 'jettisoned' by activating a metal lever when you were close to landing. The pack was connected with a strong four-metre rope to your harness and would hit the ground first, after which you would follow and land close to the pack.

Course 8617 went on to complete another ten static-line parachute jumps at the Kenilworth DZ, seven of them Dakota jumps, one of which was at night. Chris remembers the night jump as the moment he learned about 'ground rush', and completely misjudged the last few metres before touchdown. It was painful! The other three jumps were from a Transall C-160 aircraft (now decommissioned), and the Dexter DZ was used due to the high number of paratroopers who would be jumping per approach.

During my first port-side exit, I was caught off-guard due to the wind speed, which can happen when you are one of the last jumpers in a stick. Chris recalls that, much to his delight, our eleventh jump was fabulous, and most probably the best of the course. Instead of a wind-forced exit from the side door of a Dak, we had a nice 'zipline-type slide' from the open-ramp tailgate of the C-160. For the first time in my life, I experienced a short moment of free-fall parachuting as the sheer force of the C-160's double propellor wash created an air pocket through which I glided. This is heaven, I thought, but then the drag of the chute pulled me back into static-line reality.

During our time in Bloem there was a rugby match one Saturday afternoon at the stadium close to town. A few of our ranked brothers decided to attend the match after consuming some 'refreshments' in the morning and early afternoon. The stadium had a normal gate entry system, but several soldiers decided to get to their pavilion seats via the risky manoeuvre of scaling the pavilion from the rear. A member of the 'sporting' party ascended the crossbeams of the 30 m pavilion; about three-quarters of the way up, he slipped and made a wagon-wheeled

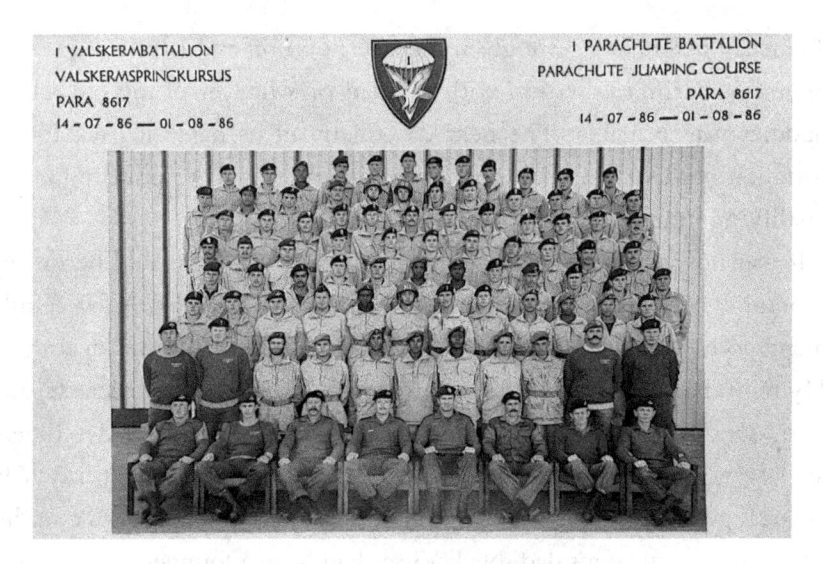

Parachute Course 86/1/7 group photo.
The author is shown second from right in the back row.

descent – his feet 'not together' – landing on a crossbeam about three metres above the ground, like a sack of potatoes. This was very close, but he escaped serious injury, apart from a very tender ribcage.

The guys finally got in from the top, and the civvies inside the stadium were flabbergasted that these 'spider-men' made it all the way to the top of the pavilion. Everyone enjoyed the rugby match, while the crowd was sporadically entertained with several Dark Phase 'freedom songs' as the day's refreshments started to take their toll. St Michael, the patron saint of paratroopers since World War II, certainly guarded them well that day.

St Michael probably watched over all of us, as the 'tricks' we got up to were hair-raising and could have resulted in serious injury or death. Grant recalls another good memory: one of the hangar instructors was a bit of an asshole, and forever had students buying him Yogi Sip drinks when they faulted or made a mistake during training. A plan had to be formulated to get him back. One day the doctors on our course laced one of the 'gifts' with a type of liquid diuretic, and the drink was duly handed to the instructor before our qualifying jump. He needed to urinate every 15 minutes or so, and therefore could not get in the plane with us on that day.

Our day for qualification, Friday 1 August, was drawing closer. On the

Thursday before, we were given the afternoon off and I rushed home to organise a drinking session with my dad or whoever of my old school buddies was available. The next day, many of us made it back to the battalion with varying degrees of *babalaas* and started to prepare for our qualifying jump.

It was not just the beady-eyed para instructors who would be on the ground watching our every move into and out of the Dak. A few family members had come to observe their sons leap into thin air from an aircraft. My mom had taken time off work to come and watch the spectacle, and Barry's mom and a few other cycle brothers' parents had travelled to Bloem for 'parents' day', to watch their sons qualify as paratroopers. It had been prearranged that Barry's mom would pin his paratrooper's wings onto his chest, in honour of his dad. Nick Visser had been a founder member of 1 Parachute Battalion before he went on to become one of the first Recces.

Also attending our passing-out parade was the legendary 'Tannie Mossie' (Joan Abrahams), a teacher at the Oranje Girls' School in Bloemfontein, who made it her life's mission to support the South African paratroopers. Her nickname came from the 'mossie' (Cape sparrow) on the old one-cent and half-cent coins, and she would hand these coins out to the troopers, reminding them that if God sees fit to watch over these insignificant little birds, then He will protect the paratroopers.

The day of our qualifying jump came and went, and most of us were now certified paratroopers. We made our way back to 1 Recce in Durban and enjoyed a weekend off. After learning how to jump out of planes, our next course, Air Orientation, would take us back to the Dukuduku training facility in Zululand.

9

AIR OPERATIONS (AIR ORIENTATION)

*Aviation is proof that, given the will,
we have the capacity to achieve the impossible.*
– Eddie Rickenbacker

Most Special Forces deployments involve fixed-wing and particularly rotary-wing aircraft (helicopters, often known as 'helis' or 'helos'). This was no different for the Recces, and we had to become au fait with many different ways of deploying with, working with and extraction by various types of aircraft. The Air Orientation course was held in the familiar surroundings of the Recce training base at Dukuduku. It was an extension of air deployment tactics with a new specialised dimension, namely, the use of helicopters in combat applications. During this training phase Master Chung joined us again for unarmed combat sessions that increased in intensity.

Our first classes covered cooperation between Special Forces and the air force, and in particular with the helicopter pilots. We learned about planning air operations, or deployments, and the difference between helo deployments, helo assaults, clandestine air operations and air logistics. We received instruction on tactical air operations and air logistic support operations, such as the dropping of door bundles from Dakotas, and rat-runs, where supplies are dropped at low level to a predetermined DZ. We also learned how to create or select fixed-wing landing strips, the marking and reporting of such strips, helicopter landing-strip selection, preparation, and marking, and arranging the reception party. We covered close air support and how to call in an airstrike during combat, something normally done by qualified forward air controllers, or FACs. We also practised parachute infiltration and helicopter cooperation during our time at Dukuduku.

One of the most important classes was on helicopter safety and how to approach a helicopter in a safe manner. This was important as the tail rotors of these machines would instantly kill you if you came in contact with them, and perhaps also disable the heli, which could have a devastating outcome during an operation. Another important safety risk to look out for was when a helicopter hovers over an incline or decline and the soldiers have to debus and move under the blades. One can easily run into the blades, especially at night and when under fire. And we learned to make sure that the barrels of all weapons pointed downwards in the heli. This ensured that any accidental discharge of a weapon would not go upwards and into the motor and rotors.

There were classes on the different types of helos, with a particular focus on the French-made Pumas and Alouettes used by the South African Air Force. The Puma was used as a troop and cargo carrier, and the lighter, more manoeuvrable Alouette was used as a gunship or to casevac wounded soldiers. We learned their capabilities, payload, number of soldiers with kit that could be loaded and safety aspects.

Next we had to learn about all the fixed-wing aircraft in use by the air force, from the single-engine Bosbok light plane, used as a spotter or 'telstar' for relaying communications, to the big Lockheed C-130 Hercules and Transall C-160 cargo/troop carriers and jump planes. The attack jets of that era were the MB-326K Impala MK II, an Italian plane manufactured under licence by Atlas Aircraft, and the French Dassault Aviation Mirage III. We had to learn how to do aircraft recognition in order to identify those that might be encountered in the operational areas, and their potential to inflict damage on own forces.

Working with helicopters and deploying with planes has a certain allure to it, but you need to know what you're doing when working with these metal birds. By now we were familiar with the venerable Dakota, and had flown in the C-160 when we did our jump course, but this was the first time a lot of us had climbed into a helicopter. It was an amazing experience. Over the years, and after I left the military, I have clocked up a great number of hours and miles in both fixed-wing and rotary-wing craft. But my preference has been for the helos, and I have been fortunate

Abseiling exercise, Dukuduku.   Abseiling from a bridge, Zululand.

enough to work with machines from all over the globe.

The next phase of our training covered the marking of landing zones for both fixed- and rotary-wing aircraft and drop zones for parachute assault or air logistic support operations. We were taught how to read the wind and how to assist the pilots to either land or drop troops in a safe and organised way, often by deploying smoke grenades to mark these areas. The classes included radio call-in procedures, and we practised talking choppers in to LZs. Then there was the use of infrared devices for night use – for the few choppers in those years with night-vision capabilities. Good ground-to-air communication procedures, either voice or signal, are critical for safe air operations, and their absence can lead to injury or even death during operations and training. Following this came tactical air operations, which was specialised and involved quite a lot of planning and logistics.

ROPEWORK

The use of ropes and ropework out of helicopters forms an important part of a Special Forces soldier's skill set. But before we could rappel out of helos we had to be taught how to use harnesses and equipment to abseil down solid structures, such as bridges in the Dukuduku area. It was great fun to descend a building or solid construction by rope using a figure-eight belaying device.

It was then time to practise descending out of a helo hovering over a DZ or target area. We conducted a lot of simulated airdrop operation scenarios, as well as rappelling out of the helos with all our kit and backpack. This proved to be slightly tricky as the pack made you pendulum backwards with your feet in the air if you were not careful.

We conducted a night exercise where we simulated a helo deployment by rappelling with full kit and then walking to a predetermined RV to plant dummy mines. I had on my full webbing and a heavy pack plus the 20 kg dummy mine strapped to the outside of my backpack, which altogether probably weighed around 76 kg – all on my back– with the chopper hovering at around 30 to 40 ft.

When it was my turn to descend out of the heli, I hooked my harness up to the rope with a carabiner and figure-eight, turned my back outwards, knees slightly bent, ready to kick away from the chopper and get to the ground quickly. I kicked out and relaxed the grip of my gloved right hand from the rappelling rope, with the weight of my kit causing me to slide downwards very fast. It was time to slow down, and as I closed my hand, it slipped off the rope. The weight of my pack caused me to tilt backwards, and I hit the ground on my back, very hard. The mine strapped to the outside caused my spine to go into a negative backwards bend – I heard the snap, crackle and pop of vertebrae and remember a sharp pain between my shoulder blades. I got up quickly and the surge of adrenaline washed away the pain. I gave the injury no further thought. I was young, tough and on a mission to become a Recce – it was no good giving in to your body's cries for help. (It later turned out that the impact had caused a hairline fracture of a spinal disc, which became progressively worse over the years due to excessive wear and tear on the spine.)

It was now time to get acquainted with 'fast-roping', a technique used to deploy soldiers quickly from a hovering helicopter if the heli cannot land. You use a thick-weave kinetic rope up to 66 ft in length that is

Air Operations (Air Orientation)

'Hot extraction' exercise, Dukuduku.

attached to the chopper frame and tossed out so that the soldiers in the heli can slide down to the ground. This was great fun, and later on, during our Advanced Urban Warfare course, we nailed it by deploying a six-man team on top of a building in less than ten seconds. The secret is in continuity and momentum, so that the soldiers follow each other within seconds of clearing the helo. You should also not be afraid and try to slow down, as your buddy above you will crash into your hands, which can make you slip and fall to the ground.

Another great exercise was the 'hot extraction', in which a similar thick kinetic rope with loops at the end is used to quickly 'hook up' four soldiers at a time per chopper and then to lift them and fly away from an extraction area, with the troopers dangling at the end of the rope. Once out of the danger zone, the helo lowers the men to the ground, where they 'un-hook' from the rope and the choppers land at an LZ.

FURTHER PARACHUTE JUMPS

The air operations training went well. It was now time to practise the static-line parachute jumps that we had learned at 1 Parachute Battalion. We conducted one daytime jump out of a Dak with battle gear but without backpacks, followed by a night-time jump with the same equipment. The second night-time jump was done with heavy packs, and there was a slight wind that caused us to 'drift' quite a bit. It was a fairly dark night and I remember battling a bit to jettison my pack. I finally got it swinging loose seconds before I hit an anthill, not far from the airstrip, hard with my feet and landed on the ground like a bloody postbag! My injured heels felt a sharp sting when I hit the ground and my back still hurt quite a bit from the rappelling accident. I got up slightly slower than I did after previous jumps but got going again, and I pulled the wire-ring 'Capewells' to release the harness. (The Capewell is a release mechanism that keeps the parachute harness attached to the body but frees it from the chute. This prevents the parachutist from being dragged by the chute when the wind picks up. It is also used to release the jumper from the harness if hanging in a tree after a jump.) Then I untied the rope from my pack and 'gathered' my chute in a daisy-chain motion as we had been taught. There was no time to lick my wounds, and I picked up the pack and continued with the exercise.

Later on, once we were qualified and were serving in the operational commandos, we got acquainted with what is known as a 'water jump' – landing in the ocean, in a dam or in a river. This type of arrival was easier on the body if executed correctly, but you had to get out of your parachute harness and out from under the canopy quickly to avoid the risk of drowning.

In all, we conducted four daytime and two night-time jumps in Zululand during this period, most of them fully operational with webbing, rifles and packs, as you would during an official mission. During one of the day jumps some of our fellow students got into trouble after exiting the plane. I was on the ground with a few other students and instructors watching the Dak do its run over the airstrip when I heard a commotion and some hard whistling with instructors pointing upwards. We saw three parachutists very close to each other, with two canopies entangled and a third close to them. These guys' chutes had not opened fully and their lines were twisted and tangled. This problematic situation is called 'a roman candle', perhaps because the tangled straps, ropes and chutes look

Air Operations (Air Orientation)

Cycle 86/01 students at drop zone before parachute jump, Zululand.

like a candle flame. These guys were falling down to earth faster than the rest due to the non-deployment of their chutes. Their distress lasted a while and they were nearing the ground too fast without fully opened canopies. There was a worried 'humming' among the instructors and we feared that our buds might 'bounce' – a term with bad connotations in parachuting circles.

They hit the ground hard, almost on top of each other, and lay still. The medics who were always on standby during these exercises rushed to the men to assess their injuries. Doc Tinus Scheepers was most seriously hurt of the trio, with a broken backbone and jaw; PP landed hard on his right side, and broke and cracked several ribs; Grant was bleeding profusely from his mouth after biting his tongue badly as he hit the ground. Both PP and Doc Tinus were immediately stabilised – Tinus on a spinal board – and loaded into a Dak, which took off for Durban, where they were admitted to the Addington Hospital. Poor Grant was sent straight back into another Dak to jump again. Otherwise, one of the instructors reckoned, he might become apprehensive about jumping.

That day, the wind was blowing at the maximum that was allowed for jumping. Doc jumped after PP and ended up in PP's canopy after he got entangled in the lines. This caused both of their chutes to collapse and for them to accelerate towards the DZ. Grant was just below them, and with them descending into his canopy he also started moving faster. Both Tinus and PP realised that they were going to crash and all three hit the DZ hard and on top of one another. The top two jumpers' boots hit Grant in the head and neck but fortunately did not cause serious injuries.

Chris, who jumped just before them, recalls it as follows: 'I was in the first half of the string (think number two or three) and they jumped after me. Once my parachute deployed I first drifted downwind but realised what the problem was and immediately turned into the wind, which was strong because I was still moving backwards. Fortunately, I was light, and the heavier men started moving in underneath me.

'The rest of the string behind me moved rapidly closer to me and someone came through my parachute carry-lines but luckily and quickly moved out of it again. PP must have jumped after me because I remember him moving towards me, turning upwind and over Tinus's canopy that was still drifting downwind. The next moment PP's canopy largely closed, while he was about 30 m to my left, PP falling through Tinus's chute and they both then fell through Grant's.

'From above it did not look good, and I estimated that it started happening around 50 ft, after which they fell hard to the ground. The three men were each lying within one to two metres of each other. After we landed, the string immediately grouped to see what the damage was to our fellow soldiers. PP complained of sore knees and ribs, Tinus held his mouth shut and complained of a sore back while the medics stabilised him on a spinal plank, and Grant could not speak with a lot of blood coming out of his mouth. We later found out that Grant had bit through about half of his tongue during the impact. I must say that I was impressed with the medical support's speed and effectiveness at the time. This incident luckily had a favourable outcome as it could easily have ended in a tragic day indeed.' This accident meant Doc Tinus had to wait for the next cycle, six months later, and he completed his training in 1987.

In between the air operations training we still had hard PT sessions, including weekly operator PT assessments, and unarmed combat classes with the wiry Master Chung. My body, and particularly my heels, were aching more often than not. I kept ignoring the pain, but it constantly reminded me that my body was protesting.

As always, time flew by, and the course soon came to an end. This was good and valid air-wing training and stood me in good stead in the years after the military when I worked around the world as a PMC. Once we were qualified operators, a few of us were sent on the forward air control course, where you were taught how to call in airstrikes from a forward reconnaissance position.

10

DEMOLITIONS AND MINE WARFARE

> *Unless you work in demolitions, don't burn bridges.*
> — Harvey Mackay

Special Forces soldiers work in demolitions *and* they blow up bridges; these activities form part of their primary skills. Calculating the amount of explosives required, handling explosives, knowing the specialised applications of explosives and detonating bombs that destroy, neutralise and disrupt enemy forces — these are specialist skills that can be deployed to devastating effect.

War is as old as humankind itself, and explosives are the most destructive force known to humankind. Bomb-making was figured out by the Chinese, who in the 9th century developed black powder — the first widely used explosive in warfare and mining. The first useful explosive stronger than black powder was nitroglycerine, developed in 1847, followed by trinitrotoluene, better known as TNT, in 1863. The 20th century saw the development of modern high explosives, culminating in 1945 with the dropping of the most powerful form of explosive — the atomic bomb.

Hand grenades also have a long history, going back to the Byzantines and Persians. The modern grenade was created by placing concentrated black powder in a casing that could be thrown by a soldier towards an enemy, with the device exploding a short period later in the midst of the foe.

The development of landmines accelerated as a result of the two world wars. Millions of these dastardly devices were manufactured and used during the 20th century, and landmines have killed and maimed uncounted innocents around the world. Millions of landmines are unaccounted for in areas such as the Iraq/Iran border, Egypt, Afghanistan and other former conflict zones such as Cambodia and Bosnia.

Demolitions and Mine Warfare

In the hands of a skilled soldier, explosives can be deployed to devastating and spectacular effect. But it takes specialist training, and a bit of grey matter, before a soldier can start blowing up things. It was now time for us to learn how to apply demolitions (dems) as part of the Recce arsenal.

The Demolitions course took place in Durban, with the practicals held outside Ladysmith, where 5 SAI was based. We stayed in the old base at 1 Recce where we had done our Basics training seven months earlier. Our cycle buddy, Lieutenant PP Hugo, who had been injured on the Air Orientation course, was now an assistant instructor, as he had prior demolitions experience at his previous unit, the School of Armour in Bloemfontein. Then there was the legendary Staff Sergeant Anton Benade (RIP), who served in the Rhodesian SAS before coming over to the Recces in 1980. Anton had a dry sense of humour, and, unlike most Recces, his tipple of choice was vodka rather than Red Heart Rum.

Our lectures took place in the auditorium located close to the gate of the new base on the Bluff. It was an impressive setting, with good audiovisual aids for lectures and presentations. Also on the course were a handful of policemen from the SAP's Railway Task Force. They fitted in quite well considering that they were from a law-enforcement background and we were soldiers.

First, we had to learn the safety parameters, which constituted a thick manual on its own. You had to pass the dems safety exam with an average of 80 per cent or higher, otherwise you would be kicked off the course and the Recce cycle. After that we learned about all the different kinds of detonators, booster charges and high explosives used in military demolitions scenarios.

HE consists of a mixture of chemical compounds that becomes unstable and explodes when set off correctly. This blast creates sound and heat, and displaces air at rapid rates so that matter caught up in the blast zone is destroyed. But to set this destructive force in motion you need to connect the explosives to a detonator, and in some cases to a booster charge. Detonators consist of a small amount (typically one gram) of a very powerful and sensitive explosive, for example pentaerythritol tetranitrate

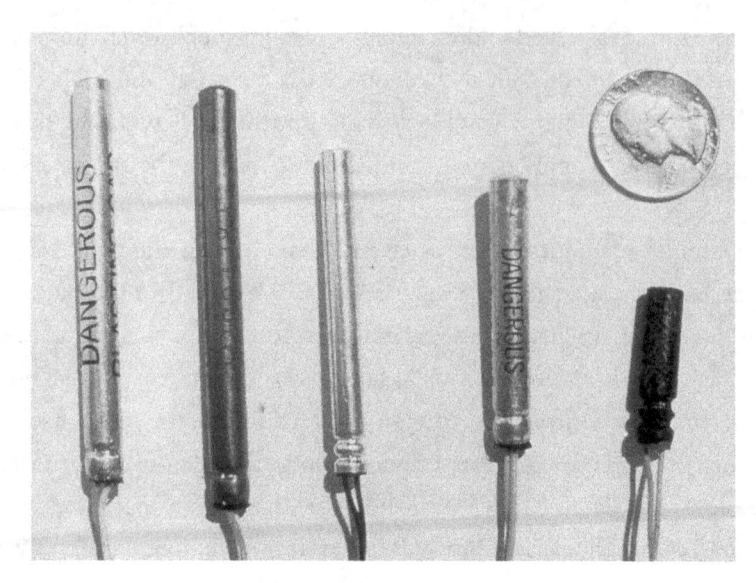

Electronic detonators (coin added for scale).

(PETN); the explosive is encased in a small aluminium tube, with either two thin wires protruding from the back end or a hole where you can attach, in dems lingo, a 'crimp' safety fuse, of varying length, to set it off.

The detonating device causes a small explosion that on its own cannot destroy much, though it can blow off your hand or a finger, or blind you. But once you stick the detonator into a larger amount of HE, this small detonation causes a chain reaction that sets off the whole lot. If you are building a big bomb, or rigging a lot of explosives to bring down a structure, you might have to make use of a booster charge, which also consists of HE but is slightly more stable than the detonating charge and less stable than the HE charges that constitute the bulk of the bomb.

There are also flexible detonating cords, or Cordtex, which are typically used in mining applications. This device consists of a very unstable, fast-detonating PETN explosive inside a plastic casing, and is supplied in rolls that look like electrical extension cords. The explosive cord-roll is used to join a number of charges over a short distance to create a 'daisy chain' that detonates different sets of explosives in sequence, or simultaneously. A small device can be clipped on to the Cordtex to create a time delay when the plastic cord detonates. We referred to these plastic squares as

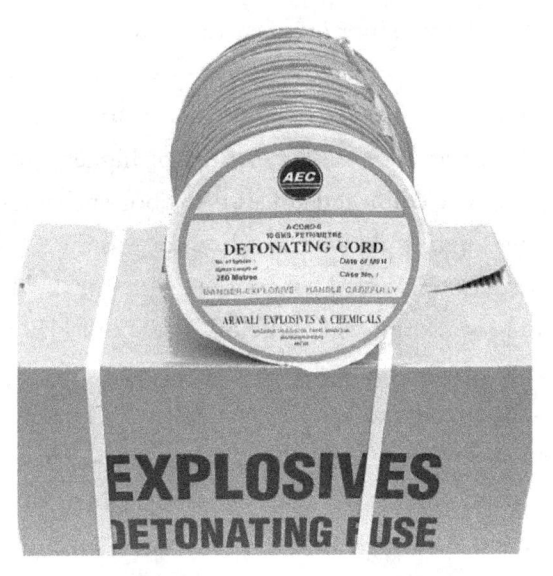

Cordtex detonating cord.

'dog bones', and they were colour-coded to indicate the different time delay of each.

But before you could connect the whole lot together and create an explosion, you first had to test your power source and wiring, unless you were using a safety fuse that burned at a steady and easily predicted rate, with a device we called a 'Vulcan head'. This was a small round-headed flat contraption, with a small amount of sulphur and two thin wires, that was set off by a spark created by your power source. It created a smell akin to matches being lit.

Calculating the correct charge loads of different kinds of explosives involves working out a lot of mathematical equations. And since mathematics and studying had been the last things on my mind in high school, I had to focus hard during these lectures and exercises. Unfortunately, some students could not get to grips with the maths and fell off the course. It was sad to see buddies who had come such a long way being RTU'd (returned to unit), but that was how high the standards were set during this phase.

We started our practical exercises down at the shooting range and the beach at the old whaling station facility, where we were taught how to handle detonators, how to insert a safety fuse into a detonator and how to connect a detonator to Cordtex explosives. An electronic detonator only requires a small amount of DC current to set it off – as little as 0.5 volts (V) will do. Therefore, an AA 1.5 V battery or higher will suffice. Then we were taught how to connect detonators to booster charges, which were made of Pentolite high explosives. The booster was the size of a fistful of tightly rolled banknotes, with a hole in the centre for the detonator.

Next we had to work out what type of Cordtex or HE you would use for the task at hand. We were shown how to construct 'knock-knocks' using the fast-detonating sheet explosive SX2, with a detonator and wires connected to a power source. This would be used to blow a door before the rest of the team entered a room containing targets or hostile forces. Sheet explosive was also very effective for constructing letter bombs. Later on, during our Urban Warfare course, we learned how to use Cordtex strips to blow doors off their hinges in order to gain rapid entry into a room where targets might be hiding. We used Vulcan heads to test our power streams and sources, and after that we started creating small explosions. It was exceptionally cool, at age 18, to be taught how to blow stuff to smithereens with HE.

There seemed to be a particular focus on how to demolish bridges, and we were taught how to work out the explosive loads for various types of bridge structures – cement pillars, metal beams, cable suspensions, and so on. One day we were taken on a trip out of the city, to a bridge that was less frequented by the public, to practise how to place charges under and around a bridge. We travelled south of Durbs in the unit's five-ton Merc trucks, with supplies for the day and training materials to simulate the attack on the structure. It was not a long drive to the exercise site. Once there, we set up a small command structure for the instructors, and then we were shown the bridge's weak and strong points, and where we were to place our carefully calculated charges. The next exercise was practising how to work under a bridge using a large green military net that you affix to stable points on the structure. It was fun trying to balance and position yourself correctly in the net. Another exercise involved affixing a mock charge underneath the bridge with strong glue. Diff recalls how

The author (left) and Japie Celliers rig an explosives ring, the Bluff.

one trooper thought it a good idea to hold the charge in place with his head, so as to free up his arms, while the glue was drying. But in doing so some of the glue ran downwards and the trooper below found his head stuck to the bridge! No names, no pack drills ... These exercises went on for the best part of the day and we learned a lot.

While were doing the Water Orientation course in Langebaan in June 1986, the ANC's military wing had attacked Magoo's Bar, a popular watering hole on Durban's Golden Mile beachfront. The attack occurred on the evening of 14 June 1986 when a car bomb exploded outside the bar, killing three patrons and wounding another 69. This incident angered us, and increased my motivation to complete my Special Forces training in order to hunt down such enemies of the state. During a weekend when we had a day off, a few of us took a trip to the beachfront to see the damage. The glass windows facing the street had been blown out and were still covered with cardboard. The place was closed and we could not really see what it looked like inside, but there were tell-tale signs of a blast. We decided to have a drink at the Why Not Bar, located in the same hotel, to take in the 'ambience' of the place after the bombing. Bombs were a fact of life in South Africa during the 1980s, and people were regularly briefed on what actions to take if they spotted a 'suspicious' parcel or item in a public place. Ironically, we were now also schooled in the art of building bombs and blowing up places. Such skills were deemed an integral part of a Special Forces soldier's training.

MINES

The Demolitions course also introduced us to mines and their application in unconventional warfare, even if the Geneva Conventions banned the use of mines in conventional warfare. These devices were used in Rhodesia, South West Africa and parts of southern Angola to attack the security forces and farmers alike.

A landmine is a devastatingly effective terror tool. It cannot be seen and it is patient, waiting for its unsuspecting prey to step on or drive over it, whereupon it detonates. And once you are aware of mines in your area of operations, you have to deploy additional resources to ensure that your personnel do not set off these hidden explosives. We had been schooled in the identification and application of various Eastern Bloc and other international mines and grenades. Later on in our Bush Warfare phase we would use these items during exercises and simulated ambushes and attacks.

And then we were also introduced to the notorious claymore mine, which is feared and respected, depending on which side of it you find yourself! The M18A1 claymore is a directional anti-personnel mine developed for the US armed forces. Its inventor, Norman MacLeod, named the mine after a large medieval Scottish sword. The claymore consists of a horizontal, slightly convex case, around 20 cm wide and half that high, filled with around 1.6 kg of HE. These fast-detonating devices are stuffed with metal bearings to create the ultimate 'shotgun' effect for maximum killing and wounding characteristics. The front end of a claymore is marked with the famous phrase 'face towards the enemy'.

Designed to counter human-wave assaults, the claymore uses a shaped PE(C)-9 charge to fire several hundred steel balls into a designated 50 m killing zone. It has two sets of legs and an 'aiming' sight with an opening on the top to the side, where the detonator is inserted. It comes with a 30 m roll of brown D10 double electric-flex wire, a low-resistance stranded/

Demolitions and Mine Warfare

tinned copper wire with colour-coded PVC insulation, used in military applications for demolitions and signals purposes. One end was connected to the detonator, and the other end to a power source, a hand-held device called a 'clacker' (due to the sound it made), which detonated the device.

Later on, we were taught how to rapidly deploy these devices, on the ground or tied to trees (around chest height), with tripwires, for when you are on the run and you want to slow down enemy follow-up forces. Claymore mines could also be used to devastating effect during ambushes: you would 'spring' the ambush by setting off a few claymore mines, perhaps in conjunction with landmines, after which you would pepper the ambush point with machine-gun and assault-rifle fire.

PUTTING IT INTO PRACTICE

We did daily PT, and Master Chung was present for us to hone our unarmed combat skills. We practised in the NCOs' car park at the 1 Recce base. These sessions generally ended with a few bloody noses or split lips. One afternoon on the rugby field at the old base, during a hard PT session, Sergeant Ian Strange (RIP) was looking for a volunteer to demonstrate some wrestling moves, and Leon Venter stepped forward. Leon was a tall and strong Dutchman, and, unbeknown to the sergeant, he happened to have Springbok colours in amateur wrestling. Ian, an ex-Rhodesian SAS soldier, was a tall, powerful man with the temper required of a Recce instructor. But during the proceedings he could not pin his student down, and the harder he tried, the redder his face became. After a valiant attempt the demo ended, and somebody in the group nicknamed the sergeant '*die groot-rooi-een*' (the big red one). It stuck for the remainder of our cycle year whenever our group referred to him.

It was now time to put our knowledge of explosives into practice. For this we moved to 5 SAI's base at Ladysmith, approximately 200 km northwest of Durban. The trusted Merc trucks transported us with all the necessary equipment and munitions for the practical phase. We were going to set up a tented camp outside the 5 SAI lines in their designated munitions training area. The unit would send field meals out to our training location. But before we took off for Ladysmith the instructors got some of our group, namely, JJ, Van and Croucs, who were full corporals already, and who also had the necessary army-issue truck licences, to go and collect a truckload of 'things' to blow up from a scrapyard in Durban. This truck, full of various metal and aluminium pieces of all kinds, including some old appliances and rail bogies, left Durban with the rest of the convoy for the practical field phase.

Once we were settled in the training area, our exercises started. We used various explosives, Cordtex, detonators and boosters to create charges of all kinds to blow up or surgically cut through the various pieces of metal we'd brought to the training site. We were taught ways of 'cutting' steel with explosives and how to make ribbon, diamond and staggered charges. It was lots of fun, but we had to stay focused to ensure we passed the practical phase of dems training. All the formulas and calculations we had been taught were applied to ensure that we worked out the correct explosive charge for each task at hand.

During the course we had been introduced to various types of charges. First, there was the shaped charge, or inverted charge, a deadly bomb that effectively concentrates the power of the explosives on a single point to penetrate heavily armoured vehicles and metal several inches thick. Three decades later, in Iraq, such devices would kill scores of US servicemen and PMCs, including South Africans. The so-called explosively formed penetrator/projectile (EFP) detonates at speeds of between 7 000 and 12 000 m per second. An EFP also creates very high temperatures, touching on 1 000°C.

We were shown linear charges, which vary in length and operate on the same principle as shaped charges. This concentrates the blast over a previously worked-out length in order to cut steel of varying thickness, including railway lines and bridges. Then there was the 'beehive' charge, used to make craters in asphalt and dirt roads. This device stands on three legs, at a height of around 10 to 20 cm, and can be positioned over a railway line or road surface. The beehive consists of between 30 and 165 kg of HE, and creates quite a blast. We blew a few craters and made some big bangs.

One bang I will never forget was when the instructors informed us that they were going to blow up a large domestic gas cylinder, filled

Demolitions and Mine Warfare

Cycle 86/01 field dems explosion, near Ladysmith.

Field dems explosion, near Ladysmith.

with liquid petroleum gas. The gas cylinder was positioned behind an old dry tree branch on a downward slope from our viewing position. We were ordered to move 1 000 m away for safety reasons. All of us assumed the prone position, with our heads sticking up like meerkats to see the spectacle. The charge was detonated, and almost instantaneously we felt the blast and saw a huge fireball mushrooming into the air – the heat was intense, and we were a kilometre away! This was impressive but also deadly serious: some of our Recce brothers had been on operations to destroy oil and gas installations, and some team members had been seriously injured or killed when explosive charges went off prematurely. In 1981, during Operation Kerslig, Captain Jacobus Petrus de Koker (RIP) was killed in action when an explosive mine detonated prematurely.

During the dems course we were also introduced to improvised explosive devices (IEDs). This refers to explosive devices that are designed to look like everyday objects. An IED blends into its environment, except that is packed with explosives. IEDs are normally detonated in a public setting, where the maximum amount of casualties and damage to property can be inflicted. Years later, many of us would lose buddies through IED explosions in Iraq, where bombs would even be hidden in dead dogs.

During the practical exercises we blew up a lot of the scrap metal that we had brought from Durban. Diff remembers how he found a *skaapsteker* (a type of grass snake) whirling around a large metal rim after one of the explosions. The snake must have been dazed, as they are normally too fast to catch. Though probably severely shellshocked, it survived the entire practical phase under Diff's careful nursing and care, to be released when we packed up our field base and returned to Durban. Some of the leftover scrap metal was returned to the scrapyard, and the owner could not believe that people could fuck metal up so badly. I wonder what he thought demolitions and explosions was all about?

When we got back to the unit, it was time for examinations and practical tests. Major Daan van Zyl, a respected senior officer of 1 Recce's operational 1.1 Commando, gave us a motivational speech on an operation the Recces had executed in October 1977. Without much fanfare, the major told us the story of Operation Kropduif, which some Recces referred to as the Battle of Eheke, on 28 October 1977. The Recces and 32 Battalion had taken part in this tough operation in southern Angola where many lives were lost in both units. We heard the stories of how our *ou manne* and everyone involved fought gallantly, and how the casualty rate was so high that the Puma helicopters that casevaced the injured and dead were covered in blood an inch thick. I remember how motivated this talk on an actual Recce operation made me feel. These soldiers were the real deal, warriors at the very tip of the nation's spear.

Our exams involved a lot of calculations and descriptions of various types of explosives and mines. We then went down to the whaling station where we rigged Cordtex loops that were detonated electronically, and with safety fuses of various lengths. We were also evaluated on constructing an IED of sorts (minus the explosives, with detonation mimicked using Vulcan heads). I rigged up an empty Cremora creamer bottle with wires hanging from the lid, which would detonate the Vulcan head when you opened the bottle and interrupted the circuit, sparked when certain wires that were connected to a 1.5 V AA battery made contact. My IED worked, I passed our demolitions course and now was the proud owner of a 'dems ticket'. It was time to move on to our next training course: Survival, Bushcraft and Tracking.

The 'dems ticket' (demolitions certificate) issued to PP Hugo.

11

BUSHCRAFT, TRACKING AND SURVIVAL

*Survival can be summed up in three words – never give up.
That's the heart of it really. Just keep trying.*
– Bear Grylls

Most elite forces are trained in the art of surviving the harsh and austere conditions that might be encountered as the unwanted and unplanned consequence of shifting battle parameters, failed operational execution or the ever-fluid nature of combat missions. Special Forces can be trained in the techniques of survival in various different natural conditions in their respective theatres of operations, for example desert survival, snow survival, jungle survival, survival at sea and, in our case, survival in the bush. The month-long Bushcraft, Tracking and Survival course precedes the aspiring Recce's last and possibly greatest challenge to becoming an operator – the Minor Tactics phase.

After the Demolitions course we started assembling all the weaponry, ammunition, explosives and logistical supplies we would need for the final three-month training period. All this equipment and materiel would accompany us on a C-130 Hercules military cargo plane to the Caprivi, and the training period would climax with our first operation into Angola. We were convoyed to the military section of the old Louis Botha Airport, ten kilometres south of Durban, from where we flew 2 000 km northwest to Mpacha in the Caprivi.

To be able to survive in the bush, mostly behind enemy lines, to be able to track your enemy, lost team members or animals, to be able to live off the land without any equipment other than a knife, to be able to use the sun and stars to determine time, direction and navigational bearing, and to be able to understand the veld and animals in the area of operations –

Bush classroom during the Survival course. The author is shown seated in front.

these were all skills that were needed by a Special Forces soldier, not only to pass the training cycle but also to practically execute and survive during operations.

We were moving to the Recces' training and sometimes forward operations base, Fort Doppies, in the western Caprivi Strip, in northeastern Namibia. The Caprivi is a vast area of southern African bush wedged between southern Zambia and Botswana. In those days, it was God's country, with magnificent wildlife inhabiting its savannahs, dense bush, forests and grasslands, pans and rivers, and thousands upon thousands of animals, including the Big Five, hippos, crocs, giraffes, baboons and all the various species of buck. The Caprivi had it all. It was a nature lover's paradise. It was also a key sector of the South West African border that had to be patrolled and defended by the SADF. It was where the fearless and effective 32 Battalion operated from their base, called 'Buffalo'. We flew from Durban to the large airstrip at Mpacha, near the border town of Katima Mulilo. All of us were excited, and I was looking forward to getting acquainted with the border, and with South West Africa in general.

When we arrived at Fort Doppies, we were shown the bungalows, lecture room, mess hall, stores, bar and other areas of concern. Unfortunately,

Teddy the lion, who used to roam freely around the facility, was no longer around, but we were told stories about him. A remarkable area at the base was a small parade ground known as Freedom Square. This was where Recces could, on occasion, air their opinions, gripes and ideas in general without being judged or bullied by higher-ranking members. What was said at Freedom Square stayed at Freedom Square. A contribution on the Recce website (www.recce.co.za) describes it as 'a square marked off in the camp. If any persons in the camp had a grievance or wished to settle a dispute, they would sound the siren on the square to call the personnel in camp. The person/s with the dispute/grievance would then be able to settle it on Freedom Square regardless of their rank or status, as all persons on Freedom Square were considered equal while on the square and could say anything to anyone without incurring any repercussions.'

Having completed our orientation, and stored our kit, it was time to move into the veld for the practical survival phase. First we were strip-searched at the chopper pad for any contraband, specifically firelighters and matches, and anything that could make things easier in the bush, for example torch lights, multitools, ropes and containers. During this search the instructors confiscated two cans of beer from Dampies' kit. Braam wondered if he had been planning to bake some 'beer bread'...

We moved to an area in the veld around five kilometres north of the Kwando River, where it snaked like a horseshoe. The 'horseshoe' was a well-known landmark for the operators who knew Fort Doppies. We assembled in a field training camp, where our first class was presented. This was on orienting yourself in the bush by finding a suitable spot to lie up and be static in order to survive until found by own forces.

Staff Sergeant Ray Godbeer was our course leader and the survival guru at the time, following the departure of Sergeant Major Dewald 'Dewies' de Beer – or 'Oom Dewies', as everyone called him – one of the 12 founding members of South African Special Forces. Ray was assisted by Sergeant Ian Strange, whom we knew well by now, and by Corporal JJ Raath, who had been an assistant instructor during our selection phase and now taught bushcraft, tracking and survival. JJ travelled to Fort Doppies with us; he had to complete the Minor Tactics training phase in

Brian Harris and buddies building a field basha.

Fire-making using sticks (Recce archives).

order to qualify, as he had been injured the year before on the 85/01 cycle.

We were told that to be able to survive in the bush, and in general, you had to be fit and have the will to survive. We learned that the human body can survive up to four minutes without oxygen, four days without water and fourteen days or more without food. Then the criteria for a good 'hide' were explained: high ground (if possible), shelter from the wind and the average direction thereof, as close as safely possible to a water source and away from footpaths.

The next subject was on how to build a suitable shelter in the African bush. The instructors demonstrated the basic principles, and then we split into two-man teams to build our own 'bashas'. The term 'basha' is used in the British Army to describe a shelter that is built in a similar way as a rudimentary tent or screen by using wooden sticks, leaves, grass and pieces of wet bark to secure it all. There are various types of bashas, defined by the type of roof you construct. Factors such as the time of year (season), position of the sun, wind direction/s and rainfall patterns had to be considered.

One major factor in surviving in the bush is being able to find water. We were taught how to dig a water hole in a dry riverbed with a piece of bark or wood, how to gather water from leaves and plants, and how to gather atmospheric water at night by using a rainproof poncho. This involves stretching the plastic coat between tree branches, or pre-cut wooden sticks, with a small weight in the middle to cause dew drops to run toward the centre. The water can be collected in the morning before sunrise. Another way of getting small amounts of water is to collect it from the stomachs and intestines of dead buck.

We were then schooled in how to make a fire using a wooden block and a stick, of certain qualities and in a specific manner. First you had to find some hard wood, which was cut and prepared as the base. Then you had to find the softest wood available and either break off or cut a rounded piece around 30 cm long that would be rubbed fast and repeatedly between your hands on the base. This was no easy task and it took a lot of hard work with your hands to create enough friction to heat up a small 'coal' and then to ignite some dry grass that you had already gathered. Once your 'kindling'

A Breed Apart

The author's survival tin.

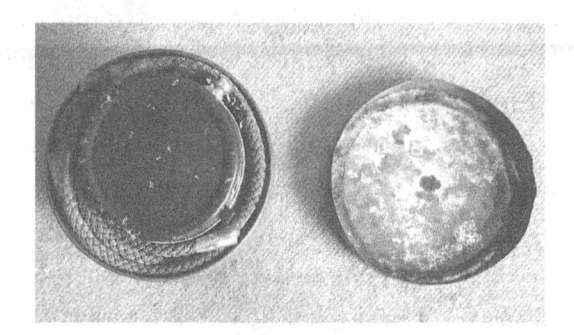

Open survival tin.

Contents of survival tin, including compass,
fishing line and hooks, and surgical blade.

caught fire you had to shield the flame with your hands and softly blow on it to make it bigger, and then add more dry grass and twigs.

As soon as you have a small fire going, you can start packing slightly larger pieces over it, and once you have a proper fire you can stoke it and add large branches or pieces of wood to the flames. It took a lot of practice, and our hands got harder as the course progressed. Another way of starting a fire was to use a piece of double-flex electrical wire connected to a power source, such as a small battery, and then 'shorting' the poles over some dry grass. You can also use the sun to start a fire: if you can get hold of a piece of magnifying glass, such as those used in prismatic compasses, you can concentrate the rays of the sun through the lens to create a beam of concentrated heat onto your kindling.

Another skill required to survive in the bush is the ability to make tiedowns by using the wet fibrous parts of tree bark. Certain plants, such as sisal, were more suitable for this purpose. The secret is to ensure that the materials you use are damp. Often you had to soak it before you could cut it into thinner strips that could be woven together to form twine. We were also shown how to use the skins of mammals to make *rieme* (hide strips).

Once we mastered the art of creating 'ropes', we were shown how to set traps for different-sized animals of various kinds. This was done by creating a slipknot, a loop that closes when one end is pulled: a bird, rabbit or larger animal such as a buck pushes its head through the loop of the slipknot, making the device tighten around its neck. The animal then strangles itself or is trapped until you can get to it. The loop could also entrap the creature by closing over its foot. The secret was to tie the non-loop end to a firm base or anchor point, to place the trap in an animal path in the veld and to camouflage it properly to blend in with the surroundings.

Another important aspect of surviving in the bush is to be able to catch fish. Part of our 'survival kit' included fishing line and a few small fishing hooks. You had to be able to find water sources such as rivers, natural pans, streams and water pits, and we learned techniques such as catching fish with a wooden spear, the correct use of 'mud streams' and

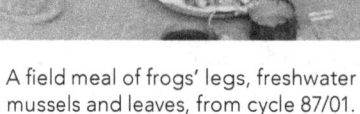

A field meal of frogs' legs, freshwater mussels and leaves, from cycle 87/01.

Brian Harris holding a tigerfish.

how to catch freshwater crabs, frogs and mussels. Brian Harris, who was a game ranger and nature lover, managed to catch a tigerfish or two, and quite a few barbel (catfish). Needless to say, he was very popular on our survival course!

To be able to survive in the African bush, you need to be able to recognise animals and birds and other wildlife. We attended many lectures, sometimes during the day but just about every evening after dark, in an open-air makeshift bush classroom where we sat on the ground with a military tent-tarpaulin rigged overhead. First there were lectures on dangerous animals, of which Africa has many, followed by lectures on the signs and expressions made by different animals to indicate danger (the way buffalos, baboons and certain birds react to intruders, for example). Animals that indicate sources of water include crocodiles and hippos – both plentiful in the Caprivi and around Fort Doppies – skunks (polecats), otters, waterbuck and birds such as the fish eagle and kingfisher. Food sources could be found by following lions, hyenas, baboons, badgers and crows.

Birds are a good source of information. In addition to the birds mentioned above, you could find water if you were familiar with birds that depend on water more than others for existence. Such birds include geese, herons, partridges, guinea fowl, ibises and *bleshoender*, or red-knobbed coots. Birds to keep an eye on for sources of food include all birds of prey – eagles, falcons and hawks. Birds are good alarms, too, if you know what to look out for and their behaviour when they are surprised, disturbed or sense danger. Such birds include kiewit, sparrows, guinea fowl and the *kwêvoël* (grey lourie).

One thing I learned quickly living in the veld was the effect of a male lion roaring at full pace close to you, especially at night when you cannot see the magnificent beast but know that he can see you. It is a sound that travels through your bones and makes you extremely wary of their presence. The Kwando and other rivers in the area were full of crocs and hippos, the latter often ill-tempered, especially when young calves were involved. Although we were armed with R4 assault rifles, our orders were not to shoot any animals unless our lives were in danger. Besides, the light 5.56 x 45 mm round would probably only upset the large dangerous game that could kill humans. We were also not allowed to hunt with assault rifles, and doing so could get you kicked off the course.

We were taught what types of insects and other small creatures could be eaten and were high in protein. These included flying ants, scorpions and the very nutritious mopane worms. I managed to catch a couple of scorpions, which I prepared by removing the pincers and cutting off the poisonous tail end (the stinger). I then pushed a small round stick with a sharpened end through each and fried these arachnids (order Scorpiones) over a small fire. It tasted a bit like calamari and was also a good source of protein.

After Rob and I built our basha, I decided to work on a strategy of 'low output' leading to 'low input' in which I lay up in the basha, conserving energy and therefore having to eat less. After a downpour or two I was able to gather a bunch of flying termites, which tasted like peanut butter once you removed their wings and boiled them a while in your aluminium dixie set. (The dixie consisted of two round pans that fit over one another, with wire-type handles that folded around the sides. It was great for frying or boiling food.)

Nicky would prepare some kind of meat in his dixie set and put it in his backpack, which was placed next to his head at night while he slept. One morning he woke to find the bag gone, and he reported it as missing. Our instructors thought that someone had pinched Nicky's belongings, and proceeded to fuck us up for a good many hours, until someone found the para bag, and some tracks, that indicated that it had been the work of a hyena.

Van recalls how Sergeant Ian Strange was the main suspect for pinching the bag, as he would sneak around at night to catch students off-guard and take their assault rifles and essential kit if they were not watching closely. Staff Sergeant Godbeer mentioned that it might have been a wild animal that took the bag, whereupon some wag muttered, 'It must be a "strange" kind of animal,' in reference to Ian's surname.

The bag was missing a chunk as big as a soccer ball, and Nicky's metal dixie set and leather boots had been bitten through. Hyenas are scavengers with humongous teeth and a bite force three times that of a pit bull terrier and double that of a lion's bite! We then heard that hyenas bite people who are sleeping on the ground in the veld in the face, crushing their skulls in the process, and then drag them away into the bushes to feed on their prey. Nicky was therefore very lucky to have not been bitten in the face during this incident.

Someone managed to get hold of a tortoise and cooked it in its shell. I was graciously offered a piece and it was quite edible. Despite the myth that it is a bit like a mix between chicken and pork, it had a distinct taste that was not bad.

Diff used to swim across the Kwando River nightly to go and set traps and snares on the other side. He thought there was less human movement there, and so his chances of catching something for the pot would be better. It was only after we spotted some crocs and hippos along the river that Diff realised the perils of his nightly excursions. He admitted afterwards that if he had known this beforehand, he might have reconsidered his approach.

Dr Tinus Scheepers, who literally 'fell' off the training cycle during Air Orientation, recalls an interesting story that played out at Doppies

Naked Recce students by the Kwando River. The author is fourth from right.

the next year, when he finished his training. During an E&E exercise, he had to work his way back to the camp at Doppies while being tracked and chased by the instructors. He came to a small branch of the Kwando. He thought long and hard about crossing the body of water, and after discovering that the water was quite deep, he turned back and walked a good four or five additional kilometres around it before getting back to his original bearing. But another student who was behind him actually crossed the river, which was about chest high. As the soldier got out on the other side, a crocodile rushed at him, snapping its jaws. The croc managed to bite the right side of his webbing, where, among other things, his pistol was situated. The bite force of the creature – the strongest in the animal kingdom, five times greater than a lion – ripped off a large piece. The soldier managed to get away, but his pistol was gone. The next day the instructors and course members went back to the same spot and threw ropes with metal hooks into the river to drag-search the area, hoping to find the pistol, but to no avail.

Our training included the identification of snakes, the different categories of snake and the kinds of poison they deliver. Not all snakes are deadly or even poisonous, but the ones that are can be divided into three categories: neurotoxic, cytotoxic and haemotoxic. We received classes in how to treat snakebites and scorpion stings. It is very important to be able to identify the type of snake or scorpion that bites or stings you or a teammate in order to follow the right course of action in treating it.

Part of our bushcraft training was to school the students in the art of tracking. This took a lot of practice and training. The types of spoor (tracks) that could be encountered in the bush and veld were explained to us. You have a spoor where there are physical marks or prints on the ground that can be seen and followed. It was important to be able to 'read' the veld and areas surrounding the tracks for signs of previous presence, for example broken twigs, stones or rocks that have been moved, and grass or brush that has been trampled on or is out of place. Then there was 'light spoor', a technique that involves the detection of slight disturbances in the pattern of grass from knee to thigh. The instructors' wisdom regarding enemy modus operandi was one of the most interesting parts of tracking, as they gave us deeper insight in how to read behaviour in the various track patterns of humans.

Towards the end of the training, the course leader, Major Jenkinson, visited us in the veld and walked around inspecting each buddy pair's basha. He saw Braam preparing some food and asked: 'Did you guys learn to live off the land?' Braam replied: 'No, Major, we are still firmly on earth and not off the land yet.' The major fortunately saw the humour and grinned while he moved on to the next buddy pair.

Two of our group, Dries and Croucs, worked out a plan to lay their hands on some morsels of food by offering to wash the instructors' cooking pots. Staff Sergeant Godbeer saw through their plan, though. He mixed river sand with a little bit of the pap left at the bottom of the pot, and sent the pair down to the river to wash the dishes. Unbeknown to them, he had set up a camera to capture them feasting on the meagre, sand-laden remnants at the bottom of the pot, which they happily gulped down!

EXERCISE EGG

One exercise that we had to pass before the course concluded was called 'exercise egg'. We were dropped off individually at last light some distance from the camp. The idea was that you had to survive the night with

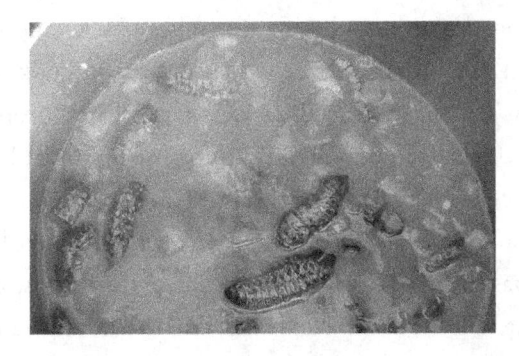

Mopane worm stew.

The author (left) and Rob Jennings in basha bush accommodation.

Nicky Fourie with para-bag and dixie bitten by a hyena.

nothing but your knife, assault rifle (for self-defence) and two raw eggs. One egg could be eaten, and the other had to be cooked by the next morning when you were picked up. After the truck dropped me off, I went down in the prone position facing northwest, towards the sunset, to listen and observe my surroundings for a while. That was when I spotted one of the most amazing things in my life: a very large herd of elephant at a distance. It was so large that it filled my entire field of vision. There must have been close to a thousand elephants, and the setting sun behind them made for a spectacular panorama. What a pity I did not have a camera to capture this beautiful African scene.

After a while I found a tree with some top growth, under which I cleared an area of twigs and bark so that I could sit with the tree behind me as a backstop. After settling in, I used the last available light to scout the area to find some grass, kindling, twigs and wood to start a fire, and for something that could help me cook my eggs. I spotted a piece of rounded metal that must have been shrapnel from a rocket or artillery shell. I picked it up and took my materials to my overnight lair.

I cut out a wooden block with the required funnel-like notch, rounded the end of a stick of softer wood and got cracking. I fervently turned the stick with the palms of my hands on the softer piece of wood in the notch to create enough friction to heat to a point where a small coal would be created and fall through the funnel onto the dry grass to ignite it. It took a while but I got my fire going, slowly stoking it with the twigs and dry wood that I had collected. I bent the piece of shrapnel until it was rounded, and then urinated in it and placed it on the fire to boil my egg. The problem was that the metal was cracked, and my urine, which was in short supply, leaked out – precious fluid wasted.

I leaned back against the tree and sat for quite a while, listening to the night sounds of the African bush. I was hungry, so I decided to eat one egg raw. I tried to carefully drill a small hole in the top end of the egg with the tip of my Bowie hunting knife. It took a while, as one must be careful not to break the shell and spill the precious contents, which represented a wholesome meal at this point. It did not seem to work, and when I applied more pressure, the egg broke. Fortunately I was holding

Slaughtering a baboon at the end of the Survival course.

the bottom section intact in the palm of my left hand, so I brought it up to my mouth, sucked up the contents and greedily swallowed it. I kept a small fire going, partly to save me from going through the process of starting another one and partly to keep lions and other predators at bay, as they are wary of light created by a fire.

I rested my body a while and thought about how I could cook the other damn egg. I had no water with me, as our water bottles had been taken from us prior to the exercise, so that was a non-starter as a boiling medium. I could wait for my body to produce enough urine again, which might take a while, or I could wander around to look for traces of water, which I did not have enough energy to consider doing. So I dug a small hole in the sand and placed my egg in it. Then I collected enough grass, kindling and sticks to keep my small fire going. I waited until well after midnight before I felt I could take a pee. Before I could urinate in the hole, I stoked the fire with a few coals and then peed in the sand surrounding the hole. I covered the egg with a thin layer of sand and packed coals on top of it. I kept this up for a good half hour to ensure my egg was cooked, even if it was going to be rubbery and hard. After about 30 minutes, I moved the fire with some sticks and dug out my egg. The shell was cracked but it seemed cooked. I did not break it open, as this had to be done in the morning in front of an instructor.

Daybreak came and we were rounded up by our mentors. My egg was opened and it was hard-boiled. The problem was that it tasted like urine, as the cracked shell had allowed the salty solution to seep into the shell while the egg was cooking. It was okay, though: my egg was cooked, I had survived the night and passed the test. In hindsight, which is always very clear, I realised that I did not have to use water – or in this case urine – to wet the sand around the egg. It would probably have cooked well enough simply by placing enough controlled heat on top of the sand. But this was how we learned valuable lessons about surviving in the wild.

During the first two weeks of Bushcraft and Tracking we received very limited food supplies, consisting mainly of pap, boiled eggs and the occasional bit of bully beef. During week three we received no food at all, and had to use the skills we'd been taught to live off the veld. I lost around nine kilos during this phase, at a time when I only weighed 80 kg, meaning that I burned more than ten per cent of my body weight.

The course was concluding and we had to be tested on the various subjects covered. The tests consisted mostly of practical exercises. We had to identify different bird and animal species, and the tracks they made. We had to be able to make a fire with a wooden stick and block, and other skills such as reading spoor and tracking ability were tested.

It was tradition to organise a form of 'veld feast' at the end of the survival course, and the instructors shot a baboon, which was slaughtered for this occasion. It was decided to take a course photo with the baboon hanging in a tree. I sat right below the hanging primate, and was also the only one looking down when the photo was taken. We were then told that there was a possibility that we could contract deadly Congo fever – in the same class as dengue fever and Ebola – if we ate the meat from the baboon. To replace it, a warthog was duly shot, and we had to settle for meat from this wild pig, which was quite tasty.

Before the end of the course we were allowed to make a 'wish list' of items that would be bought for us in Mpacha by the instructors. One of the items on my list was a tin of condensed milk. Lo and behold, when we got back to the base at Doppies, I was handed a tin of the sweet nectar, which I finished in no time at all. It was one of the biggest treats of my young life up to that point, but afterwards I had the 'shakes', as my body probably overdosed on all the sugar after a three-week period of malnutrition and near-starvation.

We took long showers to scrub the month's accumulated dirt from our bodies and wash our hair. It was a weekend, and we had to prepare for the final gruelling course in the Recce cycle – Minor Tactics, or the unconventional warfare phase.

We had survived the African bush and learned a lot in the process. The Survival course was a well thought-out and very practical training period, and the techniques learned here would stand many of us in good stead for the rest of our lives. Many of the Special Forces operators who later went into the private security sector became involved in nature conservation and the fight against rhino poaching. Some of our brethren to this day still present this type of training to groups nationally and globally. The Recce survival course is revered by everyone who understands such training. Above all, the course taught me that survival is a state of necessity to subsist.

12

MINOR TACTICS (GUERRILLA/ UNCONVENTIONAL WARFARE)

―――

The conventional army loses if it does not win.
The guerrilla fighter wins if he does not lose.
– Henry A Kissinger

After the conclusion of the Bushcraft and Survival course, we stayed on at Fort Doppies for the last stretch of our training, which was to last seven weeks. If you have served in the Recces, or understand their doctrine and training, and the outcomes of such instruction, then the words 'Minor Tactics' will be spoken with respect and reverence. Minor Tactics, the final training hurdle, and the culmination of a year's specialised training, involves the intense progression of the South African Special Forces soldier's skill set. This phase of your schooling occurs at the end of the training cycle, before you qualify to wear the coveted Special Forces/ Recce insignia – the laurelled dagger, with a unique once-off number engraved on the back, known as the 'Operator's Badge'.

During this period, all the skills that the soldier has been schooled in and passed after the main selection are put to the test in simulated operations and attacks in the vast African bushland of the Caprivi. These exercises test the soldier's agility in bushcraft, tracking, living off the land, survival in the bush and weapon skills, including the use of platoon weapons such as 60 mm high-mobility mortars, RPGs, 40 mm grenade launchers and LMGs. In addition, you use explosives, mines and grenades, conduct water-crossing exercises and kayaking attacks, and practise parachute operations, ambushes, snatches, raids, reconnaissance and an array of specialised warfare tactics, day and night. All of this is combined in one intense course – Minor Tactics. And do not be fooled by the description – there is nothing 'minor' or 'smallish' about these months in the bush. I once spoke to an ex-Recce colleague in Iraq about our training days; we were discussing the Minor Tactics phase when we were overheard by an older ex-Delta Force member, who drily commented: 'Nothing we did in Delta was minor!' We just shook our heads and smiled, knowing that nothing the Recces ever undertook was 'minor' either, least of all one of the hardest specialised military/Special Forces courses out there at the time.

Our first lectures, in the bush classroom on the western side of the camp, were about Special Forces operations in unconventional deployments. We learned about revolutionary and guerrilla warfare and the phases of each, and how our operators could infiltrate, exploit, sabotage, disrupt, neutralise and deliver such strategies on our enemies.

KIT PREPARATION

During the year we learned a lot about preparing our kit, from fitting rifle slings to packing our webbing and Bergens properly in a logical, easily understandable and tactically efficient manner. It was now time to be taught the finer points of how to prepare our kit. Special Forces operators are issued with specialised gear and cannot afford to lose it. This gear is expensive, and losing it can compromise your operation and detract from your overall effectiveness. We were first shown through practical demonstrations, and then practically executed and experienced, how to camouflage all our kit with olive green, sand brown and black paint. It took a bit of practice and finesse to get the camouflage patterns right for the different areas of operations in Africa.

For training purposes, we still used the Niemoller webbing, but we were now shown how to construct our own battle vests, consisting of a yoke and hip belt, the different types of pouches to fit on the belt and the preparation of chest webbing. All equipment had to be non-traceable to South Africa, and any serial numbers or markings had to be removed and painted over. Certain items, such as windproof matches and boots, were procured from other countries, but still had to be camouflaged.

An important aspect of packing webbing is how to secure items that you will use often. Such items include the following:

- compass
- pencil flare
- Betalight
- helio mirror (used to signal to aircraft)
- Day-Glo panel (for identification from the air)
- penknife
- hunting knife
- whistle
- lighter
- '*skaap-teller*' (clicker to count steps)
- field dressing
- Sosegon ampule (a morphine-like opioid) in a plastic sleeve with syringe and needle.

We attached these items using strings pulled out of parachute cord, the 'sleeve' of the paracord strings, or by using paracord tiedowns.

A handy aid for this exercise was to use fishing swivels (two rings connected to a pivoting joint), which we sewed on to our webbing with a heavy-duty kit needle, with the inner parts of the paracord again used as thread to secure the swivel. You attached your string or cord to your piece of equipment with another swivel, which could clip on to the one on your webbing, enabling you to detach the item from your webbing when needed.

All metal clips had to be removed from rifle slings, and the sling was reattached to the weapon using paracord. This was done to prevent the metal clips from rattling against the rifle, which could give your position away or compromise movement when sneaking up on the enemy. We were then shown a very neat trick, which stood me in good stead after my military career when I worked as a PMC: you use the sleeve of the paracord to create a loop around the safety catch of your assault rifle to be able to pull the flat metal safety clip away from the frame when you place it on 'fire'. This avoids the 'click' made when you disengage the safety and helps to prevent detection in situations where silence is required, such as lying in wait in an ambush position. It is a very handy way of preparing an

Minor Tactics (Guerrilla/Unconventional Warfare)

AK-47's safety catch, as the weapon does not have a counter-safety switch knob on the other side to disengage the safety with your right thumb while holding the grip with your master hand.

Once we knew how to prepare our rifles and kit, it was time to be taught what equipment to choose and how to pack it into our Bergens for deployment on bush operations. Standard deployment equipment included the following:

- two-litre water bottles
- sleeping bag
- groundsheet with holes on the corners and in the centre – mostly used as a 'bivvy' to sleep under in damp or wet conditions
- personal medical bag, containing tourniquet, field dressings, foldable splints, eyepatch, IV saline drip and daily meds (eye drops, painkillers, anti-diarrhoeal tabs, plasters, various first aid items)
- small gas stove
- food rations – tins camouflaged with paint, moving parts taped down and placed in a brown sock to prevent rattling
- camouflage net to cover your face and neck
- green, brown or camo bush hats or caps.

The squad would split up other equipment required in a team deployment, such as spare radio batteries, claymore mines and additional ammunition for the platoon equipment (mortars, RPG-7s, PKMs and perhaps claymores and other mines), depending on the mission parameters.

The TL and senior soldiers in the team would carry the maps of the deployment area, a pigskin notebook (with pencil) and binoculars, and the dedicated team member responsible for communications would carry the HF radio set, typically a Racal Syncal 30 (weighing five kilograms, with the battery another ten kilograms). All team members would carry spare socks, PT shorts (worn as underwear), a spare T-shirt or two and waterproof olive-green oilskin jackets. Your type of clothing and boots would be determined by the area where you would operate, and the Special Forces stores held a range of different types of military camouflage uniforms, boots and headgear.

These items listed above were the basic equipment that a Recce would deploy with, but the basic kit was often augmented by special types of gear that were required for success on the mission, for example explosives, cameras with lenses, climbing equipment such as ropes and a variety of other 'spes' (specialised) equipment available to operators. Every piece of equipment had to be camouflaged, nothing could rattle and everything had to be waterproofed. Your equipment, and its selection and preparation, played an important part in guaranteeing mission success and personal survival.

MOVEMENT AND PATROLLING

Although we had learned patrolling techniques during basics, Special Forces orientation and the individual cycle courses, we now received new instruction on how Recce teams moved and operated. We practised different patrol formations, such as single file, extended line, vee, triangle, scorpion and box shape.

Each patrol and team would deploy 'scouts' at the front of the formation. These were generally local nationals (LNs) from the area of operations who had been turned or recruited by the SADF. The Recces trained to operate with LNs due to their skin complexion and language skills. Scouts are the eyes and ears of the patrol or team and will most likely draw fire first when contact is made with the enemy. If you worked in an area where a dedicated scout was not needed, then the TL could rotate and alternate the scouting duties.

Effective patrolling is not a function of presence in the area of operations alone. It involves the correct movement of the formation, the use of cover, correct spacing between members (depending on the terrain), working in buddy pairs when resting, going down in an 'all-round' defensive position when you rest during the night, the correct use of the terrain for concealment and cover and a slew of other requirements when working behind enemy lines. Patrols could be used for offensive purposes, tactical reconnaissance, detection of enemy presence from tracks and spoor, to escort and assist with the infiltration of teams on sabotage missions, to conduct raids and ambushes, and to 'sweep' areas for enemy bases.

Methods of patrolling could be achieved through the fan, river-line, plus area and base-line methods, which we practised often. An important part of patrolling is the correct use of hand signals, as well as how to cross obstacles, including river-crossing drills, actions on making contact with the enemy, how to embus and debus from helicopters and how to cooperate with mobile infantry units that might have to assist you during your mission or during the exfiltration phase.

Navigation forms an integral part of patrolling in the bush and we practised this in teams and individually. All exercises where we had to move to a point on the vast training terrain were done by the instructors' giving us a grid reference coordinate, or a specific point such as a bend in a river or a road. We then had to use our maps, compasses, protractors, pieces of string and knowledge of navigation accrued during the year's training to navigate to the designated point.

One morning we were tasked to navigate from the camp at Fort Doppies to the shooting range, which was around four kilometres away. It was a cloudy and humid day in the Caprivi. The senior ranks on the course took charge of the routing to the range, where we were due to practise contact drills and conduct fire-and-movement exercises with platoon weapons. We departed with heavy packs, all geared up for the day's battle drills. After about an hour's walk, we realised that we were nowhere near the shooting range, and our leaders did some recalculating. We roamed the bush for approximately another hour, at which point the squad realised that we were lost. Some serious calculations were done, and sometime later we made it to the range, where we were received by the fuming course leader and instructors.

They started our punishment without delay: we were going to do fire-and-movement drills over a 1 000 m distance with heavily loaded Bergens on our backs – hit the deck hard, shoot, check mags and reload if required, get up, hastily move ten metres or so forward, and fall down again with a pack weighing more than 50 kg starting to chafe your shoulders and back. And it was November in the Caprivi, with the summer sun beating down relentlessly. Our overalls were soon sopping wet from the perspiration and full of sand from assuming the prone position so often. I was carrying the

60 mm mortar on top of my pack and the damn pipe kept hitting the back of my head whenever I hit the ground.

Conducting fire-and-movement over a hundred or so metres is strenuous enough, but doing it with a heavy backpack and over hundreds of metres per session is hard going. We only stopped a few minutes at a time to reload and drink water before the whistles and shouting started again. We did not stop for a lunch break either, and at one point I felt the watery contents of my stomach pushing up into my throat. I had to concentrate hard not to vomit. This fuck-up session went on all day long, until the start of sunset, which is late in the summer months. Our bodies ached and my heels were on fire. I could feel the burning sensation between my shoulder blades from when I had fallen on my backpack while exiting the chopper during Air Orientation.

Our individual and team battle drills, which we had practised throughout the year, were now honed to perfection. Fire-and-movement, quick attacks, flank attacks, withdrawal under fire, breaking contact, sweeps after an attack and regrouping exercises were done continuously. Our use of all weapons required to work in a Recce team, including grenades, squad weapons, explosives and pyrotechnics, was sharp.

The training was intense, and the instructors kept our revs in the red. We got little sleep, and spent many nights in the bush. One day, during a patrolling exercise, Sergeant Ian Strange called us to gather to talk to us about our tactics and techniques. We formed a circle around the sergeant with the buttstocks of our weapons resting on our feet, as we had been taught to do – in order to not leave marks on the ground, which could give your enemy an indication of how many and what type of firearms the group is carrying. I watched Mark playing noddy, with his head bobbing up and down as he started to fall asleep. The next thing, he toppled over with the LMG in one hand, but before he hit the ground he woke and managed to (barely) stay on his feet, shaking his head and taking a step or two forward. It was hard to contain our laughter, but nobody dared to laugh in front of the very serious instructor.

During another day patrol, Van's stomach played up. He jumped two metres to the right, getting rid of his backpack and webbing and

White phosphorous explosion during fire-and-movement drill.

unbuttoning his overall in record time, before going into a squat position to empty his aching bowels. After a minute or two the formation was halted to wait for the team member. The next thing, Brian came past me and commented: 'Jislaaik, old Van is shitting like a rhino!'

During a patrol on a dark night, one of our officers, Rob, walked into an object, hitting his forehead against something solid. It turned out to be the belly of an elephant, which was quietly standing asleep in the bush, as these massive mammals tend to do. It was decided to silently backtrack, and the team had to navigate around the elephant. Elephants are generally not aggressive towards humans, but will trample you to death if they have calves and think that you might pose a threat to their young. It is advisable to stay away from these beasts as they can kill you in a flash.

Part of deploying in teams was to be able to clandestinely infiltrate or penetrate target areas. Anti-tracking was an integral part of infiltration, and we were shown how to cover our tracks and the methods that could be deployed to confuse the enemy. These techniques were more difficult than they first appeared. There are many things to bear in mind when anti-tracking – the number of team members, the direction of movement, the weight and equipment you carry, the type of terrain and your direction of travel. Anti-tracking was particularly effective with infiltrations, and necessary when entering an ambush position or being pursued by the enemy.

The Recces had many tricks up their sleeves when it came to anti-tracking. One of these was 'elephant boots', which were made of a soft cushion-like material in the shape of the foot of an elephant, and which you pulled over your normal boots. You had to know the spacing between an elephant's steps and had to camouflage your other tracks between the creature's natural strides.

Another important aspect of our training was how to work in buddy pairs, in a 'buddy system'. This system included covering for each other when you took a break or took off your rucksack, and when you ate, urinated, took a shit, maintained weapons or prepared sleeping bags. It also included how to work the night-time guard shifts required when lying up and going into a hide. This was in an era long before fancy headsets and interpersonal communication devices. We were taught how to use a length of paracord, normally fixed to your thumb with a slipknot, that was connected to your buddy's thumb or other finger, in order to wake him up soundlessly when there is danger. Sometimes the buddy pairs would extend a ring-loop of paracord to the next buddy pair; pulling on the cord would raise the alarm or get their attention to further coordinate through hand signals. It was a primitive system, but it worked well.

RIVER CROSSINGS

Africa is full of rivers, streams and runoffs, and a team might have to cross one to get to their objective. River crossings were an important part of our training, and had to be done in a specific manner. A reconnaissance would be done to identify a proper crossing point – preferably a spot not deeper than chest height, and not too wide either. It was important to ensure that your backpack, or at least the contents of it, was waterproofed. Then it was advantageous to build a raft out of sticks (as a flotation device) on which to place your Bergen, wrapping it in your groundsheet. If the river was deep and wide, the soldier crossing would take off his boots and clothes and place them on top of the pack wrapped in a groundsheet on top of the raft. Your waterproof poncho could also be used for waterproofing and to create a float. This would allow the person crossing to swim more easily and not be dragged down by his boots and clothing. It was important to place your rifle on top of your flotation device, pointing forward, so that you could engage enemy forces (if required) while crossing the river. The groundsheet helped to make it float, and the float and pack could be tied to your body to prevent the current getting hold of it. Empty water bottles could be affixed to the frame with cord to make it more buoyant, but empty bottles needed to be refilled afterwards. On deployment, operators would carry thick black binbags, which are also useful for wrapping your sleeping bag and kit, to help make the pack float.

The strongest swimmer in the team or group would be on standby, without gear, to assist anyone in difficulty. It was important to cover the members that crossed, making sure they were not too close to each other. As soon as they crossed, they had to take up defensive positions behind their packs and give cover, in both directions, to their teammates that followed them. The gear would be recovered in buddy pairs while the rest of the team covered you in all-round defensive positions on either side of the river. Once the team had crossed and retrieved their Bergens they would get up in the formation that the TL would communicate to them and continue with their tasking.

Another important move was to lob a couple of grenades into a river before crossing it, to scare away dangerous animals such as crocs and hippos. It did not really give away your position, as the water dampened the sound of the explosion, but the shockwaves would be felt by animals in the water. We practised this drill going through the Kwando River, which was infested with crocs and hippos, and where lions, elephants, Cape buffalo and other dangerous animals would come to drink.

AMBUSHING

It was now time to be schooled in ambushes. We were waiting in the classroom one morning when Sergeant Strange entered and opened his lecture with words that have stuck with me: 'Morning class, today we cover ambushes. There is only one thing you need to know about this – ambush means killing and killing is fun! Let's go.'

We followed the teacher, and were shown how to position stopper groups, the main killing group and the support groups. It is important to choose your ambush location well: it should be an area where the enemy is slowed down and channelled, with good cover for the ambush team, as you will probably take incoming fire until the enemy has been neutralised. Stopper groups are positioned further away with vehicle convoy ambushes than with foot patrols. Ambushes are normally initiated with claymores and mines, and a high volume of fire is required when the ambush is sprung. Machine guns and RPGs were very handy and deadly during these destructive events, but mortars were equally handy in cutting off enemy forces trying to escape, or when there might be reinforcements in the area.

We received training on all platoon weapons, but somehow I developed a knack for operating the 60 mm commando mortar effectively and accurately, and more often than not I deployed on patrols and exercises with the mortar as my platoon weapon. This meant carrying a heavy load, as our Bergens were normally packed with 50 to 60 kg of gear. The mortar pipe weighed around ten kilograms, and the bombs another two kilograms each. You would carry four bombs as first-line ammo and another four in your pack as your second string.

At the beginning of the course, we were issued 'softie' earplugs, but I often lost them while moving or when conducting fire-and-movement. This meant my hearing took a pounding, as firing our weapons – assault rifles, machine guns, mortars and particularly the RPGs and claymores – hurt your eardrums without proper ear protection. One evening, during a last-light ambush exercise I was positioned next to the RPG gunner as his buddy and in a pair. I somehow did not have my softies in place, and when the RPG was fired next to me my ears hurt quite a lot and I could not hear well for a while. This phenomenon occurred regularly, and I developed a ringing in my ears that sounded like sun beetles. It came and went when I was exposed to loud booms and bangs. Later on in life, it turned out to be a permanent problem, as I have done a lot of shooting in my life and career, and have been close to many loud explosions. The medical term for this problem is tinnitus, and most of our older Recces either have tinnitus or cannot hear properly. Hearing loss is a global trend

River-crossing exercise.

among combat soldiers, and there are only limited ways to prevent it. You need to be able to hear your teammates shouting instructions during battle, as well as to listen for enemy movements and incoming fire.

WATER DISCIPLINE

Part of patrolling and bush warfare for Recces is conserving water and maximising its use. We learned how to track and find water sources during the Bushcraft course. There are, however, certain drills that need to be followed when replenishing your water supply at a source. The team cannot gather around a water hole or water point as there is a risk of ambush while they are concentrating on filling water bottles. The drill was to go down in an all-round defensive position in buddy pairs some distance away from the water hole, and then to send a buddy pair to the water point to check it for signs of enemy activity, dangerous animals or poisoning, and then to start filling the empty bottles to take back to the team. Sometimes a few trips were required to resupply the team. It was important to look for signs that the water was not bad or infected – dead insects, a foul smell or a lack of animal tracks close to the water point were all indications that the water should be avoided.

Water discipline is hard on the mind when you are constantly moving and sweating in the bush. The guideline was to limit yourself to around two litres of water per day, but never less than one litre. This may decrease when you are stationary in an observation post, or when you are on a reconnaissance mission and statically observing your target. We always carried water purification pills as part of our medical kit. You mixed the tablets in a litre of water; it did not taste very pleasant, but at least it killed most of the germs and bugs present in the water. Often, you could not find clean running water and had to 'resup' (resupply) with murky, muddy brown water, which had to suffice. Your body does not ask which flavour of water it wants; it needs H_2O in any form, as long as it does not contain E. coli or other bacteria.

We were shown how to filter water through a piece of parachute material, taken from the small chutes of the 1 000 ft flares. These valuable pieces of silk-type cloth trapped sand, mud and other solid particles in the water, so could be used when filling your water bottle or placed over the bottle opening to drink.

There is a famous phrase from the Minor Tactics handbook: 'When on patrol don't concentrate on your thirst, stay alert. It is better to be alive and thirsty than dead with a full stomach!' I enjoyed the ambush training. It was fast and furious, and I ended up presenting lectures and practicals on the subject a few years later when I worked in the Special Forces training wing.

CONCEALMENT

Working in a Special Forces team in enemy territory is an intricate subject. Your walking speed, the attitude of the local population – or 'povo' (from the Portuguese), as the soldiers referred to it – obstacle crossings, drills when halting and many other tactics had to be factored in. It was time to be schooled in 'hides' and 'caches'.

A hide is used when a team is working clandestinely, and where concealment is critical. Hides are used for eating or resting purposes, and can also serve as temporary bases. It is important to choose a spot for a hide well. Ideally, it should be on high ground, to help with observation,

Lying up in an ambush position.

radio communications and sight for the entire team when in an all-round defensive position.

It is important to deploy a 'dogleg' route into a hide, where you walk back in a half-circle on your route to cover your tracks in case enemy forces are tracking you. It is also important to place claymore mines on the route into your hide. These can be connected to a tripwire-type detonating device and will afford you protection in case the enemy are aware of your presence and sneak up on your position. Mines also act as an alarm when they detonate.

When setting up a hide, specific contact drill orders are issued, and escape routes and emergency RVs must be known by all team members. While in a hide at night, you must sleep behind your rifle with your webbing and boots on your body, ready to fight and move at a moment's notice. No movement is allowed in the hide unless the TL deems it necessary, but if you have to move, then you might have to leopard-crawl to where you are needed, to maintain a low profile. If the team is deployed for a long period, normally longer than two to three weeks, then a resupply route for people or vehicles, or a DZ for air supply drops, has to be considered.

Caches are points where you store equipment, arms and munitions.

A cache is normally waterproofed, buried, covered, camouflaged and booby-trapped. Caches can be used to supply rebel forces with equipment and arms or can be emplaced by a team prior to a long-term operation where the operators will use the cache for resup purposes, or for use by teams during follow-up operations.

It was a tradition for all students to box against each other during this final course. The ring was set up next to the classroom at the edge of the camp, close to the bush. We were teamed up against our opponents – how they worked it out I did not know at the time, but I was pitted against the fit and athletically built Julian. During the year we had observed him doing well with his kicks and punches during unarmed combat sessions, and were told that, prior to his military service, he had earned a black belt in some Eastern fighting discipline.

I knew that I was going to be in for a good fight. From the outset we pummelled the daylights out of each other. My dad's boxing lessons and my youthful bar skirmishes stood me in good stead, but Julian was fast and landed a few punches in my face. This enraged me and I managed to land a lot of hard blows but could not knock him out. It was a good fight, and our buddies cheered and roared.

Another interesting encounter was when Corporal Dampies was teamed up to fight against Lieutenant Hannes Lintvelt. Poor Dampies came to consult me before the bout, as he was afraid of the older ex-32 Battalion bush fighter with the cold eyes. I advised him to 'bob and weave' like Muhammad Ali used to do, and that he would be fine. The bout started, and to my amazement the light-footed Dampies did indeed float like a butterfly. Every now and then he would throw a fast straight jab at Hannes's head, which slowed his ever-aggressive advance a bit. Hannes wanted to knock his opponent out cold but could not get to him, and he tired sooner than Dampies, who kept jabbing him in the face. The bout ended, and the corporal survived the war-fighter's onslaught. I discovered afterwards that Dampies was a skilled amateur boxer, which made sense after seeing him floating like a butterfly and stinging like a bee. He probably could have knocked out the lieutenant but was afraid of the consequences …

Throughout the year-long training cycle the instructors would dish out punishment for wrongful actions, from dirty rifles and wrongly packed kit to messing up a certain drill or exercise. This was known as a 'dirty'. You could accrue a couple of dirties during the week's training, and the punishment was usually to be dropped off far from the base to walk the extended distance back in your off-time – normally a Saturday afternoon or a Sunday. At Fort Doppies we were dropped off at a point next to the Kwando River, approximately 20 km from the base, with a fully loaded Bergen weighing around 50 kg, and a case of 60 mm mortar ammo that weighed between 25 and 30 kg, depending on the type. The terrain was sandy, and it was hard going with the heavy pack plus your webbing and rifle.

But, in true innovative Recce style, some of the mortar bombs, and the other ammo used for dirties, could end up in the river *if* you befriended the storeman or perhaps accumulated some extra ammo during the week's training to replace the missing munitions as soon as you got back to base. It was still a long slog. The lure to walk fast was that if you made it back before supper time, you could join the braai before all the food was packed away. If not, then you had to settle for whatever food (leftovers) the chef or your buddies could arrange for you. And the instructors were not shy about dishing out dirties: if you made a wrong move, you could end up on the Botswana border having to spend your scarce free time lugging a very heavy load back to base.

RAIDING

Another part of Minor Tactics that I enjoyed was when we were schooled in carrying out raids. A raid is a surprise attack on enemy forces or installations inside or behind enemy defence lines. A raiding force does not occupy an objective, but exfiltrates as soon as possible after the objective has been achieved. Raids are executed by stealth, and success depends largely on the element of surprise. A raid is executed mainly after dark, or during bad weather, or on terrain that is considered unnegotiable by the enemy. The aims of a raid are to damage or destroy logistics and supplies, equipment or installations, command posts, convoys, communications centres, depots, radar stations or other key points. Other aims are to loot equipment and key personnel, or to cause losses to the enemy, draw attention away from other operations (deception), deepen the enemy's 'off-balance' factor, harass the enemy and force him to deploy additional units to protect his rear areas.

It is important to have good intelligence and a clear aim regarding the base or target you are about to attack. Your force may consist of an assault group, a special task group – to blow up fuel depots, for example – and a protection or cut-off group that must prevent the enemy from escaping, interfering or calling in reinforcements. Raids normally occur during night-time hours when enemy activity is minimal and the element of surprise is in the raider's favour. It is important for the assault team to work through the objective after the assault to search and collect all documents and other sources of information that can help you to glean insights into the enemy's organisation, weaponry and battle plans.

Part of a raid may be a 'snatch' operation in which a targeted person needs to be captured. Snatches should be conducted covertly if possible but can also form part of a raid operation if you cannot conduct the snatch silently and clandestinely. Equipment used for such missions could include chloroform, anaesthetic darts, batons or clubs, knock-out gas and handcuffs. It is preferable to keep the target awake and force him to walk on his own instead of carrying him, as this will slow you down and tire the team sooner.

We covered a lot of other specialised subjects such as how to conduct vehicle operations, which was mostly the job of 5 Recce, with their fleet of Casspir armoured troop carriers with heavy machine guns mounted on top. The Recces actually have a long history with using light armoured vehicles in Sabre operations. In the mid-1970s, these involved various LMGs mounted on Land Rovers. Later on, the weaponry was upgraded to heavy weapons such as 23 mm anti-aircraft guns, 106 mm recoilless guns and 81 mm mortar pipes mounted on rugged Unimog flatbed 4x4 vehicles.

Other subjects such as the reconnaissance of targets and close cooperation with rebel forces in the theatre of operations were extensively covered.

Being able to work with indigenous people and rebel forces is a vital part of a Special Forces soldier's training. We had classes on the command-and-control structures to be used when working with opposition forces, where it was important to take charge and overall command but also to ensure that the rebel forces understood all commands well and filtered them down their respective channels to the combatants. Many older Recces had acquired Portuguese language skills, and we also had Portuguese classes once stationed in our respective commandos.

One exercise we had to do was to conduct a recon of the St Michael training base, where Unita forces were trained by the SADF, under the guidance of the legendary Colonel Jan Breytenbach, the founding father of the Recces. Founded in 1966, Unita was the second-largest political party in Angola. It had fought alongside the MPLA in the Angolan war of independence, and then against the MPLA in the ensuing civil war, which lasted well over three decades.

During our upcoming operation in Angola, we were to be teamed up with Unita forces to assist us with the logistics and infiltration of the mission. For the purposes of the exercise, we were divided into small teams and had to infiltrate on foot to the St Michael area, which was five to seven kilometres away and to the north of Fort Doppies. Prior to the operation our course leader, Major Jenkinson, gave us a lecture on combat orders. He created a detailed model, also called a sand-table model, with sandy hills complete with rocks and twigs to indicate particular spots or areas, and water sources indicated by blue washing soap. He stood over the sand-table with a long pointer, indicating how an attack force could infiltrate and move. I enjoyed this demonstration and instruction, and later incorporated it into the Bush Warfare courses I presented at the training wing.

We infiltrated toward the rebel training base in the late afternoon and sneaked into position during the hours of darkness, applying anti-tracking and camouflaging techniques. The next morning, at sunrise, we started making notes and drawings in our pigskin notebooks, using the shortened pencils tied to the notebooks with paracord inner string. We spent the best part of the day in our recon position, which turned out to be quite close

Vehicle operations – contact drill.

A roadside explosion during a vehicle contact drill.

to the camp. I remember observing the Unita troops going about their business in the tented camp. Every now and again a sentry would look our way, and I wondered what their reaction would be if they spotted us with our blackened faces. Apparently, they were not warned about our presence, to make the exercise more realistic. Later in the afternoon we exfiltrated stealthily, walked back to predetermined pick-up points and went back to our base.

The next phase of our instruction was in minelaying operations, and we often practised laying mines. A critical factor in minelaying is having a security team to protect team members who are planting the mines. Otherwise, the soldier executing minelaying duty will be exposed and not have his rifle in his hands. This was achieved by placing stopper/early warning elements at a distance on both sides of the road or area where the mines had to be planted. The minelaying component always worked in buddy pairs: the number one would dig the hole and the number two would act as his eyes and ears and prepare the mine.

The location of a mine is important for the success of the mission. A good location is just around a bend or in an area where vehicles or foot patrols have to slow down, and the ground should not be too hard, rocky or compacted. It is important to keep the topsoil as it is. Topsoil is first placed on a groundsheet, and the sand or soil dug out of the hole must be kept separately on the sheet so that it can be carried away afterwards and dispersed over an area in order not to draw attention to it. Tools used for laying mines include your hunting knife, panga or a small foldable military-style spade. It is important to accurately plot and record where a team has laid mines in order to prevent future teams and operations being compromised by your own munitions.

BREAKOUT AND ESCAPE

A very important technique for a Recce to be familiar with is 'breakout-of-encirclement', an escape move when you are pinned down and surrounded by enemy forces. When encircled, you can break out by stealth or by force. The latter requires quick planning and proper execution to succeed. Rain, darkness, fog and adverse weather conditions can aid you in escaping by stealth. With both methods it is important to identify the weakest point in your enemy's defence so that you can exploit it.

When you break out by force, the team will wait until the last minute, when the enemy is closest to your position, before initiating contact. While you wait for them to close in, the TL ensures that every team member knows the locations of the predetermined emergency RVs, and the team will discuss the use of grenades and the deployment of smoke to create cover to escape. Once the team starts firing towards the identified weakest point, the volume of fire needs to be high to put the enemy on the back foot, and to create a breakout point in their defensive formation.

Then there was the 'bombshell' manoeuvre, in which the team breaks up and splinters like the fragments from an exploding bomb. Each team member flees in a different direction and then backtracks when possible to an emergency RV. It is important to create a password or code that members have to call out before joining the rest of the team at an emergency RV. This prevents enemy forces from entering and attacking you while the team regroups. This move will be deployed as a last resort to prevent team members being captured or killed, and is designed to split up the enemy search force by forcing them to follow more different tracks than they would when tracking a team.

There is an old Special Forces saying: 'Retreat now to fight tomorrow.' There is no honour in trying to be the last man standing and letting your country and team buddies down, nor is getting captured an honourable option. It is your duty as a Special Forces soldier to avoid death or capture, but if you are captured then it is also your duty as a combat soldier to try and escape as soon as you can.

This led to the E&E part of our training, in which we were taught how to react when captured, and how to break out and make a run to a safe area as soon as possible. E&E by military personnel is nothing new. Throughout military history, units and individuals that have been cut off from their parent organisations, or that have operated behind enemy lines, have employed E&E techniques. 'Escape and evasion' was not recognised as an operational military term until World War II. Previously, it was accomplished by individuals without pre-planning or organisation. During the two world wars, prisoners of war (POWs) were not actively interrogated for useful information, and were mostly confined to detention camps, where conditions were often harsh. But during the Korean War, the North Koreans, and their Chinese backers, took interrogation for specific information to new levels.

After the Korean War, the US and British armed forces decided to train their personnel, especially special operations forces, to resist interrogation and to try and escape whenever possible. I paid very close attention to the lectures on E&E – in May 1985 a Recce, Captain Wynand du Toit, had been captured during a covert operation to attack fuel storage tanks in Angola's Cabinda enclave. The team was discovered by a force of more than 100 Fapla soldiers, and two Recces were killed and another six wounded. Du Toit, the TL, was held as a POW. This event shook the Recce community, and such an outcome had to be prevented at all costs in future operations.

During Special Forces operations behind enemy lines, the chance of getting captured is much greater than it is for normal infantry units.

Minor Tactics (Guerrilla/Unconventional Warfare)

Special Forces troops must constantly train in E&E techniques, which must be part of any special operation planning and preparation phase. Every soldier has an obligation to himself, to his country, to the men who preceded him and to those operating with him to be trained in evading capture, and to apply such tactics when required. The challenge to a man's courage and valour is greatest when he faces the enemy alone. His normal obligation does not change, regardless of his situation. One of the greatest moral commitments of a soldier is to evade capture if possible, and to escape from the enemy once captured. Remember the international law on uniform: Act 29 of the Hague Convention on the Laws and Customs of War (1907) states that a soldier is classed as a spy when acting clandestinely.

We received lectures on the will to survive, exercising your endurance levels, the need for patience, faith (in whatever or whomever you believe in) and the correct timing for attempting an escape. It was said that the memories of family and home needed to be a motivating factor, as well as the creation of anger, hate and vengeful thoughts against your captors and enemy. Factors to be wary of are panic, loneliness, inaction, lack of planning, low self-esteem and prolonged exposure, all of which can weaken your resolve to escape.

Communist doctrines found in documents captured from enemy forces indicated that escapees would be treated no better than animals. In war, *any* action is justified to avoid capture. And to escape from capture in the bush warfare theatre you needed to understand the principles of breakout-of-encirclement, as well as bush, fieldcraft, anti-tracking techniques, the tactics used by the enemy (covered in Dark Phase) and the correct use of your minor tactics training.

Over the years, I have learned that the mainstream techniques, tactics and procedures in specialised security are the easier parts of a mission, but the operators who can pay attention to small but critical details are the ones who obtain a high mission success rate. And this holds true in your personal life as well: pay attention to the small things and this will make the bigger principles in life easier.

We were taught that the golden rule of escaping captivity is 'Go now'.

This means that you must use the first opportunity available to break out and evade. The longer you are in captivity, the more difficult it becomes to escape. This was the second rule I maintained throughout my life after the wise words and demonstration of action by the captain on the Water Orientation course: 'He who hesitates dies' and 'Act now' on challenges or difficult situations (where possible). I admit that with some challenges you should take a bit of time and think it through, but with immediate security challenges one cannot hesitate and must react quickly (or be dead – my motto). We were taught how boot laces, belts, buckles and other items that can be concealed on your body, such as flat knives, garrottes and blades, can aid you in your escape effort. After Minor Tactics, and in later years while working in hostile environments and conflict zones, I used to wear a double-thread piece of paracord tied around my waist and under my belt. If you know the correct technique to kill someone effectively and quietly, this two-metre cord could be deployed as a garrotte. It could also be used with a piece of wood to splint a limb, or to tie something down. I also used to carry a square, straight, one-sided razor blade duct-taped to the inside of my belt behind my back. If your hands are tied behind your back with tape, rope or plastic cuffs, you can use a hidden blade to free yourself.

We learned the importance of looking for escape routes and how to detect discord in enemy ranks, which could offer a window for escape. One point that was hammered home was to avoid, for as long as possible, giving up the exact nature of your mission, what unit you served in, what rank you held and your operational tactics and plans. Before an operation, always prepare the 'cover story' you will give the enemy if captured. Over the years, I learned that it was best, when accosted by hostile forces, to create a false narrative as close to the truth as possible. That way, you give them something to think about and buy some time to gather your thoughts and strategise on how to get out of the situation.

After the lectures and talks by the older experienced instructors, it was time to practise E&E. This also formed part of the final 'selection' phase, as students over the years threw in the towel during the E&E exercise, especially after being waterboarded – a regular feature. We were rounded up, with only our webbing and rifles, and driven to points on the Botswana border. We were dropped off just after sunrise, individually, and at unknown spots somewhere in the bush. We had to start running immediately as there were vehicle teams with trackers, instructors and other soldiers looking to pick up our spoor and hunt us down to be captured and bullied.

I was dropped somewhere in the training area, probably 25 to 30 km from the base (I only worked it out afterwards). I was determined not to be caught, so I decided to use the 'bombshell' technique and first broke away to the west, away from the base. I made a dogleg and turned, and then started running like a cattle thief ahead of a lynch mob. I could hear vehicles roaming the area, and at one point I heard shouting and a commotion in the distance and assumed that some of my fellow soldiers had been caught.

Later on, I learned that two of our 'colourful' buddies had been caught shortly after the start of the exercise. The instructors made them strip naked, leaving them with only their boots and rifles. I always joked that I wanted to die with my boots on, and in this case the older operators let the ones who got caught at least keep their footgear! These soldiers arrived back at the camp with scratches, cuts and abrasions from top to toe, including on their dicks and nuts!

Once I had an idea of the direction of the camp, I used my newly acquired knowledge of navigation to determine the right way to go, which in my case was slightly north of eastwards. I tried my best to apply anti-tracking, but it was time-consuming and I could only cover my tracks occasionally on the more open areas where the tracks were most visible. I also tried to move in shaded areas and where the ground was firmer in order to leave less of an imprint. I ran for about an hour until I could no longer hear the sound of voices and follow-up vehicles. I decided to take a break. My heels were on fire, so I found a tree under which I could lie on my back with my feet in the air against the trunk. I drank as little as possible from my one-litre water bottle in order to conserve my supply. After about ten minutes I heard some noises behind me and started running again.

It was almost December and the midsummer heat in the Caprivi was high. I was perspiring a lot and sipping on my precious water supply, and I ran out in the early afternoon when the sun was at its hottest. I heard occasional sounds and noises from the tracking teams, but it seemed that my bombshell technique and anti-tracking had worked, as the capture squad never really got close to my location.

I was very thirsty and started feeling weak due to lack of food and fluids. I looked for sources of water but found none. Sometime later in the afternoon I spotted a dark pool of liquid and hastily moved towards it, hoping to be able to drink from it. After looking for signs of dead insects or small animals, I smelled the puddle and realised that it must contain urine of sorts, perhaps the excretions of an elephant or other large animal. I made the decision to scoop the liquid into my empty water bottle and use my square of parachute silk to filter it. The first sip almost made me vomit, but I swallowed the vile, hot, muddy, salty concoction. I knew my body required liquids or I ran the risk of severe dehydration. I was even willing to drink my own urine, but I had none as my body was already fairly dehydrated after being on the run for more than eight hours.

I kept moving northeastwards until I heard the faint sounds of vehicles, which I assumed were close to the base. It was late afternoon. I saw pieces of shrapnel and metal and realised that I was near the shooting range. I could now find my way back, but I had to be careful. There were vehicles patrolling and quite a lot of activity, and I knew that our hunters and possible captors would be close to the base because the aim of the exercise was to get back before sunset. Afterwards, I learned that Braam had been captured by one of the 1 Recce corporals who had arrived to deploy with us on the planned end-of-course operation in Angola. Braam was stripped naked and had to make his way through the thorny bushes surrounding the camp in his birthday suit.

Just before sunset I sneaked into the camp, as I did not trust the instructors. I had made it without being captured! I reported back and immediately went to the bar/canteen where I acquired three cans of ice-cold Fanta and downed all three in quick succession. I was thirsty beyond explanation, and the cold, sweet fluid tasted liked honey. I remember how I almost vomited, as the Fanta must have been a shock to my system,

Students are briefed before an escape and evasion (E&E) exercise.

but I prevailed. I went to the bathrooms to rinse out my water bottle and refilled it at one of the water points. During the night, and after a long shower, I sipped sensibly on the bottle, but had to refill it a few times as I woke up thirsty on a few occasions. By the next afternoon my urine was a healthy colour again and I was rehydrated.

EVALUATION

Throughout the course we wrote weekly tests that we had to pass with a 60 per cent margin. Our shooting exercises, which included 'snap-shooting' and 'jungle lane', were scored throughout, and most of us passed with flying colours, as we had done a lot of shooting during the year. We were continuously evaluated during the practical field exercises – ambushes, patrolling, hides, formations and all the other battle and Special Forces drills we were taught.

At the end of the Minor Tactics course, the instructors would get together and talk about each student's progress, aptitude and overall performance working in a team. They would then make a final decision whether the student had what it took to become part of the elite and operate with them in the commandos. It happened on occasion, and indeed with two of our buddies that year, that a student passed all the tests and practical evaluations but was still pushed out of the training cycle due to something the older operators detected that made them hesitate to qualify the individual. It was only much later, when I worked at the Special Forces training wing, that I realised how this principle worked. Only then did I fully understand what at the time seemed like a harsh and unfair decision to two of our buddies. But, at the end of the day, all individuals need to be accepted by the teams, who rely on the judgement of the Special Forces School's instructors to ensure that they receive the best possible candidates, with whom they would risk their lives during operations.

Around a week before the planned operation into Angola, we were briefed and started preparing for the mission. The team of qualified operators who had flown in from Durban, and who had assisted with hunting us during the E&E exercise, were going to test their 81 mm long-distance mortaring capabilities, and the rest of us had to practise with whatever weapons we were going to carry on the operation. We were going to deploy with Russian weapons, as was the case with most operations conducted by the Recces behind enemy lines. We had to shoot in and sight our assault rifles, and certain members would carry PKM machine guns, 60 mm mortars and 40 mm grenade launchers – both the single-shot and multi-chambered versions. I was issued with a 60 mm commando mortar, which I was quite familiar with by now.

On the whole we were sharp, and our weapons handling, including of platoon weapons, was of a very high standard. We only needed practice to work in our dedicated ambush groups and to gel as an attack team. Shortly before our movement westwards to Fort Rev for the operation, we were told to assemble in the classroom at the edge of the base. Colonel Jan Breytenbach, who was commanding the St Michael training base across the road from Fort Doppies, walked into the classroom to give us a motivational talk. We were chuffed to be able to meet this legendary soldier, and the founding father of the Recces, in the flesh.

Colonel Jan was a staunch man, with hard, focused eyes, and he did not mince his words. He spoke about cooperation with rebel forces, in this

Colonel Jan Breytenbach, founder of the Recces.

case the Unita soldiers whose training he oversaw. Van remembers a tale he told about working with the rebel force. Colonel Jan, a Unita general and some other high-ranking soldiers were sitting on a hill watching Unita soldiers carry out an attack against Fapla forces. The Unita infantry were moving forward and building good momentum when suddenly there was increased fire from the Fapla positions. The Unita troops turned around as one and ran so that you could see the soles of their feet! But, according to Colonel Jan, when working with indigenous forces, you must be diplomatic in your choice of words – as I have learned over the last three decades. He said to the Unita general: 'That was a very tactical withdrawal, but now you have to attack again.' The Unita leadership immediately reorganised their fighters and attacked the enemy lines with everything they had.

This attack did not go exactly as Colonel Jan wanted, but that is sometimes how it goes in operations and battles. He told us that cooperation with partisan forces is a test in itself, with many additional challenges of language, logistics, training, courage, motivation and quality of troops – to name but a few. After this talk, the colonel said in Afrikaans: 'The enemy is the devil, and fuck the devil, when you see him you shoot and kill him!' I was very impressed and inspired, and had visions of killing many of our country's enemy forces.

Our preparations were coming to an end, and it was great to mingle with the already qualified operators and instructors who were going to deploy with us. The three-month Bushcraft, Survival and Unconventional Warfare phase was now concluded. It had been a challenging time, and the period in my life when I learned the most about warfare, and about African fauna, flora and matters in general.

All our equipment, weapons and gear were packed and moved to the Mpacha airfield, from where we departed in a C-130 for Ondangwa. Operation Nigel, as recounted in the Prologue, was about to get under way.

13

URBAN WARFARE

Some people think city fighting is all the same, but I can tell you that it isn't. In Vogen we had to fight the rebels in the streets, in buildings and in the gutters. We were ordered to clear strongpoints, to capture city blocks and hold buildings at all costs, and every mission was different. There were more ways to fight than there were planets in the Imperium and even more ways to die.
– Anonymous

We flew back to Durban after completing our bush warfare training and Operation Nigel. Once we got back to civilisation, after an almost three-month bush deployment, we had to round off our initial Recce training by learning how to fight in built-up areas in cities and towns.

Urban warfare has many faces. According to the Modern War Institute at the United States Military Academy (West Point): 'In the context of both a counterinsurgency and deliberate assault, urban combat is the most difficult form of warfare because the environment is both the most physically constraining and also involves the most constraints from a policy perspective.' Over the years I learned that fighting in an urban setup is mostly fast and furious. Unlike fighting in the bush, jungle, desert, mountains or snowy plains, in urban warfare your enemy is only a metre or two away behind a wall or around a corner, and has many places to hide and ambush you. Because of the much shorter distances and possible ambush positions, a soldier does not have much time to react to assault or counterassault when in action in a built-up area. My motto for both urban warfare and self-defence situations: 'Be quick or be dead.'

By the mid-1980s the Recces had gained invaluable knowledge and experience of urban warfare operations. Such operations included infiltration and sabotage missions, raids on enemy facilities and offensive warfare tactics to eliminate enemies of the state. The techniques taught to us were gained by operators the hard way, through blood, sweat and tears, during operations that were highly challenging.[5]

The urban warfare training facility was situated on the private non-accessible beach area on the eastern side of the Bluff, below the 1 Recce base situated on top of the massive sand dune. The buildings were leftovers from the whaling station that operated there from 1907 to the mid-1970s. Whaling in Durban began with a few steam-driven whalers hunting migrating whales off the Natal coast and eventually became the largest land-based whaling operation in the world. At its height, in 1965, the whaling station processed 78 000 tons of oil from 3 640 whales.

The buildings were large and strongly constructed, ranging over almost a mile of property, and included large drainage tunnels, many pipes and large storerooms, office buildings and processing warehouses. This was an ideal setup to practise urban warfare, as it had it all – steps, hallways, rooms and all sorts of areas where the Recces could construct 'killing houses' and 'clearing rooms'. A 50 m shooting range was built at the entrance to the facility and an urban warfare combat course range at the other end. The beach area could be used to fire heavy weapons out to sea, and there was enough space for choppers to land to load their pax (passengers), who would either jump or fast-rope/abseil down to the buildings to simulate attacks. Until the disbanding of 1 Recce in 1996, it was the premier urban warfare facility in South Africa.

Our first class was held at the old whaling station in a classroom without windows and with just a few wooden school desks with attached seats. We were shown the equipment we would use for urban fighting. The R4 assault rifles were now replaced with the shorter, more compact R5. The R5 had exactly the same working parts and calibre, but was easier to manoeuvre in close combat. Our chest and bush-rig webbing was replaced by a tighter, slimline combat vest with various pockets and magazine pouches. These urban combat vests were worn over thick green flak

---

5   For more detail on these operations, see the 1 Recce trilogy by Alexander Strachan (Tafelberg), and Iron Fist from the Sea by Douw Steyn and Arnè Söderlund (Jonathan Ball Publishers).

jackets, incorporating 11 layers of Kevlar and with neck and overlapping side protection. These jackets were heavy and bulky, though. We had to wear Kevlar helmets for head protection when moving through tight spaces and to ward off shrapnel, which often flies around buildings when there are booms and bangs. We switched to soft-soled boots with better grip patterns so as not to lose our footing on the concrete steps and floors, which could get very slippery due to the humidity and salt mist from the ocean and beach.

Other new equipment to get acquainted with was the 'flash-bang' concussion-type grenades, tear gas grenades and gas masks. Most Recce urban offensive operations took place during the hours of darkness, so we were trained in the use of a bracket to attach a large Streamlight torch to the bottom of a rifle barrel, for illumination in dark rooms and hallways.

We had classes on the typical layout of cities and street blocks. A range of new hand signals was shown to us for urban applications. Once an attack or raid was in progress, loud, clear and effective verbal commands had to be employed, as the sound of grenades and 5.56 mm rounds going off in rooms and enclosed areas was much louder than in the bush.

Movement in an urban setup needs to be fast and silent. We were shown how to walk in soft-soled boots, rolling our feet from the outside inwards, and how to silently and steadily climb up stairs without crossing our legs. There are specific procedures to peep around corners and then move while the team provide cover to the front and rear of the formation, which in most cases were four-man clearing teams with a command and stopper group element behind and outside the building to cut off any escapees. Next we were shown how to safely check if a door was unlocked or not, and then how to kick in doors by deploying the 'donkey kick' method backwards. This involves standing to the side of the door where it opens to expose as little of your body as possible in front of the door.

Door entry drills are very important during urban operations and room clearing, as the door is a 'known' factor: the enemy behind knows that you have to enter and thus they can funnel their fire to this area. The drill was to lob in a concussion grenade and count out loud from one thousand to four thousand until the grenade went off. You would then immediately

General view of the Bluff military complex in Durban, showing 1 Recce's base and the old whaling station.

Close-up view of 1 Recce unit lines and the whaling station training area.

The old whaling station was the venue for urban warfare training.

pivot into the room low and fast by placing your foot in the doorway and propelling yourself inside, while staying low in the kneeling position to create a smaller target area. The two shooters inside are the numbers one and two in the team, with a third and sometimes a fourth member outside the room entrance on both sides in the kneeling position, with their rifles at their shoulders, affording cover down both sides of the hallway of the room location. Once the numbers one and two finish neutralising any and all targets in the room with 'double-taps', they have to start searching the room for any enemy hiding under beds, in cupboards and behind fridges and other furniture. This involves a very specific set of drills and movements where each member covers the other while they move around. One will fire a couple of shots into mattresses and cupboards before ripping them open to see if there are hidden targets.

These urban warfare moves demanded serious concentration as bullets were flying around you in close proximity to the shooter next to you. But I really enjoyed it and found that this type of fighting generated a lot of adrenaline in a short space of time. But it is very hard on the ears, even with the softie earplugs that we used, as all the explosions and assault-rifle shots were amplified inside the buildings. I felt my ears hurting, especially after the hammering they had taken during the bush warfare phase and Ops Nigel. But it did not matter at the time – the adrenaline overrode the pain in my feet, back and ears. I was here to learn to fight in any and all ways required to eliminate our enemies.

We were taught how to move past doors and windows in a manner that concealed your profile and exposed you as little as possible. The taller guys had to bend more to conceal themselves. During one exercise we had to fire at targets in a room from the outside of a building where the windows were quite high as the area outside the building was slightly sunken. When Nicky realised he could not see the target, he jumped up and down, firing a salvo of shots at the target each time he was in the air. This was effective but comical. The legendary Major Jack Greeff, who was a guest instructor on the course, just shook his head when he saw this spectacle.

We were then taught how to work in buddy pairs to overcome this problem. The first soldier would stealthily approach by staying below the window, turn his back and lean against the wall while squatting, while the second soldier would sneak closer, position his rifle at his shoulder, and in one motion step up onto the upper legs of his buddy and fire through the window.

We also practised a lot of urban movement while giving cover to our teammates in streets, through alleyways, into buildings and through windows and doors. The instructors laid out an urban obstacle course where you had to move at the best speed possible through a number of buildings, pipes, narrow ledges and small windows with all your kit, helmet on and rifle in your hands. This was fun but tough going. Fighting in an urban environment tires you quickly as it is like doing sprints instead of a long-distance jog. It was just as well that we were as fit as we were, and having done thousands of pull-ups throughout the year helped a lot, as we often had to pull ourselves up while climbing over walls and higher obstacles.

It was also time to review our basic ropework and abseiling techniques. Special Forces teams deploy these techniques to attack buildings, most notably the SAS hostage-release operation during the 1980 siege of the Iranian embassy in London. It was good fun abseiling down the side of the higher buildings and then shooting through the windows at targets placed inside the rooms below. We were shown how to 'blow' open doors using shortened Remington 870 Wingmaster shotguns where the number three in the team will shoot off the door hinges or lock for the number one and two to enter and clear the room. Methods of rigging Cordtex and sheet explosives to make 'knock-knock' charges to blow heavier doors open were demonstrated to us, but it was only during the Advanced Urban Warfare course the next year that we actually rigged the explosives and used them extensively in an urban setting.

Precision shooting is an absolute requirement in urban warfare. There was a combat pistol and rifle range, complete with different firing stations – through windows, door entrances and mocked-up alleyways – where all students got drilled with both pistols and assault rifles. The course included magazine-change drills where you had to take cover behind a wall or door entrance, and risk losing points if you exposed yourself to enemy fire. You had to hit certain targets in the centre of the chest, and

Nicky Fourie during urban warfare training.

with some only headshots counted. It was a challenging run where speed and accuracy combined to work out your 'combat factor'.

This is a very good way to train with any firearms instruction, as I learned first-hand and presented later on in my career. The man who shot the best score in the fastest time was the top achiever for the exercise. Anybody who has had some proper firearms instruction can fire five shots into the heart or brain of a target if they take their time (say, 12 seconds), have a proper aiming picture and squeeze the trigger correctly, and thereby obtain a full score. But the person who can make all shots count in six seconds, or half the time, has a combat survival factor 100 per cent higher than the man who takes his time. My motto, 'Be quick or be dead', rings much truer in urban warfare and self-defence situations than in the bush or rural warfare. This combat course was referred to as the 'Israeli Combat Course', probably in reference to an exercise developed by Israeli soldiers, but the operators just referred to it as 'the Israeli'. I personally enjoyed it, and we all did very well in terms of time and accuracy, and learned a lot about close-quarters combat with both pistols and assault rifles.

The PT and fitness tests for the urban warfare phases were also slightly different, and focused a lot on upper body strength and agility in your lower back and hips to cope with the fast pace and challenging moves involved in combat in built-up areas. We practised pull-ups, dips, 16 m shuttle runs, 20 ft rope climbing, fireman's carry, sit-ups and two-kilometre sprints in full battle gear. We were fit but had to get used to the darn heavy flak jackets and different helmets in the heat and humidity of Durban in midsummer.

The urban fitness tests were scored differently to the fitness tests we'd done in basics and pre-selection. Then, you had to do a certain amount of reps, but now you had to carry on until you could not do any more, in other words MAX reps. Your score was worked out according to a predetermined table where the more reps you did, and the faster you could move, the higher your average percentage of fitness would be. You had to ensure that you obtained at least 60 per cent of the group average, which was very high due to our extreme fitness levels.

We all passed this phase and reached the end of our training cycle. It almost seemed unreal. The ones who were left were going to be 'badged' and would receive the coveted Recce badge with unique operator number. We were the biggest cycle to qualify, due to the amalgamation of troops who'd made it through basics, two other selection courses that had joined us, a bunch of 2 Recce civilian members who had to complete a few courses with us and the large number of good men who were interested in joining the organisation that year.

A small ceremony was arranged at the NCOs' mess hall. The unit OC, Colonel Andre Bestbier (RIP), RSM Pep van Zyl (RIP) and others from the unit were present. The date was 19 December 1986. We were called forward by the unit OC according to rank and age, and when it was my turn I marched forward, halted and very enthusiastically saluted the colonel. My silver dagger with laurel wreath around it was pinned on my chest. I was now a qualified Special Forces Recce in the SADF, and my unique badge number was 369. I could not have been prouder. It was one of the best days of my life. It was a double celebration for our buddy PP Hugo, who had another reason to celebrate. He left the proceedings still in his uniform to get to Addington Hospital on Durban's South Beach, where his wife gave birth to their first child, a son.

After the ceremony we went to the NCOs' bar at 1 Recce, the Riff-Raff. It was a place where serious parties and hard drinking sessions took place. We could finally, as youngsters, enjoy the nectar of the war gods with the older and experienced Recces. It was a good and hard session on a Friday afternoon where the RSM called his traditional 'RSM's parade' together, which meant the NCOs in the unit were called up for drinks and snacks at the bar. The Red Heart and Coke flowed strong and fast, like the Kwando River in the Caprivi.

Life could not have been better. I was as happy as could be, and full of Dutch courage from the amount of liquid refreshment I threw down my throat. I remember that at one point I wanted to ring the brass bell mounted against the side wall close to the bar, but was sternly warned by Staff Sergeant Justin Vermaak that such a move would land me in serious trouble. The bell was controlled and operated by the RSM, and he alone, when he called the bar to attention, or if someone offered to pay for a round of drinks.

We were given a week's leave, after which we had to report to the units we were being seconded to. Along with a bunch of other fellow basics buddies and 'youngsters', I was posted to 1 Recce. I was happy with the decision. Earlier in the cycle, we had been asked to indicate our choice of unit. I had asked to go to 4 Recce first, as most of my basics buddies wanted to go there. 1 Recce was my second choice, but in the end I was very happy that I ended up in the 'mother' unit of the South African Special Forces organisation.

SFO QUALIFICATION PARADE – 19 DECEMBER 1986

86/01 Operators Roll (names according to SADF force number allocation and age):

1. 68376318PE   Capt B.W. Harris
2. 71248751PE   SSgt W. Faul
3. 74239013PE   Capt W.J. Mutlow

4.	744616178T	Cpl A.L. van der Spuy
5.	75277343BG	2Lt P.A. Human
6.	753779298T	Lt P.A. Swart
7.	76238773PE	Lt R.G. Jennings
8.	76316314PE	Capt R. Hugo
9.	78323037PE	Lt J.B. Lintvelt
10.	79468187PE	Lt S. van der Spuy
11.	80283732PE	2Lt C.J. Roelofse
12.	81095531PE	Cpl E. van der Merwe
13.	81266124PE	Cpl M. de Villiers
14.	81352262BG	Cpl J.J. Raath
15.	822157578G	Cpl H.C. van Wyk
16.	82248303PE	Cpl H.J. Croukamp
17.	82353145PE	Cpl A.C. Coetzee (RIP)
18.	82462912PE	Lt C.J. Serfontein
19.	83290262PE	Cpl B.R. Visser
20.	83317768PE	Cpl N.J. Fourie
21.	83382291PE	Cpl D. Human
22.	834757498G	Cpl G.W.J. Schaefer
23.	83485474PE	Cpl M. de Wet
24.	83495036PE	Cpl S.A. de Beer
25.	B3540260PE	Cpl C.L. Leppan
26.	84421361PE	Cpl T.D. Bezuidenhout (RIP)
27.	84589290PE	Cpl J. Raath
28.	85702421PC	LS J.A. Masella

14

LIFE AFTER THE BASIC RECCE CYCLE AND BEYOND

1 Recce unit emblem – 'Through Stealth Our Strength'

Never give in except to convictions of honour and good sense. Never yield to force; never yield to the apparently overwhelming might of the enemy.
– Winston Churchill

The South African Special Forces qualification recognises operators as being among the elite of global special operations forces, and rightly so. During the basic training year, we were selected, trained, pushed to the limits and honed into some of the most effective special operations machines ever created. An operator was trained to gather intelligence (intel) and find, neutralise and eliminate any person(s) or organisation(s) deemed to be the 'enemy' (see 'South African Special Forces Mission and Vision' at the end of this book). This could be done in many ways, from the use of knives and garrottes to weapon systems ranging from the smallest-calibre handgun to heavy-calibre machine guns and sniper rifles, and everything in between. It also included the use of bombs, mines, grenades, rockets and mortars, and then some more.

But the reader should bear in mind that a typical Special Forces or special operations soldier's main purpose is not always necessarily to kill. If that was all that was required, then the generals could have called on the infantry or paratroopers, or units such as 32 and 101 Battalion, or the police counterinsurgency unit Koevoet, to deploy and win firefights. These fighting formations were highly effective in tracking, finding and killing enemy forces. 32 Battalion took it even further by establishing their own Reconnaissance (Recce) Wing, which was tasked with finding enemy bases for the main force to attack and destroy.

In our case, the cost, time and effort of selecting and training a Recce was a more expensive and intensive exercise. Because of the small numbers of qualified Recces, these soldiers were mainly used for very specialised tasks: to infiltrate the enemy by air, sea and land, and to operate for extended periods behind enemy lines. Such operations could be in the form of small teams specialising in long-range deep penetration reconnaissance (recon) that might lead to direct action to disrupt enemy logistical lines and manpower through very specialised means. Other tasks might be the night-time infiltration of enemy territory by advanced HALO/HAHO parachuting from altitudes up to 35 000 ft, where the operator must use oxygen and 'fly' up to 30 km towards the target area. Seaborne operators could reach target areas far from South Africa aboard navy strike craft, submarines and small boats, making use of closed-circuit diving suits to swim close to and infiltrate enemy positions. Or perhaps the enemy area could be infiltrated on foot by pseudo teams whose members look like locals and speak the same language, and who use the same weapons and tactics as enemy forces in order to penetrate their area of operations. The Special Forces soldier's skills are numerous, very specific and expertly delivered. Therefore such soldiers are too valuable to be used as cannon fodder in straightforward attack missions, although the Recces, and particularly the early ones, fulfilled this role superbly when the politicians and generals called upon the men of the laurel dagger.

I was happy to be joining 1 Recce for a couple of reasons. First, as the Recces' mother unit, 1 Recce was where it had all started and where the great older operators had begun their careers.[6] Second, the unit's specialist

---

6 For more detail on the early years of 1 Recce, see Volume 1 of Alexander Strachan's 1 Recce trilogy.

function, over and above the bush warfare operations that all three units were trained in, was urban warfare. I had really enjoyed the urban warfare phase of our training, and a few years later I would teach the subject at the Special Forces School.

The young, newly qualified corporals who were seconded to the unit were given the option of moving into the infamous 'E-Block'. From the time the new Recce base was constructed in 1979–1980, E-Block became known as the NCOs' block. Some of the older guys who lived off the base also had rooms in E-Block, where they stored their contraband and changed into their uniforms when they arrived at the unit or after PT. (The operational 1.1 Commando guys had to do PT after morning parade and up until teatime, with the training sessions lasting anywhere from an hour and a half to two and a half hours.) E-Block was the barracks closest to the front and edge of the Bluff in the 1 Recce base location, with a perfect view of the Indian Ocean. You could hear the sound of the waves breaking on the private beach area down below, where the old whaling station and the 50 m shooting range were located.

My room was on the first floor and Barry Visser occupied the room next to mine. Sergeant Gary Yaffe, who had qualified a few years before us, was on the other side. Many of the corporals who had completed the Recce cycle with me – Barry, JJ, Dries, Croucs, Bez, Nicky, Henk and Grant – moved into the rooms available on the first and second floors. We were a lively and energetic bunch. Out of the original group that had arrived in Oudtshoorn a year earlier, four of us (out of eight who made it through the cycle) were now serving in 1 Recce. The other four – Mark, Braam, De Wet and Craig – were sent to 4 Recce at Langebaan, alongside Rob, Diff and Van from our cycle.

The first order of business was to get kitted out with the operating gear and weapons required by members of 1.1. Commando. Much of this tactical equipment was known to us from our training cycle but was newer and less dated. Our handgun was the Browning Hi-Power 9 mmP. Our main bush-warfare assault rifles were AK-47s in various forms and sizes. The standard weapon for urban fighting and warfare was the R5, the shorter version of the R4, which in turn is the South African version of the Israeli Galil assault weapon. There were, of course, many other different and specialised international weapons available for operations, when such weapons were needed to blend in behind enemy lines, or when particular specs were required. I was happy – no, very happy – as we were now part of one of the greatest Special Forces Commandos in the world, and being issued the same gear and weapon as the older, experienced and battle-hardened Recces. And we were placed in different teams within the Commando, with each team having an officer and senior NCO taking charge.

The first week in 1.1 Commando was also when we went through the initiation process for new operators. This involved a serious bout of partying, where the newcomers had to tell the *ou manne* their life stories before downing the official nectar of the war gods – Red Heart Rum, laced with tequila or other strong liquors. Our initiation party was held one early evening at the old base in a large empty storeroom prepared for the occasion, complete with a small podium for the initiates to tell their stories, and a bunch of chairs for the Commando guys to watch the spectacle and to question and heckle the storyteller a bit.

Although we were already aware of this, it was again made abundantly clear by the older operators that the unit's, and the organisation's, drink of choice was Red Heart and Coke. This was served in a very large 'mug' – a cut-down artillery shell with handles that could probably hold at least two litres of fluid. The mug was half-filled with Red Heart, with a touch of Coca-Cola and some other strong 'shots' mixed into it, and you had to sip from it while standing on the podium and telling the Commando members your history and reasons for wanting to be in the Recces.

The nectar of the war gods was flowing and everybody was extremely jovial. I remember the pride and feelings of elation that were running through my veins during this initiation ritual in which us teenagers were welcomed by the tough-as-nails and battle-hardened Recces of 1.1 Commando, including quite a few ex-Rhodesian SAS soldiers and men who had been awarded the Honoris Crux (equivalent to the US Medal of Honor).

After each of us new boytjies told their stories and answered a few questions, you had to down the contents of the shell, which was constantly being topped up while you talked. After this, you had to jump off the podium and execute a classic static-line parachute landing – feet together, arms in the air, knees slightly bent and kept together while falling on either your right or left side and rolling with the fall.

My turn was coming up and I was already well oiled by the time I got to the podium. I stood there with the shell in my hands, looking at the Commando guys, wondering what an 18-year-old could tell these hardened soldiers about his life. And out of the blue I found myself saying, in a serious and focused manner, 'Hi all, my name is Johan Raath, but my friends call me Killer!' I have no idea where that came from, but the next thing the whole Commando was in stitches with laughter and applause. When the laughter died down the questions came: Killer, tell us where are you from? Killer tell us this, and Killer tell us that. The questions took a while, and then I had to down the contents of the artillery shell and jump off the podium. I landed, rolled and was welcomed as a member of the elite 1 Recce's 1.1 Commando.

What a night. We were so bombed that we could barely stand. Later on, someone organised a five-ton Merc truck to come to the old base to collect the barely breathing newcomers, or 'youngsters', as we came to be known in the Commando, to take us back to E-Block to sleep it off. And, of course, the nickname 'Killer' stuck for many decades.

1987

For the soldiers who qualified at the end of 1986, and who were seconded to serve in 1 Recce, 1987 turned out to be a busy year. We were now promoted to full corporals, and had the choice of short-term service for three years or joining the Permanent Force. I chose the latter.

After our initiation into 1.1. Commando, and early in January, our first assignment was to complete the Mountaineering course, which included rock climbing and rope techniques. The theory of mountaineering, the equipment used and introduction to climbing techniques were covered at 1 Recce's training wing, on the second floor of the unit's HQ building, at the old whaling station and at the climbing wall situated on the side of the blockhouse behind the car park. We were taught the principles of mountain operations, the types of climbs and cliff walls that might be encountered and how to prepare our equipment for such ops. Then there was the climbing equipment, which included climbing helmets, harnesses, kernmantle ropes, climbing boots, carabiners, figure-eight descenders, ascending/descending mechanisms, crampons, pitons, chock-and-friend devices, slings, belaying tools, climbing bags with chalk and a few other necessities for playing Spiderman on rocky cliffs. Our instructors included the legendary staff sergeants Jaap 'Kloppies' Kloppers and Neves Mathias – both recipients of the Honoris Crux medal.

The practical climbing and ropework phase was done about 50 km northwest of Durban in the scenic Valley of a Thousand Hills. There were various cliffs here, and it was a popular rock-climbing spot. This course was something out of the norm of soldiering and was great fun. It took serious concentration, as any slip-up could cause a fatal fall. The first order of business when we got to the climbing spot was learning how to create secure three-way 'anchor' points by rigging slings and ropes around trees and rocks or by hammering sturdy pitons into crevices.

One exercise I remember well was the 'over-handed' cliff move. You had to insert your left hand into a crack under an overhanging rock, jamming it in the rock by making a balled fist while reaching (leaping) with your body and right hand above the overhang to grab on to a thin ledge. Then you pulled your left hand out of the crevice at the same time and swung it above the overhang to grab on to another small rock ledge, with your legs dangling free while you pulled yourself up. This move was a bit of a 'cliff-hanger' as there was quite a drop below. It took me a while to master it, and I had to endure a couple of 'falls' when I slipped and fell a good ten metres downwards, only to be saved by my climbing rope and equipment.

Another exercise was where we climbed quite high up a rock face and then had to let go to grasp the feeling of 'falling' down a rock cliff in order to learn to 'trust' your equipment and ropes. It was scary at first to deliberately fall down a mountainside, but it was also exciting. The harnesses, ropes and anchor points, held up well and we learned to trust our gear.

Then there was the mountain rescue exercise, where we mimicked a situation in which a fellow soldier had fallen and needed to be saved. The soldier to be rescued abseiled to a ledge on the mountainside, took off all his equipment and lay down. Then two climbers abseiled down to the narrow ledge where the student lay, strapped him to a flat rescue plank and attached it to ropes. Then a team of guys hoisted the injured man upwards to their position, after which the rescuers climbed back up to the rescue point. We learned a valuable lesson during this exercise: placing the rescue rope around a tree, or rock/anchor point and then pulling it upwards reduces the load by 50 per cent. Off course, this was only demonstrated to us after we had tried to pull the evacuee straight up, like a dead weight, using muscle power alone. Croucs and I fared okay, as we were strong, but it was a battle to pull our fellow combatant upwards using our body strength alone.

We were taught how to survive in cold mountainous areas, and took part in exercises where you had to climb with your webbing and rifle, and, once you were at the top, to reel up your backpack. We also abseiled down the cliffs with our kit and packs on our backs. This was good training and I enjoyed it immensely. We were graded on the type of climbs we could conduct, and I was rated as an F2 lead climber, and a K2 follow climber, which indicated the level of difficulty of climb I could execute as a lead climber, securing the devices and ropes on the mountainside for another climber to follow, or following someone with a higher climbing grade up to K2 level.

LIFE AS A RECCE

Life in 1.1 Commando was great. When we were not deployed on operations or on a course, the routine in the unit would be to wake up at around 05:30, shave, get into our browns (uniform) and be on the parade ground around 06:30, when the 1.1 Commando members would fall in for roll call conducted by the Commando Sergeant Major. At around 07:00 the well-known and respected RSM, Pep van Zyl, would conduct a unit parade, after which we would be dismissed. After the 'fall out' command we would go down to E-Block and change into PT gear, which consisted

A member of 1 Recce during a mountaineering exercise.

of running shoes, PT shorts and a brown T-shirt. At around 07:45 we would congregate next to the duty room for warming-up and stretching exercises, and at 08:00 we would start PT. The sessions usually lasted for about two hours, until 10:00. This included at least a five-kilometre run and military body-weight exercises such as pull-ups, dips, sit-ups, shuffle runs and sprints.

There was a sewage treatment plant at the eastern bottom end of the Bluff that the guys in the unit referred to as '*die kakplaas*'. Every so often a 'honey-sucker' sewage truck would pass the running squad and spill some of its contents when driving over the speedbumps. The sight and smell of the raw sewage was at times a bit much for certain members of the squad, who would stop, run towards the bushes and vomit before rejoining the squad. The other drawback was that occasionally, when the wind turned northeasterly, the smell from the treatment plant could pervade the unit.

Some guys went to the unit gym to train with weights in their free time, but none of us was really into serious bodybuilding. Our focus was on agility and stamina. Besides, large muscles and heavier bodies slowed you down and led to injury.

After a shower we would get back into uniform to enjoy the 20-minute teatime break at the NCOs' hall, where there was always an array of sandwiches available. At 10:30 we would be in our team rooms on the first floor of the HQ building. As with the other ranks, we corporals were now divided into teams within the commando, with an officer and senior NCO as team leader and team NCO, respectively. Our commando rooms typically had a large table with a few chairs, and quite a few metal cupboards for the team members to lock up their webbing, kit, ops clothing, boots and any special equipment issued to us.

During the day, the commando teams would go to the shooting range or the whaling station to practise urban combat drills and improve on their weapons skills and marksmanship, which was already of a very high standard. Every so often, we would get the kayaks and Zodiac inflatable boats out of the boat stores and conduct rowing and small-boat drills in the surf off the beaches of Durban. Once, Major Chris Greyling came up with a scheme to take the unit kayaks and row to Langebaan to surprise the 'sea Recces' (4 Recce) and pitch there in their domain. The plan was to have a land-based support team travel along the eastern and southern coastline in a couple of Merc trucks to support the operators, who would row around 50 km a day. The Commando guys were fit enough to finish the exercise, but in the end the plan was canned. The unit OC rejected it, perhaps fortunately so, as it would have been a long rowing stint – well over 1 500 km and around the Cape of Storms and southern tip of Africa.

Sometimes we would take out the sniper rifles and we shot from the blockhouse downhill at targets in the old whaling station, between 300 and 400 m away. We also sharpened our night combat skills and trained two nights a week at the whaling station or shooting range. We also sometimes conducted clandestine surveillance exercises in central Durban, where we would have to sneak up a high-rise building, after reconnoitring it, to surveil the city below and make appropriate recon notes.

We would work until 16:00, after which most of us went for PT sessions of our own, even though we did two hours of hard PT in the morning.

1.1 Commando members in their team room (Recce archives).

After a good session and a shower, we would hit the NCOs' bar to enjoy a healthy starter portion of our favourite brew before switching over to the nectar of the war gods. On Fridays the entire unit would run, jog or walk the five-kilometre route around the complex as part of the 'unit PT' session. The faster you completed the distance, the sooner you could get to the bar and start drinking, so the fit Commando guys ran the distance in well under 20 minutes.

We were all familiar with the story of how, sometime in the early 1980s, the 1 Recce NCOs' bar consumed more Red Heart Rum in one year than all the hotels along the Golden Mile combined, and we made sure that this tradition was maintained. There were Red Heart ice buckets, ashtrays, coasters, and so on – the signs of the Special Forces' favourite were visible for all to see.

After the bar doors closed – often under protest – most of the younger single guys would end up going to town to drink more and to seek out the fairer sex. And true to our forefathers and tradition, we would bar-hop, but most often we would end up in our second headquarters, the Father's Moustache bar at the Malibu Hotel on Durban's beachfront. This was where I spent most of my salary, and consumed great volumes of alcohol,

Life after the Basic Recce Cycle and Beyond

Nicky Fourie and Neil 'Bez' Bezuidenhout during a kayak exercise.

1.1 Commando members during a sniping exercise at the old whaling station.

but also where I pursued other interests … It was at this venue that I met the woman who would eventually become my wife, after I lost my ID book during some fisticuffs with some civvies one night. I went back to the hotel the next day to fetch it, and it took another two and a half years before we got together.

From time to time, the commando teams would go on realistic training exercises outside the unit lines. Sometimes we would go to Dukuduku, but towards the middle of 1987, 1.1 Commando travelled to the Ithala Game Reserve in northern Natal. We stayed in the veld for a week, conducting patrols, recon and search-and-destroy exercises in which teams sneaked up on other teams and 'ambushed' them. During this exercise we had many close encounters with both white and black rhino, as the reserve was home to many of these magnificent beasts. It was cold, though. One night, during a lying-up exercise, it even started sleeting. It was one of the coldest nights of my military career.

My feet were still killing me, and I was thinking about asking the medics and doctors at the sickbay to look into the problem, which had been bothering me for eight months. But sometime towards the end of January, and right after completing the Mountaineering course, we were told the best news ever – we were going on ops! This was music to my ears. Finally, as newly qualified operators, we would be going on two operations in Angola with the *ou manne* – the experienced war-fighters. I was excited by the news and decided to can the idea of sorting out my feet. I would do it when I got back from our deployment.

After a general briefing in the commando lecture room, the first order of business was to fill the thick black plywood crates that were used to pack weapons, ammunition, gear and all the kit required for the mission. These boxes were large and particularly heavy when packed with weapons and ammo, but the sturdy handles ensured that a four- or six-man team could carry them. Getting them on the back of the Merc five-ton trucks was another challenge, but with a bunch of young and strong corporals and sergeants, anything is possible. We then had to pack our own gear in our Bergens: the mission parameters dictated what uniforms, boots, webbing and personal kit were required. Once everything was loaded, we

The Father's Moustache bar at the Malibu Hotel was a favourite Recce watering hole.

moved to the air force side of Louis Botha Airport, where 15 Squadron's choppers were parked. All the heavy boxes and gear had to be transferred into the bellies of the C-130 'Flossie' aircraft that would fly us north to the operational area in northern South West Africa.

It was a long flight – just under 3 000 km – from Durban to Ondangwa airfield. After five to six hours in the air, we spiralled down a couple of thousand feet to approach the runway. I described this type of descent in *Blood Money*: 'As we approached the airport, the pilots put the plane into a downward spiralling dive, much to the horror of the passengers, who thought we were going down ... The idea was to avoid approaching the runway in a straight line for too long, as this would allow attackers to take aim more accurately with surface-to-air missiles, rocket launchers and small-arms fire. Instead, they would take the plane down in a corkscrew motion, then level out shortly before touching down. It was a very scary manoeuvre when you experienced it for the first time, although I understood the value of it.'

We were due to deploy from Fort Rev, the Recce base at Ondangwa. Fortunately, we were familiar with both the airfield and Fort Rev from Operation Nigel, which had served as our 'fire initiation' operation. We

1.1 Commando Tac-HQ team during an exercise in Ithala Game Reserve. The author is shown standing, fourth from left.

were due to take part in two operations in which the youngsters would be led by older senior NCOs and officers in order to learn the ropes and gain experience. I was placed in a team that would work under the guidance of WO2 SW Fourie, and included my cycle buddies Barry, Dries and Julian. Dave Hall and Gary Yaffe, from our previous year-end ops, joined us as well. We were joined by some paratroopers and a few members of 102 Battalion, an operational unit of the South West Africa Territorial Force.[7] To our delight, Craig Davies, who had done basics, selection and the entire training cycle except Urban Warfare, was now stationed at 102 Battalion and would deploy with us.

It was good to see my old basics buddies again and we soon caught up on our respective news. Our 12-man team was going to patrol a part of southwestern Angola known as the 'black mountains', to the northwest of Epupa Falls, where there was a South African forward operations base manned by Koevoet and SADF members, around 330 km northwest of Ondangwa. Our mission was to be on the lookout for a Swapo 'special forces' brigade, and to search-and-destroy these enemy forces. Intelligence

---

7   The South West Africa Territorial Force was an extension of the SADF. The leader group consisted of white males with infantry training, with the other ranks recruited from local people in the operational area of Kaokoland and northern Ovamboland.

Gary Yaffe, CJ Oosthuizen and the author keep the cold at bay during the Ithala exercise.

indicated they were hiding in and operating from this mountainous area.

It was early February 1987, and the two-week operation took place during the season when rain pounded the area. Our gear and Bergens were heavy – my pack weighed in at 85.5 kg, and that was without my webbing and rifle, which added another ten kilograms or so. Once again, I was appointed the team mortarman. This was another reason why my pack was so heavy: I was carrying the 60 mm mortar pipe and eight mortar bombs, plus 14 litres of water (at least one litre for each day), a fortnight's rations and all my field gear and spare ammo. It all added up.

We deployed from the base just south of the falls and flew 50 to 70 km almost due north, and were dropped by the Puma helicopters in an area in the mountains that was suitable for an LZ. We went into an all-round defensive formation until the choppers left. There were heavy clouds gathering and the sky turned dark. Late in the afternoon it started raining heavily, and the rain did not let up for almost the entire two-week operation. Our sleeping bags, spare T-shirts and equipment that needed to stay dry, such as the radio and medical supplies, were placed in waterproof plastic bags. But after a few days in the constant rain, everything turned damp, and being constantly wet for days on end has the tendency to depress a soldier's spirit and mood. But this was also part of soldiering and had to be endured.

An aerial photo of Fort Rev, the Recce base at Ondangwa airfield.

Another view of Fort Rev.

Fort Rev supported Recce deployments on the
border and in operations in Angola.

Life after the Basic Recce Cycle and Beyond

We moved at a slow pace in the wet mountainous terrain, probably not more than two or three kilometres per hour. We could not find spoor or any other signs of enemy activity. The terrorists often mounted attacks during the seasonal rains as the rain hampered follow-up operations and neutralised their tracks.

The days started to drag, and my body, particularly my Achilles tendons and heels, was aching a lot. We hoped and prayed that we would make contact with the enemy, but this was not on the cards for our team on this mission. During a patrol, one of the parabats, a tall fella, could not hold out any more and lit a cigarette to take a few puffs. Our TL, SW Fourie, was on him in a flash and angrily removed the ciggy from his mouth and stomped on it. The parabat was read the riot act right there and then, in a low but intense whisper from the sergeant major. I was glad that I was not a smoker. Some of the older operators, as we learned, carried small (camouflaged) containers or flasks in their packs containing Red Heart or Old Brown Sherry, which could warm a soldier's body quickly at night, or when required in an emergency. But the smokers had a hard time, unless the operation was an open, non-clandestine vehicle-advance-movement where the teams could lie up overnight.

Our two-week mountain patrol came to an end a day or two earlier than planned due to the adverse weather conditions, and the Pumas came and ferried us back to the base on the other side of the border. We were tired and I was hungry, but we did not have much time to relax as there was a Dakota on its way to transport us back to Ondangwa. We loaded our packs and gear into the Dak, and it took off and turned southeast, flying very low to the ground at 'treetop' level (around 120 m). This was done in order to dodge surface-to-air missiles, which were a real danger at higher altitudes. The low-level flight was very bumpy as the plane flew through pockets of hot air rising from the ground. The instability and bumps soon led to nausea; when you come back from an operation, your stomach is empty and 'unstable', to say the least. Some of us grabbed the paper bags that were available and vomited into them. No wonder the Daks used in the operational area were called '*kots-koets*' (vomit coach).

After we got back to Fort Rev, we went through the normal after-ops

Recce operation in Angola's 'black mountains'. The author and Barry Visser are standing at rear in the centre.

drills where we cleaned our weapons, our kit and ourselves. Then we had a warm meal and some 'refreshments' that very quickly went to our heads. The majority of 1.1 Commando's members were at the base, and we enjoyed chatting and catching up with our buddies and fellow soldiers. The gathering became slightly raucous. The next morning, we were told by one of the senior officers that the bar would be off-limits for the rest of the deployment. This did not go down well with some of our ranks. Staff Sergeant Wayne Ross-Smith (RIP) took it upon himself to get hold of some pineapples and yeast, and started brewing his own beer behind one of the barrack buildings.

We had a few days spare before the next mission, to the Kuvelai area of central-southern Angola to disrupt enemy logistics. During this lull, the powers that be called us in to discuss our futures. A three-, five- and ten-year career path was discussed with each member, including the courses required and performance needed to get promoted. Commandant Daan van Zyl told me that my first year in the army would count towards promotion, as I had joined the Permanent Force. After serving three years I would become a sergeant, after passing at least two courses that counted towards promotion. Thereafter I would have to serve another three years as a sergeant and pass the necessary courses in order to move up to staff sergeant. It sounded like forever, but what came next was downright funny, although I did not dare show it to the commandant. I was told that after becoming a staff sergeant, I would have to serve another three years before I would be eligible to become a Warrant Officer Class 2 (WO2). We were talking about almost a decade into the future, but I listened intently and remember the scene to this day, 36 years later! I honestly did not think that I would reach the age of 30, and I almost did not – the same with 40 and then 50. I should have perished on a number of occasions, but life decided to play a trick on me, and here I am. At the time it just sounded odd that I should plan my existence that far ahead, but it was part of the military planning process. It was good because it gave the soldiers a clear picture and direction of what was expected from them, and the rewards their actions would bring.

The next operation was designed to disrupt enemy supply lines through the use of certain explosive devices. The team was led by Captain Roy Vermaak, and the senior NCO was Gary Yaffe. Barry, Henk and I were in the team along with some other 1.1 Commando members. We were dropped by the Pumas some distance south of Kuvelai, and the plan was to trek for about a day to a secondary road south of the town. On our previous mission, where we patrolled the mountains, we expected to run into Swapo forces, as the area was sparsely populated, but now we had to watch out, not only for Swapo insurgents but also for Angolan government troops, as well as the local population. Any contact could compromise our location and operation.

I carried the mortar and other team members had to lug the heavy explosive devices, weighing between 20 and 25 kg each, that we were going to plant. We got close to the target area and had to lie up until the next morning in an all-round defensive position. It was late afternoon on 18 February 1987, and it was my 19th birthday. I heard the grass rustle and saw Sergeant Gary Yaffe stealthily approaching my position. He had a rat-pack 'Tarzan' energy bar in his hand that he presented to me and whispered, 'Happy birthday, this is your gift from the captain.' I was chuffed, as I was hungry, plus it turned out to be rum-and-raisin flavour, which seemed appropriate.

We spent the night in our lying-up position, doing two-hour shifts of guard duty in buddy pairs. We prepared to move at first light, which was around 05:15. After a few hours of slow, careful navigation through the bush we arrived at the road where the explosives had to be placed. Once the devices were in position, we used tree branches to remove our boot prints. During the exfiltration somebody mentioned to be careful of tripwires that might be connected to a POMZ, a deadly Russian anti-personnel mine mounted on a stick. I remember how my mind went into overdrive to move very carefully and cautiously, and to focus hard on the grass and shrubs underfoot.

After about half a day of walking south, the team seniors earmarked an area suitable for an LZ, and we went into a lying-up position to wait for a Puma helicopter that was going to do a night-time pickup and fly us southwest to Ondangwa airfield. The time seemed to drag but we eventually heard the sound of the heli blades cutting through the air. Comms was established and the chopper was guided in to our position. As the bird descended the pilot decided to switch on the landing light on the underside, as somehow either the crew's NVGs did not work or they were inexperienced. The light was excessively bright after our eyes had grown used to the darkness, and I remember the TL and senior operators being very upset about this, as we were not far from a village where Fapla troops and possibly Swapo insurgents were stationed. The pilot only switched the light on for a few seconds before touching down, but it felt like hours. We bundled into the helo and it took off in the dark of the night and we were on our way back to Fort Rev.

We stayed in the forward operations base for a few days to debrief and to pack all our weapons and gear back into the large black boxes. During this period, we received notice that the Intelligence section had intercepted enemy radio chatter indicating that the devices we had set up had destroyed enemy trucks and supplies. It was good to receive confirmation that the mission had been successful.

We left Ondangwa for Durban sometime late in February, and once back at the unit we demobilised, or 'demobbed', as the operators called it. Life returned to the normal 1.1. Commando routine. But we did not hang around for long. In May an order came through for a raiding-type operation to be conducted by 1 Recce in a southern African state. The raid was to take place in a built-up area where enemy targets had been identified that we had to eliminate. All the newly qualified 86/01 cycle corporals (youngsters) deployed on this mission, along with a number of senior NCOs and a few officers from 1.1 Commando. We flew up to Fort Doppies, and it was much more pleasant to visit the Recce base not as a student but as a qualified Special Forces soldier, and as part of the team and organisation that created it.

Mock-ups resembling rooms were constructed on the shooting range at Doppies, and we practised room-clearing drills. Prior to the operation, a Recce team deployed with bicycles to 'blend in' with the population. The plan was for three teams to infiltrate with scrambler motorbikes. The three motorbike teams would be flown by helicopter straight to their targets where they would execute their direct-action assaults. On the night of the operation five 1.1 Commando teams left Doppies, and a few of us moved to the Mpacha airfield for deployment by chopper to the different target areas. The team that I was in would be dropped close to the target buildings for quick penetration and execution, with stopper groups deployed to cut down any escapees.

We got to the airfield after dark and had to wait a while for confirmation from sources that the targets to be eliminated were indeed in the earmarked buildings. Teams one, two and three deployed, and we were waiting for the final confirmation that our targets were where they were supposed to be. It was quite an apprehensive moment, and I remember our TL, Staff Sergeant Johnny 'Guava' de Gouveia (RIP), walking up and down the runway in the dark like a caged tiger while listening to radio traffic from the other teams. Then the disappointing news came over the radio that our targets were not where they were meant to be, and the mission was called off. I thought that Guava was going to blow a fuse, but we all shared in the anti-climax. To complicate matters, the Impala fighter jet that was supposed to be acting as a telstar (comms relay) broke down, and a Super Frelon heavy-lift helo was dispatched to execute this task. Unfortunately, this is the way things go with Special Forces operations – the weather,

Cycle 86/01 'youngsters' at Fort Rev in 1987.
The author is standing second from left.

location, presence or absence of the targets, unexpected local population and many other factors can prevent teams from executing their missions.

It took a good couple of hours for our buddies to return, but at least we could monitor their progress and successes on the radio and root for them. We got back to Fort Doppies early in the morning and the guys demobbed and enjoyed a few cold beers to toast the success of the two teams who had completed their mission. We departed for Durbs in the C-130 a day or two after the ops. When we got back to the unit, we unpacked all weapons and equipment, cleaned and maintained all items and handed them in to the stores to be locked up.

Back at the unit, our next task was to take part in the six-week Advanced Urban Warfare course, scheduled to start early in May. This was good news, as I had looked forward to further training after the urban orientation course before we qualified as operators. The course was highly specialised and practical, drawing on years of operational experience gleaned by the Recces, and was one of the best advanced warfare courses in the world. This was one of the 'spes' courses that qualified operators could do to increase their readiness and efficiency for operations in urban environments.

The orientation course we had done six months earlier was still fresh in our minds and formed a good platform for the advanced course. First we

Life after the Basic Recce Cycle and Beyond

Urban warfare training: practising movement between rooms.

Urban warfare training: abseil and fire through windows.

did some revision on equipment and how to prepare urban battle gear. We also revised subjects such as urban movement, house clearing and obstacle crossing, but with more intensity and longer, more frequent exercises. We were now taught how to work in multiple teams, with a number of teams going into buildings and clearing rooms and buildings, together with search teams equipped to look for hidden targets or to follow the clearing teams to collect items for intel.

We were also introduced to a 'killing house', a large apartment-sized room with many different working parts – moving and pop-up targets, cupboards, beds and old appliances such as fridges, stoves and washing machines – around which targets were arranged. It was good training, but you had to focus hard and be precise in the execution of your actions. The Special Forces at the time were not earmarked to act on hostage situations within South Africa. This task was the responsibility of the SAP's elite Special Task Force (STF), which were the cream of the crop when it came to hostage situations. We did, however, often find hostage-type targets in the killing house and buildings where we practised urban fighting and clearance drills.

Most of the soldiers on the course were very good shots by now, and everybody passed these 'hostage' shoots where you had to take a split second longer to ensure that you engaged the correct target. We also conducted 'dark' killing-house drills at night with infrared filters fitted over the torch of your weapon's lens, while wearing a set of NVG. This was in an era when such equipment was still fairly bulky and infrared laser aimpoints were few and far between. But with practice you could figure out how and where to aim while looking through the infrared lenses of the NVG.

Part of the Advanced Urban Warfare training was how to infiltrate cities clandestinely and how to conduct urban reconnaissance. It is easy enough to become a 'door-kicker' and learn how to clear buildings and rooms, but you first have to get to those areas before you can take direct action. It is therefore very important to know how to infiltrate urban areas. Such infiltrations could be done as low-profile/undercover missions in which you infiltrate by foot, truck, motorbike, bicycle or perhaps parachute. The last-mentioned requires a high degree of planning and coordination, and landing on top of buildings in the dark from a high altitude is something the Recces had already started to practise in the early 1980s. Only a handful of experienced 'sky-gods', as we referred to them, could pull this off, but it was an option.

Another infiltration technique is to make use of the stormwater drains and tunnel systems beneath the city to sneak into position. We took part in a night-time exercise in which we had to row across Durban harbour, between all the ships and port traffic, to the outlets of the city's large stormwater drains. We were teamed up in buddy pairs in kayaks and departed from a quiet location close to Salisbury Island, the naval base on the eastern side of the port, near the western side of the Bluff military complex. The layout of the port and piers meant that it was not a straight-line rowing exercise. This distance to the sugar terminal, where the stormwater pipes drained into the harbour, amounted to around four kilometres. It was important to work out the best time with respect to the tides and weather conditions, as the year before a man had drowned during this exercise – RIP Corporal Pedro.

The trip across the port was done in legs where you had to navigate to, and then turn towards, a new bearing on a few occasions. Navigating stealthily through the ships and port traffic was interesting, to say the least. But the next phase was outright challenging to the mind. At the city end of the port, close to the sugar terminal, the massive pipes that ran into the harbour discharged stormwater drainage from the city's catchment area. We steered our kayaks into these massive pipes and rowed through them for a short distance, until the point where we could get out of the kayaks and walk knee-deep in the water through the tunnel below the city. Once we entered the tunnel, the front member in the kayak would switch on a low-light torch, as it was pitch dark. As soon as the torch went on, fish began jumping out of the shallow water towards the light source. It was freaky to see these thin mullet fish jumping towards you. Some ended up in the kayak and had to be thrown out, and one fish hit me in the head.

Once we were under the city, the pipes became smaller and narrower, but still big enough for us to walk in a crouching position towards the

A Breed Apart

Urban warfare training: drills in smoke-filled room.

Urban warfare training: movement and assault wearing gas masks.

city centre. We had to use precise (underground) navigation to get to an area close to Greyville Racecourse. We had to count our steps and work out the average distance travelled in this claustrophobic setting. Once we reached the area, we looked for manholes close to the racecourse. The first team member would act as a scout, lifting the manhole slightly and peeping out to see if there was any movement or traffic before we would open the hole for the team to get above ground. We gave each other cover when climbing out of the manhole and deployed an all-round defensive position once all team members were out.

We were also taught how to conduct urban surveillance and reconnaissance operations to gather intel that could be applied strategically or tactically. This training included how to infiltrate high-rise buildings to conduct area surveillance. We were shown how office and residential buildings are constructed and their layouts. The lift system and shafts are areas of importance to a Special Forces team, for various reasons.

Escape and evasion in an urban environment in a foreign country is an important subject, and we received a lot of instruction about this. The unit's training wing had an arrangement with the SAP dog unit in Durban, and the students on the course were exposed to police dogs and the way they operate to 'hunt' suspects. Such training is of importance for an operator who has to flee a city if things go wrong on their mission, or if they have to escape and evade enemy or foreign forces. We went to the dog unit's training facility and donned special padded suits. Then you had to run and the dog handler would release the dog to 'tackle' you. This was quite an exciting drill but also slightly nerve-wracking, as these police dogs were aggressive and bit non-stop. In the evenings and at night, students would individually be teamed up with a dog unit patrol car to go out and work on actual crime calls. It was good training, and we learned how the police's flying and dog squads operate to hunt suspects down. The idea was to identify possible grey areas and ways to escape if you were ever in a position where you had to evade the authorities in a foreign country.

Maps, and the preparation thereof, are a very important part of E&E, particularly in urban areas. You need to know street and block layouts,

A Puma helicopter drops students on top of the water tower, Salisbury Island.

A student abseils 30 m down from the water tower, Salisbury Island.

danger areas and possible safe havens, possible escape routes that are quieter and less likely to be patrolled by foreign forces, plus a slew of other considerations that must be applied to and indicated on your map/s. It is important to hide maps properly and to have a decent cover story with the right supporting documents. Choice of clothing is also a consideration, and grey neutral colours with soft-soled shoes work better. Extra knee and elbow padding in your clothing are helpful, as you use your knees and elbows more often in getting over walls and urban obstacles.

Concentration of population and certain areas need to be studied, as well as the language and customs of the area of operations. Other training included night flights with experienced Puma pilots in urban areas. One intense exercise was when we had to fast-rope down to a multi-storey high-rise residential building. You had to trust the chopper pilots and their crew looking out the door to ensure you didn't miss the building and become pulp on the pavement below.

Another exercise that got the adrenaline going was abseiling down the water tower at the naval base on Salisbury Island. The tower, a pillar-type structure with a large cement reservoir on top is around 30 m high and holds 310 000 litres of water. We ascended the tower via the fixed ladder inside the column until we could exit and stand atop the structure. Here an instructor from the special techniques branch would hook you up to the abseiling rope with the figure-eight and carabiner on your abseiling harness. You had to slowly walk down the slanted side of the water reservoir to where it starts angling back down towards the column. Then you had to kick yourself away from the structure and give slack on the rope to descend past the concrete side of the reservoir below your feet. Many students who hesitated to give it a good kick, and who hung on to the rope with their master hand, ended up with bloody noses and foreheads after hitting the side of the structure.

The six-week course concluded, and we were now qualified to take part in urban operations, although some of us youngsters had already gone on an urban operation on foreign soil before the course started. We learned a lot about specialised fighting techniques in built-up areas, and I enjoyed it immensely. I did not know that a few years later I would end up presenting this course at 1.2 Commando – the Special Forces training wing.

After the urban course I was earmarked to go on to the next 'spes' training phase – free fall and HALO training. However, the pain in my feet was killing me, and I was withdrawn from the course, which allowed Tinus de Klerk to move into my spot and do the training. This was the last time that free fall and HALO training was done at 1 Recce. The next year all this training was moved back to 1 Parachute Battalion.

By now the medical staff at the 1 Recce sickbay knew me and the challenge posed by my Achilles tendons and the soft tissue of my heels. After the urban warfare course I decided to address this problem once and for all. I was referred to Brigadier Etienne Hugo, the top military-medical orthopaedic surgeon, who visited the provinces each quarter. Brigadier Hugo recommended cortisone injections on the bottom of my heels, straight into the affected soft-tissue areas. These injections hurt quite a bit and did not seem to help much.

The next assignment for us newly qualified corporals was the Regimental Signals course, which would equip you for deployment as the team signaller during operations. The course involved specialised training presented by experienced signallers, some of whom had served in the Rhodesian Bush War until 1979/1980. We were taught how to operate an array of radios, from VHF, UHF and HF to ground-to-air. We were taught how to send and receive Morse code, which took a lot of practice. The most important part of the course for bush operations was to know how to 'cut' the HF radio set's antennae to the right length and position them for maximum range and effectiveness.

During the second half of the year, 1.1 Commando's operators were called up to conduct operations in support of the last three main operations in the Bush War theatre. The 1.1. Commando teams were briefed on deployment to southeastern Angola, where a major MPLA offensive against Unita was developing. The SADF's overall objective was to support Unita against the Fapla forces, who were bolstered by large amounts of Soviet-supplied equipment and thousands of Cuban, East German and Soviet advisors. The strategic town of Cuito Cuanavale, on the Cuito River, was to be one of the hinges of the offensive. SADF planners rolled out operations Modulêr, Hooper and Packer, with Operation Modulêr starting 13 August and ending on 5 December 1987. Operation Hooper commenced on 2 January 1988, and the 1 Recce team that deployed the year before stayed on over the Christmas and New Year period.

I asked Brigadier Hugo if I could deploy with the commando on these operations. He strongly advised against it, and I informed Major Frans van Dyk, the OC 1.1 Commando, that I was booked off on 'light duty' and would not be able to join the deployment. My heart ate shit about this development, but I knew it was a sensible decision by the surgeon. My old cycle buddy, Corporal Dries Coetzee, was also booked off on light duty as he had broken his leg badly in a motorbike accident a little earlier in the year. It was an open fracture, and he had to hobble around the unit with metal pins and a rack sticking out of the cast.

The commando deployed and we were left alone on the first floor of the HQ building to look after the offices, which were locked up, except for the reception desk, or 1.1 Commando duty room, as it was known. We manned the telephone, but there were not many calls, as the rest of

1 Recce members and an intel officer, Cuito area, Christmas 1987.

The damaged bridge over the Cuito River, blown by 4 Recce members, 1987.

the unit and the families knew the teams were out on ops. RSM Pep kept us busy with some punitive tasks after the two of us tried to drown our non-deployment sorrows in the Riff-Raff bar on a number of occasions.

Between 24 and 28 August, a team from 4 Recce was sent on a mission called Operation Coolidge. Its objective was the destruction of the bridge over the Cuito River, which Fapla used to move supplies from Cuito

Cuanavale to the Fapla brigades located on the Lomba River. Teams from 5 Recce working in the area would assist as support and infiltration/exfiltration element. The Recce team were dropped off by helicopters 40 km north of the bridge and rowed down towards the bridge in kayaks. They hid the kayaks and donned closed-circuit diving gear to infiltrate underwater to the bridge in the dark. After partially detonating their demolition charges, the team was discovered but managed to escape, leaving the bridge damaged and unable to be used by enemy vehicles.

The attack took place during the night of 25–26 August 1987. When the team was discovered, they took incoming fire and the TL, Captain Fred Wilke, was shot through the arm and bled profusely. Another one of the team members, Staff Sergeant Anton Beukman, was attacked by a crocodile, which he had to fight off with his hunting knife. He stabbed the crocodile several times while underwater, after the beast repeatedly rolled him over, and managed to get the blade of his diving knife, which he carried around his ankle, into the eye socket of the animal to kill it. The team struggled for quite a while to escape and evade the enemy forces but made it out alive.

Two members of our cycle, PP Hugo and Diff de Villiers, were involved with the extraction of the team members, who had to split up. Diff, who was posted to 4 Recce, and a team of Unita soldiers was involved with the casevac of one of the wounded team members. He recalls how they ran with the improvised stretcher and wounded soldier placed on their already heavy rucksacks until his shoulders started bleeding from the chafing of the pack and poles. PP Hugo, who was stationed at 5 Recce, oversaw the lifting of the members, including the operator shot through the arm, and their subsequent escape from the enemy. Both teams went through some hairy situations with enemy forces on their heels, Russian Mi-24 gunships circling the area and serious incoming fire from BM-21 Grad rocket launchers. The entire scuba-attack team was awarded the Honoris Crux for bravery by then State President PW Botha. He also handed Anton a unique trophy: a mounted crocodile skull, with the knife Anton had used to kill the croc through the eye socket. Diff received a Military Merit Medal for his actions.

Life after the Basic Recce Cycle and Beyond

The 4 Recce team met State President PW Botha to receive medals for bravery, 1987.

The trophy presented to 'crocodile man' Anton Beukman.

Dries and me were informed that I was earmarked to travel to Pretoria to undergo combat medical training at the military's elite 7 Medical Battalion (7 Med), which had been formed to support the Recces and other combat units within our military setup. This was a productive development and led to my acquiring a lot of new and very useful life-saving skills that would serve me well for the rest of my life. This was intense medical training. By the end of our training cycle, we were familiar with buddy aid, how to stop bleeding and how to run the contents of an IV bag into a wounded soldier's veins. But this course took medical assistance to new levels.

A number of police STF members joined us on the course. We assisted with autopsies in the morgue at the academic hospital in Pretoria to learn about the human anatomy, and the frailty or resilience thereof, and assisted doctors in the emergency ward of a busy hospital in a township north of Pretoria. Here we had to treat people with gunshot and stab wounds, and a few that had been attacked with pangas, which gave us a lot of opportunity to practise our suturing skills.

The course ran for two months. I had to return to the unit by train as I wrote off my car – the first one I ever bought – after a hard party session with the STF members, or 'Taakies' as they were called, one Friday night after work at a police canteen in northern Pretoria. We saw the year out alone, as our buddies were still deployed around Cuito Cuanavale as Ops Modulêr ended and Ops Hooper began.

CONCLUSION
(1988 TO 1990)

The year 1988 was a strange one for many reasons, and it was a very tremulous year in our country's history. The SADF launched Operation Hooper early in the year, which would lead to Operation Packer, which in turn led to the conclusion of the eight-month battle of Cuito Cuanavale, where the SADF won the battles but lost the (political) war. Several bombs went off in cities all over the country, and the security forces, including Special Forces, hit back at enemy bases and locations in Gaborone, Botswana and Maputo, Mozambique. A faction planned a coup d'état in the then homeland of Bophuthatswana, which failed. There was a lot of internal political strife, with supporters of the Inkatha Freedom Party and the ANC clashing violently. Right-wing activities were also at a high. A right-wing fanatic killed eight black people in a public location in Pretoria.

After operations Hooper and Packer, and the final battle of Cuito Cuanavale, the conflicts of the Bush War officially came to a conclusion later in the year, and there was a big shift in politics in South Africa that also affected South West Africa. Late in the year, peace accords were signed to end South Africa's 73-year administration of South West Africa, which would go on to become independent Namibia the next year. FW de Klerk took over the position of state president from PW Botha, and began to lead the National Party on a different course, leading to the unbanning of the liberation movements and negotiations for a democratic constitution.

I was now well settled at 1 Recce and in the operational 1.1 Commando, and was looking forward to seeing new cycles coming through 1 Recce, qualifying and ending up in the unit. But my feet finally reached a point where I battled to put any weight on them, and the doctors at our unit medical facility sent me to the Natal Command sickbay, close to Durban's northern beaches. I was admitted and told that I needed to rest for two weeks with my feet in the air. I was placed on strong non-steroidal anti-inflammatory drugs (NSAIDs), and I also had some physiotherapy sessions.

All this seemed to help with the pain, but once I was back on my feet again the pain returned. During my time in the army medical facility, I turned 20. I had done well on the Combat Medical course and the powers that be thought it was a good idea to send me on the Advanced Medical course, also in Pretoria at 7 Med. I was excited about this upcoming training, which would qualify me as a level 5 paramedic equivalent in the army.

The idea of training qualified Special Forces soldiers in advanced medical techniques is nothing new. During most overt and even some clandestine operations, 7 Med could supply combat medics, and doctors if required, to support the Special Forces teams. But certain missions were so sensitive that only the qualified operators had the necessary security clearance to take part, or the team configuration did not allow for it. During such missions it was always preferable to have an operator who was trained as an advanced emergency medical technician (EMT) on your team.

This time I was the only 1 Recce member on the course. In the end there were only five of us, with the others consisting of Staff Sergeant Billy Erasmus and three other black members of 5 Recce. The six-week course took medical training matters much further, and we worked a lot in the emergency ward of the academic hospital. We now assisted the doctors with surgical operations, amputations and births, and we covered a lot of different types of wounds and how to treat them. We also learned about various illnesses and diseases, and I learned a lot about medicine and its applications. I had taken well to medical training the previous year, and I enjoyed both courses immensely. These medical training courses enabled me to work later on as an EMT and combat medic in conflict zones after my military career ended, and I often used these medical skills to tend to casualties, particularly when working in Iraq.[8]

We followed the politics of the day and realised that the war in Namibia was going to come to an end, and furthermore understood that the

---

8   See Blood Money, pages 44, 45 and 82.

Conclusion (1988 to 1990)

role of the Recce units and the military in general was going to change dramatically. The routine when we were not on course or deployed was still the same - early-morning parade, PT, teatime, work until 16:00, then your own private PT or to the pub (or perhaps both). We did night training on Tuesdays and Thursdays, mostly urban warfare techniques at the old whaling station. We also paddled the kayaks and used the Zodiac inflatables on a regular basis.

During one of these exercises, I hook-turned the inflatable too quickly while we were exercising 'man-overboard' drills, and nicked Nicky with the propeller blade in the crack of his butt as he dove downwards when he saw I was going to hit him. Thankfully, there was no other damage than a deep gash in his butt, but it caused him a lot of discomfort and he had to improvise ways of sitting and shitting for a while.

We shot a lot and I developed good skills with a pistol during combat shooting scenarios. I made the 1 Recce four-man practical combat pistol shooting team. We attended some trials and a few of us received our Natal SADF provincial colours in the sport. I was part of the team that went to the national championship in Pretoria, and it was great fun shooting in combat competitions. I did not fare too badly for my first outing and ended in the top third of shooters countrywide. I was looking forward to taking part in future championships, but soon my work in the training wing kept me too busy to enter contests.

In the second half of the year a bunch of youngsters and cycle buddies, from both 1 and 4 Recce, went to Pretoria to undergo advanced combat medical training. Many of the students on this course would end up deploying in South West Africa the next year prior to the final battles and eventual conclusion of the Bush War. I was sent on two more courses, the first being the military's version of driving heavy trucks, armoured personnel carriers and motorbikes, and the field maintenance of such vehicles. This was fortunate as sometime in the early 1990s we could apply for the conversion of our military permits to the civilian equivalent of motorbike and heavy truck licences. The second course was called 'Methodology' and dealt with the techniques required to present military classes. I did well on this course and it helped me a lot when I was

The author as a sergeant, 1989.

transferred to the training wing towards the end of the following year. During the Methodology course we were shown how to put together course programmes, curricula and classes, and how to prepare different training aids, in an era before PCs and PowerPoint presentations came into widespread use. Notes for instruction, including diagrams and line sketches, had to be done by hand on 'transparencies' – thin clear plastic sheets on which you could write and draw – and placed on an overhead projector, which would project your notes and illustrations on to a white pull-down screen.

1989

In January 1989, I was promoted to sergeant. I was still only 20 years old, and my 21st birthday was a month and a half away. The ANC announced the end of their guerrilla campaign in Angola, but a number of explosions still rocked the country, including one outside Natal Command on the Durban beachfront.

Under the New York Accords, South Africa and Cuba agreed to withdraw

Conclusion (1988 to 1990)

South West African Police ID card as used by 1.1. Commando members, 1989.

their forces from Angola, and a date was set for Namibian independence.[9] United Nations forces were going to be deployed to Namibia to oversee the transition to independence, in line with Resolution 435 (1978). This would eventually lead to a peaceful handover of the country from South African control, and all-inclusive democratic elections.

With independence looming, most SADF forces were withdrawn from South West Africa. Border patrols were downscaled and became the responsibility of the South West African Police (Swapol). The Swapol counterinsurgency unit Koevoet was still ready to react to any possible hostilities if Swapo fighters crossed the border, breached the peace agreement and committed acts of terrorism.

Our headquarters in Pretoria, Speskop, was tasked to deploy some Recces to the border to gather intel and assist the government in getting accurate information on the transition process in South West Africa. A number of cycle buddies who had undergone combat medical training at 7 Med, plus a few of us who were qualified ops medics at 1 Recce, were earmarked for this mission. The plan was to deploy the Recces as 'medics'

---

9   The Tripartite Accord between Angola, Cuba and South Africa was signed in New York on 22 December 1988. The agreement is widely known as the New York Accords.

with the Swapol territorial forces at different bases along the border in Ovamboland's sector 1.0 (one-zero, a term referring to the Namibia/Angola border area from Ruacana eastwards to Rundu).

I was chosen as one of the group from 1 Recce who would deploy, as I had already done the ops medic and combat medical courses in 1987 and the first part of 1988. Apart from me, the 1 Recce group consisted of Lieutenant Tinus de Klerk, staff sergeants Abel Erasmus and Gary Yaffe, Sergeant Barry Visser and corporals DEM Laubscher, Harry Caarstens (RIP), 'Dup' du Plessis, Dolf van Tonder (RIP), Raymond Archer and Ernesto Bongo (RIP). Another group, from 4 Recce, would deploy to sector 2.0, which lay east of Nkongo base and towards the Caprivi. This group consisted of Lieutenant Rob Jennings and sergeants Eugene van der Merwe, De Wet Human, Mark de Wet, Braam de Beer and Johan Ferreira. In all, eight guys from the 86/01 training cycle – Barry, Braam, Wetta, Diff, Rob, Mark, Eugene and me – would be deployed on this mission.

We were pre-briefed at our respective units on our roles during the mission, which we referred to internally as Operation Saga. It would run in parallel with the wider Operation Merlyn, which involved the deployment of Koevoet and Swapol forces in the run-up to the elections planned for later in the year. We then moved up to Speskop for final preparations, and flew from Waterkloof Air Force Base to Windhoek, the capital of South West Africa.

In Windhoek we stayed outside the city at a Swapol security branch training facility, where we underwent induction training on how the Swapol system worked, the political situation in the country, the status of Swapo, what our roles would be and how we were to integrate into the Swapol teams. We were even given Swapol identity cards as part of our cover.

The training went on for about a week, after which we were due to travel to Oshakati by bus for the deployment. We departed the morning of 18 February 1989, on my 21st birthday. The festivities, however, had started the night before at a braai and get-together that was arranged at the police base after our final day of induction/orientation. We delved into the beers and Red Heart that evening, and I arranged a bottle of the nectar of the war gods for my birthday celebration the next day. Needless

Conclusion (1988 to 1990)

to say, it was a bunch of very hungover Recce corporals, a few sergeants, a lieutenant and an intel officer from HQ who boarded the bus to travel northeast to the operational area. It was a long trip in this vast country, and we had to cover close to 800 km. The trip took the best part of a day, but it was exceedingly jovial. The buses did not have air conditioning in those days, and I remember smelling of rum as I perspired in the summer heat. At one point I 'fell asleep' only to be woken when we approached Ondangwa, about 35 km south of Oshakati.

We arrived at Oshakati around sunset and were dropped at the Swapol barracks. We offloaded our gear, which was mostly civvy clothing. We could not wear uniform because the SADF had officially withdrawn from South West Africa. After this chore was done, we were invited to go to the Koevoet bar, which was situated close to the barracks and not far from the safe house we were given to stay at when we travelled to Oshakati from our outpost positions along the border.

My 21st birthday party then proceeded further. The funniest part was trying to maintain our cover as security personnel attached to Swapol, as the entire town somehow knew that we were Recces. It was okay as this was not a covert or clandestine mission, more like an undercover cop setup. We got hammered with the Koevoet members, joked about the UN force that was slowly starting to appear around the area and eventually made our way back to the barracks.

We stayed at this location for a couple of days before we were posted out to the various forward operations bases along the border. We were briefed a bit more about the operation by the intelligence officer, and we learned a lot from hanging out with the Koevoet and Swapol guys. Corporal Ernesto Bongo (RIP) and I were shipped off to Nkongo, the easternmost base in sector 1.0. We were teamed up with some police members, a warrant officer and a constable, who had been called up from South Africa, and hitched a ride with one of the Koevoet teams that operated in the eastern part of the sector. When we got to the base, we saw the following motto displayed at the entrance: 'Nkongo base, where men are men and sheep are nervous.' It summed things up nicely, as the base often got 'revved' by insurgents.

The author with fellow Recce Ernesto Bongo, at Nkongo base, on the border, 1989.

We worked on the border for almost six weeks, observing, gathering intel and occasionally patrolling the *kaplyn* (cutline) that marked the border between Namibia and Angola. Whenever I could, I hitched a ride to our safe house in Oshakati, where Tinus was stationed, in the hope of running into some of my buddies. Occasionally, this led to serious 'reunion' bouts after we discussed the mission and shared intel.

Towards the end of March, the United Nations Transition Assistance Group (UNTAG) forces arrived in the operational area to oversee the handover and upcoming elections. They were to be stationed in the country from April 1989 to March 1990. It was the first time any of us had seen UN troops, and it was quite a spectacle. Soldiers from Indonesia, India, Malaysia and other countries were stationed at different bases along the border. All their aircraft, combat vehicles and other equipment were painted white! How the hell did they plan to conceal all this equipment in the Bush War scenario? But after what took place in April, I realised that these dudes were not interested in camouflage or concealment. As a matter of fact, they were not geared for fighting a war.

On the morning of 1 April 1989, more than a thousand heavily armed Swapo insurgents crossed the border from Angola into Namibia in

Conclusion (1988 to 1990)

Ops members at the safe house in Oshakati, 1989 (author at rear, with cap).

initiating what became known as 'The Nine Day War'. The UNTAG forces were nowhere to be seen. The Swapol and South African forces had to do the fighting.

Around noon the first contacts between Koevoet teams and the insurgents started coming through on the radio, and all the bases in the area were alerted. There were fierce contacts and heavy battles between the Koevoet, Swapol and Swapo forces. Some Recces were embedded with the Koevoet teams. On 4 April, one of our buddies, Corporal Herman Caarstens (RIP), was killed in a contact with enemy forces, alongside 21 Koevoet members killed during the nine days of fighting. He was the last member of the SADF to be killed in action in the Bush War. Sadly, but perhaps fittingly, he would be classed with Lieutenant Fred Zeelie, the first casualty of the Bush War (March 1974). Both men were from 1 Recce. Johan Ferreira, one of our cycle buddies, received a Military Merit Medal for his actions during this operation.

After I got back from Namibia, toward the middle of 1989, I was informed that I was earmarked to be transferred to 1.2 Commando, the Recce training wing. I was excited about this prospect. I moved up to the second floor of the HQ building, where the training wing was situated, towards the end of the year and settled in quickly. My commander was Major Willie de Koker (RIP), and I was earmarked to present the Minor Tactics and Advanced Urban Warfare courses. The Methodology course that I had done the year before helped me a lot in drafting lectures, compiling training aids and developing training models. I enjoyed giving instruction and quickly developed a propensity for it, perhaps because I hail from a family that has produced many teachers throughout the generations. At the end of July, I moved to town and settled in with my future wife (and life partner), though I kept my room at E-Block.

1990

The start of the new decade brought a lot of changes in southern Africa. Most importantly, South Africa embarked on the process of ending apartheid. On 2 February, President FW de Klerk unbanned the African National Congress, the South African Communist Party and the Pan Africanist Congress. The ANC abandoned the armed struggle somewhat later. Political prisoners were released, including Nelson Mandela, who had served 27 years behind bars, including 18 years on Robben Island. PW Botha resigned from the National Party in protest at De Klerk's new direction. The various apartheid laws were repealed and the process of negotiating a new constitution began.

At the training wing I did a lot of reading about methods of instruction and how to fine-tune presentations in class. I assisted Major De Koker in overhauling the Advanced Urban Warfare training manual when I was not out presenting courses, and it kept me gainfully busy. The training wing commander at the time was the legendary Commandant (Lt Col) Andre Diedericks, or 'Diedies' as he was known. He was a highly professional soldier and a perfectionist when it came to training matters.

I was the weapons sergeant at the wing and had access to the urban stores, including the ammunition store. I often went down to the whaling station to shoot and test different weapons and calibres with all the types of ammo available. It was great fun, and I learned a lot about the penetration, ricocheting and performance of the different weapons, calibres and types of ammo. One of the most important points I learned

Conclusion (1988 to 1990)

when shooting through car windscreens was the significant deflection of the 9 mm round downwards when firing out of a vehicle, and upwards when shooting through the windscreen from the outside. In contrast, the heavier 230-grain .45 ACP bullet fared much better and maintained its flight path. It was the start of my love affair with the Colt 1911 .45 ACP pistol, which was incidentally also designed by John Moses Browning, the inventor of the 9 mmP pistols we used on operations at the time. I shot at stoves, metal cupboards, fridges and all sorts of household furniture to see what weapon systems and ammo worked best for urban fighting, and to study the penetrative and ricocheting characteristics associated with each system, ammo type and furniture variety.

The Recces' premier bush warfare training facility, Fort Doppies, was closed down in 1988 as part of the SADF's withdrawal from South West Africa. Towards the end of that year, and in 1989, a few courses were presented at the Hellsgate training base, which was also in the woods of northern Zululand, close to a missile testing range. This was only a temporary arrangement, and eventually a new bush warfare training facility was created at Madimbo, against the Limpopo River, which forms the country's northern border with Zimbabwe, and close to the northern gate to the Kruger National Park at Pafuri. The SADF had a large piece of land at Madimbo, with units stationed there to patrol the border.

The new base was built next to a military runway and had to be constructed from scratch. I was part of a team of instructors from the training wing who travelled to the area to present the Minor Tactics phase to the cycle that came through that year. Sergeant Major Pep van Zyl was moved from Hellsgate to oversee the construction of the new base with a bunch of his 'special troops', national servicemen who could not be deployed in the infantry or other combat units due to certain personal restraints, and who were used by the old weathered sergeant major to assist with construction and other 'odd jobs'.

We stayed in army tents as the barracks and facilities were not yet built. One night, while four of us lay on our stretchers, somebody heard a noise and shone a torch at the roof of our tent, where we spotted a bunch of large black scorpions. There must have been close to 50 of these creatures,

Harry Caarstens and DEM Laubscher having a bush lunch, 1 April 1989.

Harry Caarstens, RIP.

Conclusion (1988 to 1990)

with their thick black tails curving downwards. It was decided to switch off the light and let them be, upon which I crept deep into my sleeping bag and pulled it over my head.

The new facility was named Fort Scorpio because of the abundance of these predatory arachnids (order Scorpiones). One of the most prevalent species was the *Parabuthus transvaalicus*, one of the biggest scorpions in the family Buthidae. It grows up to 15 cm in length, is dark brown to black in colour and has a thick tail and thin pincers. Thick-tailed or fat-tailed scorpions generally have potent venom, and *Parabuthus transvaalicus* is considered to be one of the most poisonous scorpions in southern Africa. Every so often one of the students on the course was stung and had to be treated by the medics.

I caught a few of these beautiful animals, which I kept in an empty ammo box. I named the biggest one Brutus. True to our competitive alpha-male characteristics, Brutus was pitted against large hairy baboon spiders, tarantulas and big centipedes. He won many fights and was declared a champ before I retired him and took him back to Durban. He lived in my room in E-Block in an empty fish tank furnished with sand, rocks and twigs. I did not have enough time to catch prey for him, which was normally geckos and spiders found on the Bluff, so the retired champ had to grow accustomed to small pieces of cold KFC, which he seemed to enjoy.

I enjoyed presenting the Minor Tactics course to new cycles of would-be Recces. The terrain at Fort Scorpio was excellent for Recce training needs, and we covered all the subjects that we had done in our training at Fort Doppies. My favourite lectures and practical exercises were those covering ambushes, trench clearing and assisting in 'fire initiation'. This was done by mounting LMGs on slightly higher ground, at 45 degrees on both sides behind the students. The students would leopard-crawl underneath low-strung barbed wire while we fired FMJ 7.62 x 51 mm ball rounds over their heads and threw thunder flashes around them to simulate explosions. The intention was to create the feeling of a firefight, and to get the adrenaline and fear going in a student to be able to train them to overcome such fears and to continue moving forward in such a situation.

Brutus the scorpion, Fort Scorpio, 1990.

Trench clearing was a good exercise – the attack team had to crawl towards the trench while their teammates on the flanks laid down suppressing fire on the trenched area. When they were close to the trench, the attack team would lob a couple of grenades into it, and after these detonated they would jump into the trench, back-to-back, and start clearing and engaging targets as they moved further away from one another. The challenge with the exercise was for the students not to overthrow, or to short-throw, the grenades and miss the trench. But as live training scenarios went, this happened once or twice, and the instructors had to hit the deck before the grenades went off or risk being hit with shrapnel from the hand-bombs.

After these courses we moved back to Durban to present the Urban Warfare orientation courses to the cycle students before they qualified. And I was also now an instructor at the urban warfare branch, which presented the advanced course to newly qualified operators as part of their 'spes' training. I enjoyed this type of warfare immensely and also learned a lot about overcoming new challenges. Each new exercise presented challenges to the students, which the instructors had to be able to help the students solve, quickly.

1991 TO NOVEMBER 1992

I assisted as an instructor on various Minor Tactics and Urban Warfare courses, and towards the second part of 1991 I was earmarked to undergo the then elite VIP Protection course at the Military Intelligence College (SAMIC) training farm north of Pretoria. Earlier in the year a few of the instructors in the training wing, with a number of operators, were earmarked to start research and development (R&D) for the formation of a new 'clandestine urban warfare' branch, as the role of the Recces had changed drastically with the conclusion of the Bush War.

There were about six of us, three of them from the 86/01 cycle – Sybie, who was a major now (and the OC of the R&D team), Dries and myself. We were joined by Staff Sergeants Adriaan Steyn, Buks van den Berg and Corporal Ernest 'ET' Pringle, and the R&D begun.

One of the reasons I was sent on the VIP Protection course was that a large part of the course focused on defensive, advanced and offensive driving techniques, which I was earmarked to research and turn into a viable training course for the new clandestine wing. I enjoyed the VIP Protection training module immensely and came first on the course. The powers that be sent me on various other advanced training courses in Natal and Gauteng. Some of the training involved high-speed racing driving techniques, and there was a lot of skidpan training – throwing vehicles around in all kinds of manoeuvres that could be used to escape ambush-type situations. I took to the training and seemed to have some talent in driving the daylights out of motor vehicles in tight situations. The training enabled me to run tactical and advanced driving and executive protection courses at a tactical training centre that I opened a few years later, after leaving the military.

In 1991, I had to participate in an advanced infantry warfare course to qualify to be promoted to staff sergeant. I was sent to the Infantry School in Oudtshoorn, where it had all started five and a half years earlier. I did the Battalion Mortars course, which ran over a five-week period at the end of the cold winter months in the second half of the year. We were taught how to operate the 81 mm South African-built mortar in various applications and with an array of different and deadly ammunition. I passed the course and was in line to be promoted to staff sergeant the next year.

The author presenting training at Madimbo 1, early 1990s.

1992

I was promoted to staff sergeant at the beginning of the year, after serving a total of six years in the military. I turned 24 in February. The new clandestine urban warfare group underwent various clandestine training courses at different branches of the intelligence and counterintelligence services. We also did training in covert intelligence-gathering, the handling of foreign agents and other covert warfare tactics with Eeben Barlow[10], a former CCB operator and 32 Battalion Recce, through his newly founded company, Executive Outcomes. One subject of the course that I enjoyed, and that has served me well throughout my life, was neuro-linguistic programming, a communication technique used in covert warfare to measure and assess possible source personnel for recruitment and to determine the accuracy of intel provided by agents. We were busy, and explored all sorts of techniques, such as lock-picking, opening and 'hot-wiring' cars, clandestine communications and surveillance methods, and other TTPs required to shape the new specialist branch and to get it operational.

Toward the middle of the year I could not take the pain in my heels

---

10   Barlow began his military career as a sapper in the Engineer Corps.

Conclusion (1988 to 1990)

The author presenting small-arms training at Madimbo 2, early 1990s.

any longer, and Brigadier Hugo decided that it was time for surgical intervention. I went up to 1 Military Hospital, in Pretoria, where he was going to try a new technique that was still classed as 'experimental'. It involved surgery to open both heels and conduct a nerve-release procedure. The brigadier wanted to do one foot at a time so that I could still walk with the aid of crutches while the other foot healed. In the end, I convinced him to operate on both heels at the same time.

When I came to after the operation I was in hell with the pain where the surgery had been done. I stayed in hospital a few days and caught a ride back to the unit with RSM Boats Botes, who had taken over from RSM Pep late in 1988. Boats was up in Pretoria on military business and he arranged a minibus van for me to be able to lie flat while he drove to Durbs. I had plaster casts on both feet and it hurt like hell. I was in a wheelchair for six weeks, and on crutches for another six, during which time I managed to write off the wheelchair after a heavy night partying with my dad, and broke a crutch on a taxi driver's head during another unsavoury incident …

After three months I returned to the unit, my feet hurting more than ever, and continued my duties at the training wing for a short while longer. My decision to resign from the military was aided by some wrong choices I

Wayne Ross-Smith, the author and Neves Mathias relaxing at Madimbo during the 1990s.

made at the time, and I left the force on the last day of October 1992.

My almost seven years in 1 Recce and Special Forces prepared me well for working in the high-risk security sector, particularly where advanced training was required. I stayed in Durban but visited the unit and my old buds often, although many of them left the unit to join Executive Outcomes in their Angolan campaign. The pain in my feet was now worse and my back hurt a lot. But in the end I made it through testing times and lived a colourful life while in the Recces.

WALLS AND TRAMADOLS

Einstein perfectly summed up the nature of existence with these words: 'Nothing in life is constant except change.' The only constant in my busy and colourful life has been pain. I have lived with chronic pain since the age of 18. After I wrote the initial chapters of this book, in early 2020, I had to undergo a complete reconstruction of my lower back. The serious and involved surgery, by a well-known neurosurgeon and lifesaver, Dr Jacques Scheltema, took almost nine hours. Two titanium rods had to be emplaced next to my spine, held in place by no less than ten large titanium screws. Another four donor bone discs replaced the worn and broken ones, held in place by ten metal pins. The operation was a traumatic

Conclusion (1988 to 1990)

event, very painful and life-changing. What drives a man to disrespect his body so much that his back starts leaking spinal fluid into his body, to the point where I collapsed and could not walk any longer? The answer is straightforward and simple – stupidity.

If you have followed my life story closely enough, you would realise that I hammered my body and ignored the warning signals almost for an entire lifetime. It is called 'sustained bodily abuse' and is almost like something out of medieval torture chambers. And I have openly and willingly engaged in this abuse of my own frame. I threw my body into everything I did – more so than I needed. For most of my life I saw walls as challenges that could only be breached by running straight through them, instead of finding smarter ways to climb over or move around them. The testosterone and adrenaline concoction in my brain, coupled with senseless machismo, made me stupidly blind and closed to alternative ways to soften the blows on my chassis.

I am sure the reader can ascertain that I should have stopped after injuring my Achilles tendons and the soft tissue of my heels during Special Forces selection, or at least after I qualified as a Recce and got my Operator's Badge, and sought medical solutions to the problem. But I kept delaying treatment for reasons that, at the time, I deemed good enough. Another example: until the ripe age of 52, and leading up to my surgery, I blindly refused to even contemplate using elbow or knee pads when engaging in activities that take a toll on the joints, such as fire-and-movement exercises wearing tactical gear, bulletproof vests with plates and other equipment. I referred to those around me who wore such devices as 'sissies'. What a moron I was. If I had taken such precautions, using kidney belts and other protective gear, and performing exercises, drills and missions with greater care, then I might have saved myself a whole world of pain.

Then there are the anti-inflammatory and painkilling meds without which your body eventually cannot function. In my case, it started after selection with 50 mg Voltaren, aka diclofenac, obtained from the medics, which I sometimes mixed with ordinary paracetamol to numb the pain in my Achilles tendons and heels. Shortly thereafter I discovered that if you add around 1 000 mg of ibuprofen, aka Motrin, to the mix, it brings some form of relief. These types of NSAIDs work better for back and muscle sprains than they did for my burning heels. I quickly discovered that ice packs were the only relief for the fire in my feet.

After years of cortico-steroid injections into the soft tissue of my heels, endless physiotherapy and eventually, in 1992, surgery to attempt to release the nerves in my heels, in the mid-1990s a clever doctor in Durban put me on strong tricyclic anti-depressants (TADs). These increase the brain's tolerance for pain, particularly nerve-related pain. Twenty-eight years later, I am still on them to quell the burning fire in my feet.

My back and neck started firing warning shots early in the 1990s and particularly into the new millennium, but I ignored these and kept going by mixing up more NSAIDs, painkillers and TADs to the point where my liver and kidneys started aching. Then I had the misfortune to dislocate and hurt my left shoulder severely in the first half of 2004 during an ambush in Iraq.[11] By then I was in bad shape, with fires burning in my feet, back, neck and shoulder. I was, however, hellbent on staying in Iraq and taking up the challenges that this damned country dished up in the early years of private military contracting in the 'Sandbox'.

My answer for the excruciating pain in my bust joints was for my doctor to inject me with cortisone mixtures every three or four months in my shoulder, and sometimes jabs for the back and neck too. I spent healthy amounts of hard-earned cash on chiropractors and physiotherapists during my breaks too – all in order to keep punishing my body even more without giving it the break and proper medical attention it needed. Of course these kinds of measures and meds do not heal; they just quell the pain and the inflammation, sometimes masking the problem. The injections and painkillers mean that you do not feel the pain as severely, and hence you push your injured limbs and body parts beyond their limits.

Then I discovered the magical properties of high doses of tramadol, an opioid class of painkiller – a heavy drug. By 2006 my work tempo and responsibilities were so demanding that I asked some of my new medic buddies in the US military and some pharmacists around Baghdad for

---

11 See Blood Money, pages 6–8.

Conclusion (1988 to 1990)

some injectable tramadol vials and low doses of Valium, which I mixed in a syringe and injected myself in my upper legs, often.

In the early part of 2007, my body started firing more warning shots. I worked myself into a blackout in Iraq, mostly because I was managing the chronic pain with concoctions of painkillers that took their toll on the body. After a very busy and intense 40-month stint in the Sandbox I returned home and worked around Africa for five years. I finally had my broken shoulder fixed in 2008: reconstructive surgery was required to sort that mess out. One thing I learned about that particular injury is that when you injure yourself, severely or otherwise, have it checked out immediately and medically managed soonest after the injury. Waiting a number of years before addressing such ailments greatly complicates the eventual medical intervention.

During my time in Africa, I eased off slightly from the NSAIDs and took painkillers less frequently. I had to continue with the TADs in order to manage the pain signals from my feet and back, and some discomfort left over from the shoulder surgery. Early in 2012, opportunity knocked for me to return to the 'new' Iraq, following the end of the US military withdrawal in December 2011. I could not wait to get back into the Sandbox, broken body and all.

The work rate in the new Iraq was not as heavy as after the 2003 war, but it was still demanding on a body that has accrued many hard miles. One of the main culprits was the endless hours, days, weeks, months and years that PMCs spent driving around wearing personal protective equipment, which in this case consisted of Kevlar vests with heavy metal plates inserted in the front and back, hence the slang description of 'bulletproof vest'. These vests with plates, combined with your chest webbing and/or battle jacket, weighed between 15 and 20 kg. It doesn't sound like a lot, but after 12-hour stints on the road for extended periods of time, it wears the body down.

My lower back became progressively worse and I increased the cocktails of NSAIDs, tramadols, codeine-based painkillers and other meds to cope with the pain levels. Then, in July 2014, while working on a project in the south of the Sandbox, I was set up and wrongly arrested. I was jailed for a couple of days in Basra, the main city of southern Iraq, where I contracted a severe viral brain infection and food poisoning, and where my back and particularly my neck was injured extensively.[12] The viral infection led to too much fluid being produced in my skull, and hence a build-up of pressure on the brain and on my optic nerves.

Early in 2015 I had to undergo surgery to emplace a shunt to drain the excess fluid from my skull to my stomach on a permanent basis. With the surgery came new sorts of pain, in addition to the severe pain in my back and now my neck. It was time to up the game exponentially on the meds side, and I managed to obtain a steady supply of 'morphine patches', which you apply to the skin. The patch releases small amounts of the narcotic into the bloodstream on an hourly basis. This, coupled with the tramadols and other concoctions of meds described above, kept me ticking over. My neurosurgeon warned me to not return to Iraq. He suggested that I should sort out my body as a matter of priority, and also that I consider a change of career …

Honestly, after I recovered from the surgery to release the pressure in my skull, I was hurting so badly on so many fronts that the words 'chronic pain', which I had lived with all my adult life, took on a new and even more intense meaning. And my warped solution was an easy one: increase the amounts of opioid painkillers and NSAIDs. Fortunately, I had stopped using alcohol altogether in 2000. My liver and kidneys were now hurting like they did in the hard-drinking days of my youth, with the only difference being that it was not the alcohol that was doing the hurting.

By mid-2017, my body had had enough. I knew that if I did not pull the plug on my career, and if I did not tend to my body's cries for help, then I would end up crippled or dead as a result of an overdose of opioids and all the other meds that temporarily quell the fires in your body. I had every intention of having my back and neck checked out, and of readdressing the 1992 surgery on my heels. But when I got home in August 2017, the final editing and preparation for the publication of *Blood Money* went full steam ahead. I therefore delayed things a bit longer. When the book was

---

12 See Blood Money, pages 247–249.

Conclusion (1988 to 1990)

launched in March 2018, I was taken up with events, book launches, radio talks, TV interviews, travelling the country to give talks on the book and all the paraphernalia that go with successfully launching your memoirs in an organised and professional fashion.

I kept ignoring the ever-growing pain signals by numbing them with painkillers and just mentally living through the pain. Then, early in 2020, as the world was in the grip of COVID-19, I basically could not walk anymore and collapsed. My wife took me to the emergency room of our local hospital. I was admitted, and the necessary X-rays and MRI scans of my back were done the next day. When the neurologist who had performed the 2015 surgery, and who had warned me to quit Iraq, saw the X-rays and MRI images and shook his head, I knew it was serious. He reckoned that according to the evidence, I should not have been able to walk at all. According to him, I should have been in a wheelchair 'a long time ago'. Reconstructive surgery was scheduled.

Then, six months after my back was fixed, I felt my arms start burning and my hands going numb. After more X-rays and MRI scans, to nobody's surprise it was discovered that my neck was in as bad shape as my lower back. Pressure on the nerves in the neck was causing me to lose feeling in my hands and for my arms to feel like they were on fire. Neck surgery, specifically the emplacement of some new steel joints into my lower neck, was scheduled for mid-2022.

Until recently, I did not address the chronic pain I have lived with in an understandable and somewhat chronological order. I certainly did not write this segment of the book to look for sympathy or to point out my near-addiction to heavy drugs to quell the pain in my body. I have jotted down these unpleasant memories in the hope of sending a message or two to young soldiers, youthful strong men/women and gents or ladies who are caught up in the world of hurt through battering their bodies for whatever reason they see fit – STOP NOW! TAKE TIME OUT RIGHT THIS WEEK AND HAVE YOUR ACHES AND PAINS CHECKED OUT. Do not rely on medication or drugs to suppress the hurt. Go and see the best doctors at the best medical facilities you can afford. If you are not entirely convinced that a particular physician is giving you the best advice or the treatment you require, then go for second or even third opinions.

Do not delay the mending process any further. Often, rest and taking a break from the activity that causes the hurt is required. Easier said than done. Many of you (us) do what you do for a living, to make ends meet and to take care of your families. This is where it gets tricky, and where a bit of financial management and insurance against injuries or temporary disabilities comes in very handy. Protect your body when possible: use belts, straps, pads, protective gear and common sense to avoid taking hard 'hits'. And if you must take a hit or fall, brace yourself and protect your head, neck and back in particular as much as you can. Find smarter ways to get hard physical work done. Use the old adage of 'work smarter, not harder'.

And, most importantly, do not let a young mindset rule an old body! Part of my problem was always that I never let go of the mindset of the 19-year-old unbreakable Special Forces corporal. Nothing was ever too hard or too difficult to get done in my later career, much to the detriment of the body. It is good to be 'young at heart' but be careful not to let this translate into overstretching your physical capabilities.

See the mending of your body and mind as a military operation or security mission. STOP THE HURT NOW, THROUGH ANY MEANS POSSIBLE.

And the truth is that all veterans pay with their lives.
Some pay all at once while others pay over a lifetime.
– JM Storm

EPILOGUE

Warriors are not the ones that always win, but the ones that always keep fighting.
— Anonymous

Over the decades since I left Special Forces, people have often asked me if my selection or the Recce training cycle was really that tough. I normally reply, 'Yeah it was kinda tough, but I did it, so it is not entirely undoable.'

When you reflect back on your life you realise that feats achieved where hardship was involved always seem easier once you have been there, done it and got the bloody T-shirt. But as I wrote this book, and as I dug out, dusted off and captured the memories of my brothers in arms and my own memories, I came to the realisation that the process of becoming a South African Special Forces operator, or Recce, was a hard and challenging mission to say the least. From the inception of 1 Recce in 1972 until the conclusion of the Rhodesian Bush War in 1980, and the Angolan Bush War in 1989, just under 400 Recces qualified out of roughly 100 000 guys who attempted the achievement. This translates to a success rate of around 0.4 per cent. I am therefore eternally grateful to God for giving me the mental and physical abilities to have been able to succeed in this lifelong goal and dream.

People ask many questions when it comes to Special Forces operators and operations. One that comes up regularly is: 'What does a Recce look like?' The questioner usually expects the answer to be in line with something out of a Rambo movie – large, muscular, menacing-looking dudes, loners who do not talk much, who cannot blend in with civilian society, who suffer from post-traumatic stress disorder (PTSD, what we called 'bossies') and who dream of wars and days long gone, and who sometimes lose it and go on crazed drinking, killing or wife-battering sprees. Another view is that they are ex-soldiers-turned-PMCs, work for bad people or evil corporations, and are all too ready to resort to violence.

What a load of bullshit. Hollywood is our profession's biggest enemy, as it creates so many misperceptions of overly muscled, aggressive alpha males who cannot control their testosterone levels, who perform outrageous military moves and who are cold-blooded killers. An old urban myth about the Recces is that at the beginning of the training cycle, the recruit is given a puppy to take care of during the year. Then, as a final test of the student's commitment and mental toughness, he must kill the young dog and eat its flesh. Another load of BS. All my fellow Recce operator brothers are animal lovers, and they wouldn't dream of harming a dog. Yes, dogs and other animals had to be neutralised during some operations, but that was only as a last resort so as not to compromise the team.

My overall perception of the operators with whom I trained, operated and coexisted is that they were of ordinary athletic ability or stocky build, but had extraordinarily strong minds. They were born with very fast mental processors that could quickly summarise, analyse, plan and execute the tactics and strategies required to successfully breach any and all challenges that might have confronted them.

These were soldiers who could push their minds and bodies beyond normal human limits, with a high tolerance for pain and fatigue, who could override the calls of hunger, discomfort and mental tiredness, and who could purge the urge to give up. Men who could think on their feet, who could quickly adapt, who were not set in their ways and who did not hesitate to conduct actions in very unconventional ways. Men who showed great compassion towards women, children, old people, victims of war and animals. And men who were unforgiving to anybody who got in their sights as part of a mission – regardless of how gory it would get and how much blood they might have on their hands, as long as the outcomes were justifiably achieved.

Humans with these characteristics and qualifications are scarce, and this unfortunately has led to many individuals claiming to have served in Special Forces, or to have been Recces. Our experience is that these wannabes are generally drunken bar fools or losers who for some unknown

Epilogue

reason seek to boost their own low self-esteem. 'Stolen valour' is the term we use to describe the behaviour of such military impostors, or individuals who lie about their military service. In years gone by, qualified operators would physically 'sort out' such pretenders. But these days, where new-gen softies try to win fights in courts and obtain financial settlement, and where anyone with a smartphone can become a social media sensation, the pretenders are now rather named and shamed. The South African Special Forces Association (SAFSA) website (www.recce.co.za) has a 'Wall of Shame' listing the details of those who falsely claim to have been operators. In a way, this is a more fitting punishment than a broken nose or split lip, as a Wall of Shame listing ensures that the perpetrator's pride and ego remains shattered as long as the website exists.

The phenomenon of stolen valour is a global one. Wannabes will claim to have been members of elite military units, such as the SAS, Delta Force, US Navy Seals and others. Such individuals are impostors of the worst kind, as they insult the units that produced men who bled for their countries, and they affront the legacy of those who paid the ultimate price. Fortunately, these units have similar approaches, and they name and shame the culprits.

Information about the Recces was formerly quite limited, and the operators generally stayed below the radar, with most people not knowing who we were and what we did. This gave rise to many rumours and legends. Fortunately, in the second decade of the new millennium, a number of books written by ex-Recces started appearing on the shelves, and the wider public could gain a better understanding of who we were and what we did. One reason it took so long for these accounts to come out was the South African military's 30-year confidentiality rule regarding disclosure of secret missions, which included most Recce operations. But after the three decades ran out, and over a period of another two decades, the men started talking, and rightfully so, as their stories needed to be told.

Talk about broken noses and split lips. It is common knowledge that the Recces never stood back from a good fight. And make no mistake, we occasionally got clobbered properly ourselves. By the time fights broke out, our reflexes were severely neutered by the excessive amounts of alcohol in the bloodstream, mostly administered by the drink of the war gods, Red Heart Rum. Or we just took on too many 'combatants' the unarmed way, much like the Recces took on superior forces during most of their operations behind enemy lines. At least they won most of those battles!

This brings me to a point that needs further explanation. Unarmed combat and the ability to fight barehanded are mostly irrelevant in most Special Forces operations. We are trained to destroy the enemy by any means necessary, and if that means plunging a combat knife into an opponent's heart or slicing through the enemy's throat with a wire garrotte, then so be it. But getting down to rumble with your enemy is not much of an option and might be the result of a failure in planning or execution on the part of the warrior. These days, there are many people who practise various forms of unarmed combat, which vary in style, method and execution. This is how MMA started. It is a very effective form of fighting, something modern-day service members receive some training in. But it remains a 'last resort' option for a Special Forces soldier on a mission, as punching or choking your enemy is not required. All that matters is the total destruction of your foe. And if you work on a protective detail as a serving Special Forces soldier, you have failed in your mission if it gets to the stage of hand-to-hand combat to protect your principal. This leads some eager young MMA fighters to believe they are superior 'warriors' because they have the ability to beat a Special Forces soldier in a barehanded fight. But this constitutes a very small part of a war-fighter's skill set and armoury, as the proficiencies required and indicated in this book and much historical operational experiences have shown.

A more serious matter is the frequent observation that Recces are mad, or 'bossies', in other words that they are mentally affected and traumatised by events that occurred in war and conflict zones, often through 'flashbacks' to traumatic events. It is a scientific fact that PTSD exists as a serious medical condition. After the publication of *Blood Money*, I was often asked about this subject, as many of us who worked internationally, and specifically in Iraq, saw blood and gore galore. My answer was always the same: the 'D' in PTSD stands for 'disorder', but I

Epilogue

beg to differ. A disorder is characterised by lack of normal functioning of physical or mental processes. The 'D' should rather be changed to a 'C', for 'condition', as I feel PTSD is more than a possible 'voices-in-the-head' state and should be viewed as a medical crisis requiring an immediate health response before it can grow and fester. Nonetheless, the Mayo Clinic describes PTSD as follows: 'A disorder characterized by failure to recover after experiencing or witnessing a terrifying event. The condition may last months or years, with triggers that can bring back memories of the trauma accompanied by intense emotional and physical reactions. Symptoms may include nightmares or flashbacks, avoidance of situations that bring back the trauma, heightened reactivity to stimuli, anxiety or depressed mood. Treatment includes different types of psychotherapy as well as medications to manage symptoms.'[13]

One group of people much affected by PTSD are soldiers who have served in combat zones and close combat situations. In the old South Africa, young white males were forced to join the military for two years of national service, or to serve in the police for four years. Many never really wanted to be soldiers or law enforcement officers in the first place. As with most armies fighting a war (of sorts), generals serving the politicians in power sent these young men (average age 18–19) into battle. I have always maintained that soldiers are the pawns of politicians, and like in a game of chess, the pawns form the first line of defence but are always the most expendable. And among the young soldiers who returned from the war on the border – in correct military terms 'the Bush War' – there were many who carried heavy burdens brought on by getting wounded or maimed, or by losing friends and fellow soldiers, and who saw warfare and bloodshed up close and personal.

But in the old South Africa it was frowned upon and seen as unmanly to talk about the demons that plagued you – at best you were described as 'bossies'. Trauma, or PTSD, was mostly swept under the carpet, and the only treatment was perhaps a quiet talk with the unit chaplain or your local dominee (pastor). Many of these young men left the military or police

---

[13] 'Post-traumatic stress disorder (PTSD)', Mayo Clinic, 6 July 2018, www.mayoclinic.org.

and went into civilian life silently suffering from PTSD on their own without receiving professional help or counselling from the appropriate bodies. In many cases this led to abusive marriages, excessive drinking and alcoholism, and to drug addiction. I personally know one veteran who turned to hard drugs, and can attest to the fact that this is a very real problem stemming from remnants and memories of the Bush War. James Starkey, who did his national service in 61 Mech (61 Mechanised Battalion Group), was involved in numerous combat incidents in 1987–1988 during and after Operation Modulêr. In one such contact, his Ratel armoured car was hit and his co-driver killed next to him. These images stayed with James and led to his PTSD and alcohol and drug addictions. He eventually overcame his addictions and faced his PTSD head-on, to the extent that he became a PTSD counsellor and wrote a book about his experiences.[14] And I know that such problems existed on the other side of the fence too, in the ranks of those we once considered to be our 'enemy'. But, in the case of the Recces, I observed a different aspect of this phenomenon.

Special Forces warriors are career soldiers who want to serve the military on a permanent basis. These war-fighters knowingly and willingly understand that they will put their bodies, minds, souls and ultimately their lives on the line in fulfilment of their duties. Unlike conscripted servicemen and people who see the military as an employment opportunity, combat soldiers are driven by something that is hard to explain to people who are not part of this brethren. The best analogy would be the moth and the flame, where the moth is drawn ever closer to the flame, even if the moth knows it might be deadly to venture closer.

Special Forces soldiers are fuelled by a sense of patriotism and professionalism. And with this approach of will, commitment and sense of duty comes a better-prepared and stronger mindset to accept, analyse and deal with trauma in a more effective way. Bear in mind that psychologists were present throughout our selection process, observing our every move and noting our reactions, interactions and overall response to being pushed

---

14 See James Starkey, *A Stark Reality: The War Within* (2020).

beyond the limits of normal human physical and mental endurance. You might somehow pass the physicality of Recce selection, but you might well fail the 'psycho' tests and evaluations if the selectors and psychologists detected a chink in your mental toughness. And therein lies the key to the fact that from the first Recce operations in the early 1970s to the end of the Bush War in 1989, during more than 250 specialised operations behind enemy lines, no Recce to my knowledge 'lost it', or went 'bossies', and none had to be treated for PTSD. And, as far as I am aware, this is still the case. I have no doubts that some Recce operators experienced their own demons and suffered silently, but, like the professional soldiers they are, they worked the problems out for themselves.

A lot of people have asked me whether, after spending a decade on the ground in Iraq, and in very tremulous times too, all the bloodshed, killing and death I witnessed traumatised me, and if I perhaps suffered from PTSD. The answer is not a straight yes or no, but I decided a long time ago to see, analyse, deliberate and accept the outcome of whatever happened, however bloody, inhumane and sad it might be. And by saying that I 'accepted' it does not mean that it did not sicken and anger me beyond measure to try and make sense of old women and young children being blown to pieces, or being executed or beheaded, by fanatical, cold-blooded terrorist killers. But that is what conflicts, civil wars and hatred of other belief systems do to humanity. Most people cannot effectively deal with it, and rightfully so, but that is where professional combat soldiers – war-fighters if you will – are different, for the reasons mentioned above.

As a PMC in Iraq, I observed the same phenomenon. Special operations forces and other combat soldiers from the US-led coalition were the tip of the spear in the fight against Al-Qaeda, Islamic State and various other terror groups. Time and time again, they turned the tide against these murderous organisations. They were augmented by reservists who were not career soldiers, and who perhaps suffered more from PTSD than the hardcore special operations forces. Bear in mind that PMCs did not go to Iraq, Afghanistan and other hellholes to fight the terrorists directly but rather to use our considerable skills to augment the forces on the ground. PMCs took over close support and protection roles that freed the combat soldiers to fight the terrorists. But we were attacked and we bled just like the regular military forces, and this was where our professional qualifications, experience and background assisted us to survive bloodbaths involving loss of life and limb. It was the same when we served our country – the same psychological and by now embedded mental combat toughness, which does not wane when you leave the military or law enforcement. The most important lessons from our training as Recces, and that later defined our characters, were how to withstand hardships, how to work as a team, how to show leadership and initiative in challenging situations, how to be flexible and adaptable, and how to work in the most challenging and austere conditions under pressure.

All I ever wanted to be was a soldier, and I am very proud to have qualified and worked as a South African Special Forces operator. The absolute quality, strength and experience of our founders, and of the Recces who came after them, forged an organisation that has become one of the most revered special operations forces in the world. Many books have been written on the Recces in recent decades, and rightfully so, as this unique military history would otherwise be lost. For me, to have looked, listened, learned and walked beside such war-fighters and elite soldiers has been nothing but a privilege. We were a unique variety of men from all walks of life, like the ones who became Recces before us. To my brothers of Cycle 86/01, and to those who followed, I salute you all. You are all definitely 'a breed apart'.

THE MEMBERS OF RECCE CYCLE 86/01

JOHAN RAATH

Johan was born in Bloemfontein on 18 February 1968. His parents were government and municipal employees, and both came from farms in the Free State districts of Harrismith and Brandfort. Johan matriculated at Hoërskool Sentraal in 1985 and was called up for national service in January 1986. Shortly after arriving at the Infantry School in Oudtshoorn, he passed the Recce pre-selection tests and left for Durban, where he underwent basic training in Special Forces. He passed the Recce selection and the year-long training cycle and qualified as a Special Forces operator in December 1986. Johan served for seven years in the SADF and left as a staff sergeant after working as an instructor in the Special Forces training wing for three years. He founded a tactical training school outside Durban, and in the late 1990s started working as a security contractor, military trainer and VIP protection specialist for presidents, generals and international signatories in Africa, and later globally. He worked in various conflict zones and ended his career in Iraq in 2017 after working there for more than a decade. His first book, *Blood Money*, looked at the role of South African PMCs in Iraq. *A Breed Apart* is his second book. Johan currently consults as a military advisor and trainer and undertakes security assessments and threat analysis for international companies wishing to enter conflict zones. He has a keen interest in community and farm safety.

BARRY VISSER

Barry was born on 30 April 1967 in 3 Military Hospital, Bloemfontein, to Nic, a founding and then current member of 1 Parachute Battalion, and Jeanette, a teacher. Barry started school in Oudtshoorn, where his father was stationed as the 2IC to Jan Breytenbach at the newly formed 1

Reconnaissance Commando. After the death of his father in the operational area, the family moved back to Bloemfontein, where Barry attended Grey College. At school he was an avid rugby player, swimmer, diver and water polo player. He matriculated in 1985, was conscripted into the SADF and completed his basic training at 1 Recce. After completing the Special Forces training cycle at the end of 1986, he joined the Permanent Force. Barry served in 1 Recce from 1987 to 1993 as a staff sergeant, and after completing the Officers Formative course in 1993, he was posted to 4 Recce, where he served until 1998. He was moved to Special Forces HQ in Pretoria, where he served until being posted to the newly formed Special Forces School, north of Pretoria. Barry returned to 4 Recce in 2008, when he was appointed 2IC, and ended his time in Langebaan as OC in 2016. Barry is currently serving at Special Forces HQ as a senior staff officer and plans to end his military career in 2027, when he will retire.

DRIES COETZEE (1966–2021) (RIP)

Dries was born on 15 November 1966 and grew up on a farm in the then Western Transvaal (now North West province). He was an avid rugby player at school, and after he matriculated he was called up to the army for national service. He decided to join the Special Forces and passed the various selection phases in the second half of 1985. He and a few other successful candidates joined training cycle 86/01 the following year. He qualified as a Recce in December 1986. Dries served in 1.1 Commando at 1 Recce in Durban for several years, then in 5 Recce in their 5.1 Commando at Fort Rev in the operational area. He did the Officers Formative course and was transferred back to Durban to serve in the Special Forces training wing. He left the military in the mid-1990s to join Johan Raath, who was running a tactical training centre, after which he got involved in security work in Africa. In the mid-2000s, Dries joined forces with Johan Raath again and worked in Iraq for a number of years as a PMC in various positions, including co-pilot of a small plane on risky missions in Anbar province. After Iraq he pursued one of his passions and completed his private pilot's licence for fixed-wing aircraft. In 2008, he started working as security manager for an oil company in the eastern region of the Democratic Republic of Congo (DRC). Three years later he moved to the town of Goma in the same region due to instability and war in the vicinity. He enjoyed the challenges of the DRC and established his own private security company, which he successfully ran until his death from cancer in June 2021. He is survived by his wife and two sons. Dries is remembered for his physical power, patience and deconflicting skills during tight situations.

NEIL 'BEZ' BEZUIDENHOUT (1968–1993) (RIP)

Known as 'Bez' to his army buddies, Neil grew up in Newcastle in northern Natal. After he matriculated, he was called up to Oudtshoorn to do his national service, where he passed the Recce entry-selection phase. He was posted to 1 Recce in Durban where he completed his basic training and passed the various Special Forces selection courses. He was part of the 86/01 training cycle and qualified as a Recce in December 1986. He was stationed in 1.1 Commando at 1 Recce and participated in several operations towards the end of the Bush War. After he left the unit, he worked at a cement plant for a while in the early 1990s with another ex-operator. Neil joined Executive Outcomes in late 1993 and was killed in action in Angola the following year. He was sitting in the rear door of an Mi-8 helicopter during landing and was shot alongside three other ex-Recces (RIP). He is remembered for his motormouth, sense of humour and athletic capabilities.

CHRIS SERFONTEIN

Chris was born into a military family on 13 February 1966 in Nelspruit, in the Lowveld region of the then Eastern Transvaal. His grandfather, a *'penkop'* during the Anglo-Boer War and after, who retired as a major general in the SADF, shaped his passion for soldiering and national security. His early years, as a son of a combat infantry commander, would take him all over the country and to South West Africa. The years at Ogongo military base would shape his love for the bush. During school holidays he was allowed to go hunting alone and disappear into the Ovamboland bush surrounding the base, navigating, tracking, stalking, anticipating, and waylaying. His military career began in 1984 with basic training at 1 SAI in Bloemfontein, followed by junior leadership training at the Infantry School, Oudtshoorn. He joined the Permanent Force on 7 June 1984 and completed his military career as colonel on 31 December 2010. As a young officer, he opted to do Special Forces selection in October 1985 and qualified as a Special Forces operator in December 1986. The Military Academy in Saldanha then became his home for three years, and he completed the BMil (BA) degree in December 1989. During the December holidays, Chris volunteered to participate in pseudo-operations to counter Swapo rainy-season infiltration from southern Angola. These were being conducted from 5.1 Commando at Ondangwa to give the permanently posted operators a well-deserved December break. He was pleasantly surprised to meet up with a fellow 86/01 operator, Sybie van der Spuy, during one of these operations. In 1990, he served in 4 Recce's operational commando. He then commanded the Northwest Command Reaction Force Company as a major from 1992, which included Operation Baccarat, when the SADF had to intervene during the Bophuthatswana unrest and conflict during the run-up to the democratic elections of April 1994. He was further posted as an officer instructor at the Junior Command and Staff Duties Branch at the South African Army College from 1995 as the special forces and peacekeeping specialist. He then transferred to the Joint Operations Division in 1998 as a lieutenant colonel to manage the dual functions as the SO1 Peacekeeping Operations in Africa as well as acting SSO Special Operations, under the leadership of Major General Andre Bestbier and in support of the then GOC Special Forces, Brigadier General Les Rudman. On completion of the army's Senior Staff course in 2000, he was then transferred to Special Forces HQ in 2001 as SSO Operations. In February 2006, he was appointed OC Special Forces School at Murray Hill but had a dual responsibility to act as the SSO Force Preparation during 2006 while completing his MBA. Chris completed the Executive National Security Programme at the War College and terminated his service in the SANDF on 31 December 2010 to take up the position of technology manager at the Council for

Scientific and Industrial Research (CSIR) as manager of Technology for Special Operations (TSO). This is the successor to EMLC, which supported Special Forces during the Bush War. Chris managed the Special Forces technology programmes at TSO until 2020 and was then requested to manage national technology programmes in safety and security, focusing on national security.

RENIER 'PP' HUGO

Renier was born in Pretoria on 17 May 1960. Shortly after his birth, his parents – who both served in the army – moved to Cape Town, where his father was one of the founding members of the then Coloured Corps. He attended primary school in the Cape and in Oudtshoorn after his father was transferred to the Infantry School. Renier matriculated at Hoërskool Sand du Plessis in Bloemfontein after his father moved to 1 SAI. He began his military career in the Armoured Corps in 1979. After Part 1 he served as an instructor (corporal) at the School of Armour. He was promoted to sergeant in 1982, went on the officers' course in early 1983 and was promoted to full lieutenant in the same year. He then applied for a transfer to Special Forces where he served in 1 Recce from 1983 to December 1986. Early in 1986 he passed the various selection courses and completed the Special Forces training cycle at the end of 1986. He was then transferred to 5 Recce Regiment in Phalaborwa and served as an operator there until April 1995. Renier resigned from the military in 1995 with the rank of lieutenant colonel. He then joined Executive Outcomes and served as the operations commander in Sierra Leone from May 1995 to December 1996. He then worked on contracts in various countries and in various positions including Uganda, Angola, the DRC, Iraq, Afghanistan, Zambia and Mauritania. Today, Renier works privately as a security analyst and threat assessment expert.

WILLIAM JACK MUTLOW

William was born in 1958 in Potchefstroom in the then Western Transvaal, attending President Pretorius Primary School and Hoër Volkskool in Potchefstroom. He was called up for national service in 1977 at 5 SAI, attending the School of Infantry after basic training. He then volunteered to join 32 Battalion, remaining there for a few years as Bravo 4 platoon commander, after which he was transferred to 3 SAI for a short while, before moving to Speskop, Section Special Medical Operations. In 1986, he joined cycle 86/01 as a captain, qualifying as a Special Forces operator. A special medical unit was born from Section Medical Special Operations due to the operational medical support requirements of Special Forces, airborne units, STF, and other special defence groups involved in the Bush War and the fight against the military wings of the liberation movements. The new unit was founded as the 7 Medical Battalion Group (7 Med), and William held the posts of training wing commander, chief of staff and OC. He resigned in 1996 as a lieutenant colonel and embarked on private business ventures in Angola and other African countries, applying his Portuguese language skills (learned during service in 32 Battalion), military planning protocols and especially his endurance, developed during Special Forces training, to succeed in his undertakings.

CHRISTOFFEL 'CHRISTO' JOHAN ROELOFSE

Christo was born in 1964 in Stellenbosch and matriculated in 1982 in the small town of Fort Beaufort. He started his national service in 1983 and did Special Forces selection in 1985. He joined the 86/01 cycle and qualified as a Recce at the end of 1986. After qualifying as an operator, he was transferred to 5 Recce in Phalaborwa and from there to 5.1 Commando in Fort Rev, at Ondangwa. He joined the pseudo teams that operated from Fort Rev. In 1988, he went to the Military Academy in Saldana, and obtained his BMil degree, majoring in industrial psychology, from the University of Stellenbosch. After the academy, he went back to 5 Recce and was transferred to Special Forces HQ in Pretoria and joined some of the covert Recce teams at the time. Christo resigned from the military in 1996, joining a private security company operating in Africa and the Middle East. He stayed with the company, which runs various international missions, and is at present the chief operating officer of the group. He is married with three children and lives in Pretoria.

SYBRAND 'SYBIE SNR' VAN DER SPUY

Sybie was born on 24 May 1963 at 2 Military Hospital, Cape Town. As the oldest of four, he grew up in a conservative yet dynamic, tight-knit family where Mada ensured a stable and loving home environment while 'Oom Sybie', always the soldier, was the OC of Hunter Group, a band of weekend soldiers that became 2 Reconnaissance Commando (later 2 Recce). Sybie is the oldest operator on record to have passed Special Forces selection. As such, he and his brother Olla, also a Special Forces operator, spent most weekends participating in Hunter Group and, later, 2 Recce activities. By the age of 15, he had probably fired each and every East Bloc weapon used in Africa. Sybie matriculated from Hoërskool Kempton Park in 1981 and joined the Permanent Force as an infantry second lieutenant after a year at Oudtshoorn. A disastrous 1983 Special Forces selection effort resulted in him heading off to the Military Academy in 1984. Sybie passed crayfishing and parachuting with distinction, with academics unfortunately lagging a bit ... This saw him back at Special Forces selection early in 1986, and he qualified as an operator at the end of that year. Sybie started his operator career at 5.1 Commando, certainly the most operationally deployed unit in the SADF towards the end of the war in Angola. It was an exhilarating and eventful four years before he finally moved from Ondangwa back to Phalaborwa. 1991 saw him transferred to the Special Forces School in Durban as Combat Branch Commander. There, under the leadership of Duncan Rykaart, they redesigned the training curricula, adapting selection and training for a post-Angolan era of operations, answering to the more clandestine/covert-facing Special Forces role requirement. During the next years Sybie acted as OC 1.2 Commando (Special Forces School), OC 1.1 Commando, 2IC 1 Special Forces Regiment and acting OC 1 Special Forces Regiment for an extended period. He was posted to Special Forces HQ in 1996 and resigned as a full-time officer in 1998. He spent 18 years as a Permanent Force officer and another seven as a Reserve Force soldier. In civilian life, Sybie has specialised in crisis and project management. He is currently the COO of a listed Canadian mining entity.

MATTHYS 'DIFF' DE VILLIERS MMM

Diff was born on 30 December 1965 in Ottosdal, in the then Western Transvaal. He is called Thysie by his parents and Diff by his military friends. Diff's father is a ninth-generation South African farmer, and his mother is a maths teacher. Both are descendants of French Huguenots, and both are very patriotic, Christian and conservative. The family located to Rhodesia in 1968 where Diff spent most of his childhood roaming the forests, rivers and savannahs of that country, acquiring excellent skills in hunting, fishing, bushcraft, marksmanship, survival and languages that would stand him in good stead in later life. The family moved back to South Africa in 1980, and Diff matriculated in 1983 at the Hoër Landbouskool in Kroonstad. Initially rejected for military service on medical grounds, Diff qualified as a diesel mechanic before managing to re-enlist in 1985 in the Infantry Corps. He completed basic training at 3 SAI in Potchefstroom, qualified as a junior leader at the School of Infantry in Oudtshoorn and made pre-selection for Special Forces at 1 Recce in Durban. After participating as an instructor for a three-month basics cycle, Diff joined his own troops on some specialised training and passed Special Forces selection in 1986 and completed the 86/01 cycle. Diff was posted to 4 Recce in Langebaan, where he became a seaborne Special Forces operator and was very successful as a small boat and attack diving instructor, and also specialised in underwater demolitions and forward air control. He left the service in 1989 at the conclusion of the Bush War and served another decade in the reserve forces, retiring as a staff sergeant. Diff became a livestock and crop farmer in Western Transvaal in 1990, and later also ran his own agricultural contracting business, as well as a small security company specialising in tracking down farm murderers. He also provided training to farmers, their families and workers on pre-empting and defending against farm attacks. In 2003, Diff was recruited to work as a PMC in Iraq, where he worked for well over a decade. He has since outsourced his skills to various militaries, private military companies and private security companies around the globe, picking up more language skills along the way. He lives in a rural district of Mpumalanga. During breaks between work assignments, Diff enjoys spending time with his family, hunting and fishing with his kids and grandkids, travelling to remote destinations with his wife and restoring vintage machinery in his workshop.

EUGENE 'VAN' VAN DER MERWE

Eugene matriculated in 1983 and was called up for national service in 1984. He did his basic training in Oudtshoorn, where he became a corporal. He was then posted to 1 Parachute Battalion, where he served until the end of 1985 when Colonel Andre Bestbier recruited a few parabats for Recce selection in 1986. In addition to Van, these recruits included Hennie 'Croucs' Croucamp. They arrived at 1 Recce in January 1986 as civilian force members, which would change if they passed selection. They stayed in the C-Block barracks where Sergeant Major Bruce Laing took charge of them, alongside a number of candidates from the Cape Coloured Corps. JJ Raath, who had been injured on his cycle the year before, took these members under his wing and orientated them in the unit before they attempted selection. Of this group, Croucs, Dampies and Van passed selection, joined the Permanent Force and completed the year-long Recce training cycle that ended in December 1986. Van was posted to 4 Recce where he qualified as an attack diver class II, served for ten years and left as an officer in 1996. He opened two small businesses in Cape Town, and became involved with the Special Forces old boys' organisation in the Cape, serving as chairman for the Cape region in 2006–2007. He emigrated with his wife to Queensland, Australia, in 2008. He joined the Australian Defence Force in 2018, serving as a gunner until 2022, when he resigned. Eugene and his wife have started a small business in Queensland, where they reside.

NICKY FOURIE

Nicky was born in Vryheid, Natal, on 23 April 1967 and matriculated from Gelofte Skool in Pinetown in 1984. He was called up for national service at the School of Artillery in Potchefstroom in January 1985, and spent his first year in the artillery. But he was interested in something more challenging and decided to prepare for Recce selection. He passed the Recce selection and the year-long training cycle and qualified as a Special Forces operator in December 1986. Nicky served a total of four and a half years in the SADF and left as a sergeant. He then worked at a financial institution. In 1993, he joined Executive Outcomes and worked in Angola for eight months. Thereafter he decided to explore the world backpacking and playing rugby. He received a rugby scholarship from a chiropractic college in Atlanta, and is now the owner of a chiropractic practice.

HENK VAN WYK

Henk was born in Vredendal, in the Cape Province, on 29 May 1966. He spent his childhood years between the diamond town of Alexander Bay and a school hostel in Springbok. After his father's death, when Henk was 16, the family moved to De Aar. He was an avid long-distance runner and rugby player and a keen off-road motorcycle enthusiast. After matric in 1984, he joined 1 Special Service Battalion for basic training in January 1985. A special platoon was dedicated to preparing for Special Forces selection in May 1985. He attended the preparation phase and spent two weeks in Dukuduku, but then decided to join 8 SAI, as he did not feel ready for the Special Forces selection at that stage. He completed his infantry training and was stationed with 8 SAI's Bravo Company in the operational area of South West Africa, first in sector 1.0 (from August 1985 to December 1985) and then in sector 2.0 (until March 1986). At this point Henk applied again to attend the Special Forces selection phases. He passed the Recce selection and the 86/01 cycle and qualified as a Special Forces operator in December 1986. He served under a short-service contract until the end of 1988. After his resignation, he started studying electrical engineering. A few months into his course, he was recruited by Mosselbaai Gas, or Mossgas, to work on their new plant in Mossel Bay. After working as an instrument technician for a few years, Henk completed a diploma in information technology (IT) and took up a new career in this field. A few years later, he started a IT consultancy business, which took him to North Africa, the Middle East, Russia, Japan and the US. While building his career in IT, Henk also expanded on another passion of his – skydiving. He owns and operates Skydive Mossel Bay (skydivemosselbay.com), a successful skydiving school and DZ in Mossel

Bay, where he is both an instructor-evaluator and pilot. He has two children, both avid skydivers. The DZ at Mossel Bay airfield is a popular hangout for ex-operators and paratroopers, and many a Red Heart has been enjoyed when old army friends stop by.

MARK DE WET

Mark was born on 17 February 1967, and matriculated in 1985. He went straight into the army from school, passed his Special Forces pre-selection, did basics in 1 Recce and successfully completed his training cycle. He was one of only eight guys who qualified as school-leavers at the end of 1986. After cycle, Mark was posted to 4 Recce, where he spent 16 years going through the ranks from corporal and ending as a warrant officer class 1. During his time at 4 Recce he qualified as an attack diver class II. He qualified in HALO/HAHO free fall parachuting, underwater demolitions and bomb disposal ordnance towards the end of his military career. He was also chief instructor at the urban wing in Langebaan. In 2002, he resigned and did his commercial class 2 diving course and started a diving career in Nigeria. After two years in Nigeria, Mark joined some of his old Special Forces buddies in the Sandbox. Mark spent ten years in Iraq, working for a number of companies before joining an old cycle mate – who happens to be the author of this book – at a private outfit. He then returned to South Africa but after two years found himself working abroad again for Eeben Barlow of Executive Outcomes in Uganda. He then joined the mining company BHP Billiton, working in Ethiopia as a security manager. Mark did a stint in anti-piracy in Mozambique for Eni, the Italian energy giant, and then returned to Iraq to work for an international company. He worked for Rio Tinto in Richards Bay before joining GSS and then GardaWorld in Nigeria. He is presently working in Kimberley, doing close protection for a diamond mine. Mark still keeps in regular contact with his cycle buddies.

SYBRAND ABRAM 'BRAAM' DE BEER

Braam grew up in the then Eastern Transvaal on a chrome mine near Burgersfort, where he finished primary school before going to high school in Pietersburg (today Polokwane) at Kuschke High. In Standard 8 he moved over to an agricultural school in Stilfontein, where he matriculated. He then went straight to the army where he completed the Special Forces pre-selection and then basic training at 1 Recce. He passed the selection phases and completed the training cycle. He was christened 'brown eyes' by RSM Pep van Zyl during his selection phase. Braam was then posted to 4 Recce in Langebaan, where he served until 1993. Braam qualified and specialised in attack diving class 2, and took part in several operations during his Special Forces career. He resigned as a staff sergeant in October 1993 and joined Executive Outcomes. He was with the company for three years, after which he moved and worked in conflict zones all over Africa, including Sudan, Liberia, Sierra Leone and Angola. In 2004, he went to work in Iraq as a PMC, and thereafter in Afghanistan. Braam settled in Brackenfell in the Western Cape in November 2009 and worked at different ventures. He started his own furniture factory from the ground up, and is still running it. The road he walked in Special Forces helped him a lot with who and where he is in the world, and he knows that without God he would not be where he is today. Like many of the soldiers of cycle 86/01, he often realised that he survived and saw the sun come up due to God's having had a clear hand in our life's journey. We fear naught but God.

CRAIG LEPPAN

From early in life, Craig wanted to be a soldier, but not just any soldier. He decided to complete the Special Forces application section when he was 15, and was called up to Oudtshoorn, where he passed the pre-selection exercises. He describes his military career as one of the most enjoyable and special experiences of his life, from the initial challenges to the individuals he met to the tight situations and actions that led to his success. These accomplishments allowed Craig to realise greater goals in life. After his military career, he went to Cape Town and qualified with a National Higher Diploma in Mechanical Engineering. From there he was employed by the Mediclinic group, assisting them to grow from four hospitals to 24 over six years. After this, Craig went abroad and studied networks and IT.

He worked as a contractor from 1997 to 2004. After travelling through Canada, China, Australia and New Zealand, he came back to South Africa in 2004 with the goal of travelling overland through Africa. This dream was realised when he left on an 18-month, 49 000 km epic journey covering most of Africa south of the Sahara. Craig is now involved in agriculture and IT, and dabbles in many other activities that interest him. The bonds he has with his fellow soldiers are unbreakable, and their common history and experiences give them an understanding that very few people encounter. He believes that life is precious and that you can achieve whatever you want to.

GRANT SHAEFFER

Grant was born in Port Elizabeth (now Gqeberha) on 14 September 1967. His dad worked at Delta Motor Corporation and his mother was a legal secretary at a local law firm. Grant matriculated in 1985 and decided from the beginning to join the Special Forces in 1986. The first step in this direction was the Infantry School in Oudtshoorn, where he passed the pre-selection for basic training in Durban at 1 Recce. He passed the Recce selection and the year-long training cycle and qualified as a Special Forces operator in December 1986. Grant served for three years and ended his service as a corporal. In 1989, he joined Murray & Roberts in Port Elizabeth, and through their bursary programme studied building surveying at Port Elizabeth Technikon. In 1992, Grant left Murray & Roberts and joined a Christian missionary organisation in Cape Town. For the next two years he travelled through Zambia and Malawi ministering the Gospel. In 1994, he enrolled at the Baptist Theological College in Cape Town where he spent four years studying theology. During this time he married his wife, Lynne, in Cape Town. In 1998, Grant and Lynne and their son Joel moved up to live in Mbala, Northern Zambia, as missionaries. They are still there today, serving the people of this small district.

JAPIE CELLIERS

Born in Ermelo in 1967, Japie Celliers grew up on the farm Roodewal and matriculated in 1985 at Hoërskool Ermelo. He joined the SADF in January 1986, travelling by milk train to Pretoria and continuing on to

Oudtshoorn. He passed the pre-selection test for Recce qualification and started basic training in Durban at 1 Recce. He passed the Recce selection and joined the year-long training cycle, but during this period he contracted bilharzia. After he recovered, he joined the following training cycle and qualified as a Special Forces operator in 1987. While waiting for the next cycle, he did numerous short courses, and was said to be the trooper who had done the most courses in the SADF at the time. Japie continued his military career at 4 Recce in Langebaan until February 1989. He then joined the family farming business in the Ermelo area, where he is today. He has been involved in various agricultural organisations which he chaired and is currently chairman of the National Woolgrowers' Association in Mpumalanga. Japie is still happily married to Minisa, and the couple have three children: Mirinka, Jacob and Daniel. Japie's motto in life is *'Wil hê om te Wil!'* (Have the will to accomplish anything in life), as he was motivated by these words the day before he started Recce selection by the then course leader, Major Kobus Human.

ANDREW 'ANDY' VAN DER SPUY

Andy did his one-year national service in January 1977, and managed to get jump-qualified in the same year, just before it changed to two years. He then volunteered to serve an additional two years, for which he received a bonus. During his jump course he met Hentie Bonthuis and Koos de Wet, who went on to become operators. The legendary Ian Strange (RIP) was also part of his intake and served in the same squadron. Ian Strange, Sergeant K****r Smit and Corporal Baker left after basics to do Recce selection. All three qualified as operators at the end of 1977. Andy was stationed in the operational area of South West Africa, in the Caprivi at Mpacha, for 19 months of his two-year service contract. Seeing operators such as Staff Sergeant Jack Greeff on a couple of occasions triggered the thought of joining the Permanent Force. The minimum term was three years, but this did not suit him as he was planning to study mechanical engineering after his national service. A friend told him about 2 Recce, which consisted of Citizen Force members and would train students while they did their camps. He was called up to do selection in January 1981.

A large group gathered in Pretoria where fitness and other psychological tests were done. Many failed this part, and the ones that passed were put on a C-130 cargo plane to continue their selection at Fort Doppies. At the end of selection, three **Citizen Force** students and five members of 5 Recce made it. In 1982, he joined the next cycle to complete the Demolitions, Bushcraft, Tracking and Survival, and Minor Tactics/Unconventional Warfare courses, which involved a four-month call-up (from civvy street). In 1984, Andy underwent the Water Orientation course, and in 1986 he joined the infamous cycle 86/01 to complete Air Orientation, Minor Tactics/Unconventional Warfare and Urban Warfare Orientation. He qualified at the end of 1986, which brought him great pride. Not many operators had the opportunity to qualify through 2 Recce as Citizen Force members, and he is grateful that he could do so. When 2 Recce closed down, all the operators on their books were divided between 4 Recce and 5 Recce. Andy went to 5 Recce as he was more airborne-qualified. He deployed on various occasions with 2 Recce and 5 Recce. He also qualified in free fall and HALO. Andy completed his National Diploma in Mechanical Engineering in 1985. He started working for Armscor in January 1986, which gave him the opportunity to conduct business with Special Forces and other airborne units. After 35 years and eight months, he finally retired from Armscor and is now enjoying his retirement.

JOHAN FERREIRA MMM

Johan grew up in a farming community along the Soutpansberg and matriculated at Hoërskool Louis Trichardt in 1985. He was called up for national service at the Infantry School in Oudtshoorn, where he passed the Special Forces entry selection in January 1986. He took part in the basic training course at 1 Recce on the Bluff, passed the various selection phases and joined the 86/01 training cycle. An illness prevented him from completing the para-jump course. He joined the next training cycle, completed his training and qualified as a Recce early the following year. He was posted to 4 Recce where he served more than three years in the maritime boat teams and reconnaissance teams. In 1990, he was transferred to 5 Recce where he served in the specialised reconnaissance teams alongside some of the great senior recon team operators. He left the force in February 1991 to study agriculture, obtaining a diploma with distinction. He worked as a farm manager for a couple of years before starting his own farming business. Since 1994 he has pursued a successful career in the pecan nut industry.

LEON VENTER

Leon was born in Roodepoort on 1 March 1966. He left school in 1984 and was called up for national service in January 1985. He arrived at 3 SAI in Potchefstroom, and after a few weeks passed selection to go to 1 Parachute Battalion in Bloemfontein. He completed his basic and PT courses and qualified as a paratrooper. At the end of 1985 he passed the Recce pre-selection and was sent to Durban. He passed the Recce selection and cycle courses up to Demolitions. Leon was then sent up to the border for the rest of 1986, and from 1987 he did camps at 2 Recce until the unit was disbanded in the early 1990s. He qualified as an artisan in 1989 and worked at several companies from 2011 to 2021. He lives on a small farm just outside Koster in North West province. Leon played good rugby, wrestled and participated in MMA. His sporting achievements include provincial and national colours.

JAMES STARKEY

James Starkey, author of *A Stark Reality*, served with 61 Mech Bn in Operation Hooper. He and his unit stayed in the Angolan bush without facilities for about five months in 1987/88. They encountered enemy forces on numerous occasions during this time. These face-to-face encounters involved enemy tanks, armoured vehicles and taking fire from artillery, MRL's and enemy aircrafts. James also took part in the Cuito Cuanavale battles. The trauma of war severely impacted James, and he acquired acute PTSD. Unable to reintegrate into society, he turned to alcohol and drugs for comfort. Thankfully, he has since recovered from his substance abuse and is still in regular treatment for the PTSD which helps him to keep 'the war within' as peaceful as possible.

REST IN PEACE (OTHERS)

Various books have presented the full roll of honour for fallen Recces. The list below includes only those featured in this book.

When I wrote *A Breed Apart* I realised after a while how many times I had to insert 'rest in peace', or RIP, for some of our Recce forefathers, instructors, operators, fellow buds and good friends who have passed on since our training year of 1986. We honour all these great men and superb soldiers who have moved on to Valhalla. Here are their names:

Sergeant Major Trevor Floyd
Sergeant Major (RSM) Petrus Paulus 'Pep' van Zyl
General (Colonel OC 1 Recce) Andre Bestbier (Rhodesian SAS)
Colonel Andre 'Diedies' Diedericks
Colonel Sybrand 'Sybie Snr' van der Spuy
Major Dave Drew
Major Willie de Koker
Sergeant Major Bruce Laing (Rhodesian SAS)
Sergeant Major Piet 'Oppies' Opperman (Selous Scouts)
Sergeant Major Gavin Christie
Sergeant Major Wayne Ross-Smith (Rhodesian SAS)
Sergeant Major Japie 'Kloppies' Kloppers
Staff Sergeant Anton Benade (Rhodesian SAS)
Sergeant Major Johnny 'Guava' de Gouveia
Sergeant Ian Strange (Rhodesian SAS)
Sergeant Ernesto Bongo
Corporal Dolf van Tonder
Corporal Herman 'Harry' Caarstens (last SADF member killed in action in the Bush War, 1966–1989)

SOUTH AFRICAN SPECIAL FORCES MISSION AND VISION

Special Forces vision: Special Forces Brigade recognises and supports the National Defence Force in its striving to maintain the National Constitution, as well as preserving the territorial integrity and sovereignty of the Republic of South Africa. Special Forces is committed to contributing to the assurance of security, stability, peace and progress for the country and its people. Special Forces enjoy high repute in the eyes of the general public, as well as on an international level, as a result of its professionalism and maintenance of standards.

Special Forces Brigade is an affordable, dynamic and effective force, which boasts specially trained personnel and is equipped with specialist equipment. The international recognition of the Brigade's capabilities makes Special Forces a credible force that must be reckoned with.

Special Forces is representative of the composition of the Republic of South Africa's population, falls under command of the South African Army, and comprises landward, airborne and seaward capabilities.

Special Forces are politically neutral, professional and just in its actions. Readiness levels are maintained in order to ensure that Special Operations can be conducted at any time and place. Christian values are maintained within a policy of freedom of religious choice.

Military ethics, personal integrity, honesty and loyalty are emphasised to support and mould the individual members' value system. All members are actively encouraged and supported to achieve their full potential.

Special Forces mission: Special Forces must be ready to carry out reconnaissance, direct offensive action, counter-terror and unconventional operations at any time and place.

Aim of Special Forces: To maximally disrupt the military capabilities of the enemies of South Africa when specifically authorised to do special operations, at any time and place, through creative and pro-active actions.

Role of Special Forces: Special Forces, as a force multiplier, is to conduct tasks to satisfy national objectives that *cannot* be performed by other elements of the SANDF without the risk of conflict escalation, utilising specially trained and equipped soldiers. Special Forces supplies specialists on full-time standby and provides specialist military support and training to allies.

Special Forces mandate (approved by the Minister of Defence on 2 February 1998): Special Forces as a strategic force carries out special operations, independently or in cooperation with other state departments or arms of service, to achieve national objectives, internally or externally in peace and war. Such operations will be executed in accordance with the Constitution of the Republic of South Africa, the White Paper on Defence, the Defence Review and international law, with oversight and approval at the highest operational level.

To execute this mandate Special Forces must be able to carry out the following tasks either independently or in support:

- **Primary tasks**, which include direct offensive actions; strategic reconnaissance and intelligence collection; unconventional guerrilla warfare; counter-terror actions; theatre search and rescue; influencing operations; peace support operations and any other tasks which in future may be assigned.

- **Collateral tasks**, which include crime prevention; humanitarian aid, support to the government's military-diplomatic initiatives and any other task which in future may be assigned.

INDEX

Page numbers in italics indicate pictures

1 Parachute Battalion 1, 32, 41, 61, 85, 103, 118–120, 124, 130, 135, 237, 275, 283, 290
1 Reconnaissance Commando (1 Recce) 1–3, 7, 11, 26, 30–31, 33, 35–38, 41–42, 48, 51, 96, 106, 130, 141, 147, 150, 194, 200, 202, 207, 209–211, 213, 218, 229, 237–238, 243–245, 247–248, 251, 260, 267, 276–277, 279, 282–283, 285–289, 291
2 Reconnaissance Commando (2 Recce) 97, 103, 206, 281, 288–290
4 Reconnaissance Commando (4 Recce) 3, 31, 33, 35, 43, 96–97, 100, 106, 207, 211, 217, 239–241, 245, 248, 276, 278, 282–286, 288–289
5 Reconnaissance Commando (5 Recce) 3, 29, 31, 35, 96, 104–107, 110–111, 116, 186, 240, 244, 276, 279–280, 289
32 Battalion 41, 61, 151, 154, 184, 210, 258, 280
101 Battalion 9, 28–29, 209

A
Abrahams, Joan 'Tannie Mossie' 130
African National Congress (ANC) 3, 145, 243, 246, 252
Ali, Muhammad 184
Al-Qaeda 273
Anglo-Boer War 5, 42, 277
apartheid 2, 47, 109, 114, 252
Archer, Raymond 248
Ashipala, Willy 113

B
Baker, Corporal 288
Barlow, Eeben 258, 285

Benade, Anton 141, 291
Bestbier, Andre 206, 278, 283, 291
Beukman, Anton 240–*241*
Bezuidenhout, Neil 'Bez' 18, 102, 208, 211, *219*, 277
Blood Money 2, 94, 106, 221, 244, 262, 264, 270, 275
Bongo, Ernesto 248–249, 291
Bonthuis, Hentie 288
Botes, Johan 'Boats' 11, 22–23, 25, 259
Botha, PW 240–*241*, 243, 252
Breytenbach, Jan 32, 187, 196–*197*, 275
British Special Air Service (SAS) 1–2, 204, 269
Browning, John Moses 253
Bush War 11, 22, 31, 110, 124, 146, 187, 238, 243, 245, 250–251, 257, 271–273, 277, 279–280, 282, 291

C
Caarstens, Herman 'Harry' 248, 251, *254*, 291
Castle, Barbara 70
Celliers, Japie 50, *145*, 287–288
Celliers, Minisa 288
Christie, Gavin 103, 291
Chung, Master 88, 131, 139, 147
Churchill, Winston 209
Civil Cooperation Bureau (CCB) 96, 258
Cockroft, Stephen 97
Coetzee, Dries 77, 104, 164, 208, 211, 222, 238, 240, 257, 276–277
communist, communism 1–2, 5, 191, 252
Croucamp, Hennie 'Croucs' 148, 164, 208, 211, 215, 283
Cuito Cuanavale, Battle of 238, 242–243

294

Index

D

Dampies, Corporal 155, 184, 283
Davies, Craig 51, 222
De Beer, Braam 20, 26–28, 42–43, 116, 155, 164, 194, 208, 211, 248, 285–286
De Beer, Dewald 155
De Gouveia, Johnny 229, 291
De Jong, Coenie 42–43, 60
De Klerk, FW 243, 252
De Klerk, Tinus 237, 248, 250
De Koker, Jacobus Petrus 150
De Koker, Willie 107, 252, 291
Delta Force 60, 171, 269
De Maupassant, Guy 9
De Villiers, Matthys 'Diff' 20–22, 42, 49–50, 60, 73–74, 83, 91–92, 115–116, 123–124, 144, 150, 162, 208, 211, 240, 248, 282–283
De Wet, Christiaan 42
De Wet, Koos 288
De Wet, Mark 23, 42, 49–51, 117, 176, 208, 211, 248, 285
Diedericks, Andre 252, 291
Donkergat 97, *99*, 102–103
Drew, Dave 107, 291
Du Plessis, 'Dup' 248
Du Toit, Wynand 190

E

Eheke, Battle of 151
Einstein, Albert 260
Erasmus, Abel 249
Erasmus, Billy 244
Executive Outcomes 102, 258, 260, 277, 279, 284, 286

F

Faul, Billy 88, 208
Ferreira, Johan 248, 289–290
Floyd, Trevor 41, 291
Fort Doppies 153–155, 160, 162–163, 169, 175, 185, 187, 229–230, 253, 255, 289
Fort Rev (Ondangwa) 9, 14, 29, 196, 221, 224–225, 228, 276, 280
Fourie, Nicky 24, 75, 78, 124, 162, *165*, 203, *205*, 208, 211, *219*, 245, 283–284
Fourie, SW 222, 225
Franklin, Benjamin 118
Freedom Square 155

G

Godbeer, Ray 11, 25, 27, 155, 162, 164
Greeff, Jack 203, 288
Greyling, Chris 9, 11, 28, 217
Grylls, Bear 153

H

Hague Convention on the Laws and Customs of War 191
Hall, David 11, 222
Harris, Brian 25, 61, *156*, *160*, 177, 208
Hellsgate 15, 253
Hugo, Etienne 237–238, 259
Hugo, Renier 'PP' 61, 78, 85, 113–114, 116, 137–138, 141, 206, 208, 240, 279
Human, Arnold 78, 208
Human, De Wet 'Wetta' 23, 33, 36, 42–43, 124, 208, 211, 248
Human, Kobus 35

I

Inkatha Freedom Party 243
iron-cross exercises 76–79, 81
Islamic State 273

J

Jenkinson, Dave 11, 18–19, 23–25, 38, 55, 60, 164, 187
Jennings, Rob 38, 44, 60, 161, *165*, 177, 208, 211, 248
Jones, Phillip 103
Jordaan, Wessel 'Jorrie' 11, 24

K

Kissinger, Henry 170
Kloppers, Jaap 214, 291
Koevoet 29, 210, 222, 247–249, 251

L

Laing, Bruce 11, 20, 22, 82, 88, 283, 291
Laubscher, DEM 248, *254*
Leppan, Craig 42, 51, 208, 211, 286–287
letra course *81*–82

Lintvelt, Hannes 61, 102, 184, 208

M
Mackay, Harvey 140
MacLeod, Norman 146
Mandela, Nelson 252
Masella, Julian 103, 184, 208, 222
Mathias, Neves 214, *260*
Mauldin, Bill 60
Mil (fellow trainee) 54
mixed martial arts (MMA) 270
Modern War Institute 199
Moorcroft, Koos 110–111
Morgan, Richard K 87
Muller, Stephan 60
Mutlow, William 61, 208, 279–280

N
National Party 1–2, 243, 252
National Union for the Total Independence of Angola (Unita) 11–13, 15, 17–20, 25–26, 29, 187–188, 196–197, 238, 240
Niemoller, Johan 70
Nine Day War 62, 251

O
Oosthuizen, CJ 'Oosie' 11, 38, 43, 56–57, 60, 73, 88
Operation Coolidge 239
Operation Kerslig 150
Operation Kropduif 150
Operation Hooper 238, 242–243
Operation Merlyn 248
Operation Modulêr 238, 242, 272
Operation Nigel 13, 30–31, 62, 65, 198–199, 203, 221
Operation Packer 238, 243
Operation Reindeer 120
Operation Saga 248
Opperman, Piet 'Gif'/'Oppies' 114, 116, 291

P
Pan Africanist Congress (PAC) 2, 252
Pedro, Corporal 233
People's Armed Forces of Liberation of Angola (Fapla) 5, 9, 13, 190, 197, 228, 238–240
People's Liberation Army of Namibia (PLAN) 109, 113
post-traumatic stress disorder (PTSD) 267, 270–273
Pringle, Ernest 257
Prinsloo, 'Swapo' 11

R
Raath, JJ 73–74, 148, 155, 211, 283
Raath, Johan
  youth 3, 5, 7–9, 275
  basic training in Oudtshoorn 33–36, 61, 275
  training in Durban 36–48, 51, 92, 275
  training at Dukuduku 48, 51–60, 63, 68, 70–88, 86, 92–93, 130–131, 134, 220, 284
  at Xangongo 13–17, 20, 22, 25, 30
  PMC (private military contractor) in Iraq 26–27, 31, 49, 55, 62, 139, 148, 172, 262–263, 268, 273, 275–276, 282, 286
  SMIND 87–95
  Donkergat, seaborne, water orientation training 96–104
  Dark Phase training at Phalaborwa 104–117
  parachute course 118–130
  air orientation training 131–139
  Advanced Urban Warfare training 135, 199–208, 230, 232, 252
  Demolitions and Mine Warfare training 140–152
  Survival, Bushcraft and Tracking course 151, 153–169
  minor tactics course 170–198
  feet and Achilles heel problems 48, 82–83, 85, 136, 203, 220, 237, 243–244, 259–263
  Advanced Medical course 244–245
  promotion to sergeant 246
  promotion to staff sergeant 258, 275
  instructor at training wing 251–253,

255–257, 275
VIP protection & R&D course 257–258
resigning from SADF 259–260
back problems 101, 136, 260–265
opioid addiction & painkillers 262–266
author of *Blood Money* 2, 94, 106, 221, 244, 262, 264–265, 270, 275
Recces (*also see* South African Special Forces) 1–3, 5, 7, 9, 11, 14–15, 22, 24, 26, 28–38, 41–43, 45–49, 51, 55, 60–61, 64, 66, 70, 72, 78, 82, 84, 88, 90, 92–93, 96–97, 100–101, 103–107, 110–112, 114, 116, 119, 122, 124, 130–131, 134, 141, 147, 150–151, 153–155, 169–171, 174, 176, 178, 180–181, 185–187, 189–190, 194, 196, 199–202, 206–207, 209–213, 215, 217–219, 221, 229–230, 233, 237–238, 245, 247–249, 251, 253, 255, 257–258, 260–261, 267–270, 272–291
Resolution 435 (United Nations) 247
Rhodesia (Zimbabwe), Rhodesian Bush War 1–3, 56, 90, 105, 114, 120, 141, 146–147, 212, 238, 267, 282, 291
Rhodesian Light Infantry (RLI) 2, 114, 120
Rickenbacker, Eddie 131
Roelofse, Christo 23, 208, 280
Ross-Smith, Wayne 226, *260*, 291
Rudman, Les 278
Rykaart, Duncan 281

S
Scheepers, Tinus 93, 137–138, 162
Scheltema, Jacques 260
Schwarzenegger, Arnold 24
Selous Scouts 2, 105, 114, 291
Serfontein, Chris 23, 60–61, 97, 122, 128, 138, 208, 277–279
Shaeffer, Grant 51, 117, 129, 137–138, 208, 211, 287
Shaeffer, Lynne 287
Sheffer, Johan 88
SMIND (Spesiale Magte Individueel) 87–95

Smit, Sergeant 288
SMORIE (Spesiale Magte Oriëntasie) 52, 61, 67–69, 73, 87, 92
South African Communist Party 252
South African Defence Force (SADF) 2, 5, 13, 25, 32, 38, 55, 58, 60, 70–72, 96, 106, 109, 113, 114, 154, 174, 187, 206–207, 222, 238, 243, 245, 247, 249, 251, 253, 275–278, 281, 284, 287–288, 291
South African Infantry School 1, 7, 32–35, 37–38, 44, 48, 86, 91, 123, 257, 275, 278–279, 287, 289
South African National Defence Force (SANDF) 1, 278, 293
South African Special Forces (*also see* Recces) 1–3, 5, 7, 9, 11, 13, 15, 22, 29–33, 35, 38–39, 44, 46, 49, 51–54, 57–58, 60–61, 69–71, 74, 83–84, 86–87, 91–93, 95–96, 98, 105–106, 109–110, 117–120, 122–125, 131, 133, 140, 145–146, 153, 155, 169–171, 173–174, 182, 187, 190–191, 195–196, 204, 206–212, 218, 222, 229, 232, 235, 237, 243–244, 260–261, 266–270, 272, 274–289, 292–293
South African Special Forces Association (SAFSA) 269
South African Special Forces Mission and Vision 292–293
South West Africa People's Organisation (Swapo) 2, 5, 9, 11, 62, 109, 113, 222, 227–228, 247–251, 278
Speskop 1, 33, 247–248, 280
Starkey, James 272
Steyn, Adriaan 257
Storm, JM 266
Strange, Ian 11, 16, 19, 25, 88, 147, 155, 162, 176, 288, 291
Sun Tzu 105
Swapol 247–249, 251
Swart, PA 208

T
Tjepeppa, Wolfgang 18, 24

U
Umkhonto we Sizwe (MK) 2

United Nations Transition Assistance Group (UNTAG) 250
US Navy Seals 96, 296

V
Van Aswegen, Barry 36
Van den Berg, Buks 257
Van der Merwe, Eugene 208, 248, 283
Van der Merwe, Marc 88, 90, 112–113, 148, 162, 176–177, 196, 208, 211
Van der Spuy, Andy 208, 288–289
Van der Spuy, Mada 281
Van der Spuy, Olla 123
Van der Spuy, Sybie 61, 83, 102–103, 115–116, 123, 208, 257, 278, 281, 291
Van der Spuy, Sybie 'Snr' 102–103, 281
Van Dyk, Frans 35, 238
Van Tonder, Dolf 248, 291
Van Wyk, Henk 82, 208, 211, 227, 284–285
Van Zyl, Daan 150, 226
Van Zyl, Petrus 'Pep' 41–42, 79, 85, 206, 215, 239, 253, 259, 286, 291
Venter, Hannes 97
Venter, Leon 104, 147, 290

Vermaak, Justin 207, *239*
Vermaak, Roy 227
Visser, Barry 24, 33, 62, 72, 82, 85–86, 99, 130, 208, 211, 222, 227, *239*, 248, 275–276
Visser, Jeanette 275
Visser, Nick 130, 275–276
Von Mollendorf, Dolf 50
Vorster, Alewyn 'Vossie' 100

W
'Wall of Shame' (SASFA) 269
Washington, George 32
waterboarding 75
Wilke, Fred 240

X
Xangongo 9, 13–17, 20, 22, 25, 30

Y
Yaffe, Gary 11, 15–16, 28, 211, 222, 227, *239*, 248

Z
Zeelie, Fred 2, 251

CPSIA information can be obtained
at www.ICGtesting.com
Printed in the USA
LVHW081337280722
724566LV00013B/374